Moral Argument, Religion, and Same-Sex Marriage

Moral Argument, Religion, and Same-Sex Marriage

Advancing the Public Good

Edited by
Gordon A. Babst, Emily R. Gill, and Jason Pierceson

LEXINGTON BOOKS
A division of

ROWMAN & LITTLEFIELD PUBLISHERS, INC.
Lanham • Boulder • New York • Toronto • Plymouth, UK

Published by Lexington Books
A division of Rowman & Littlefield Publishers, Inc.
A wholly owned subsidiary of The Rowman & Littlefield Publishing Group, Inc.
4501 Forbes Boulevard, Suite 200, Lanham, Maryland 20706
http://www.lexingtonbooks.com

Estover Road, Plymouth PL6 7PY, United Kingdom

British Library Cataloguing in Publication Information Available

Library of Congress Cataloging-in-Publication Data

Moral argument, religion, and same-sex marriage : advancing the public good / edited by
Gordon A. Babst, Emily R. Gill, and Jason Pierceson.
  p. cm.
  Includes index.
  ISBN 978-0-7391-2649-3 (cloth : alk. paper) — ISBN 978-0-7391-2650-9 (pbk. : alk.
paper) — ISBN 978-0-7391-4119-9 (electronic)
  1. Same-sex marriage—Law and legislation—United States. 2. Gays—Legal status,
laws, etc.—United States. 3. Constitutional law—Religious aspects. I. Babst, Gordon
Albert, 1961– II. Gill, Emily R., 1944– III. Pierceson, Jason, 1972–
  KF539.M67 2009
  346.7301'68—dc22
                                                                              2009020014

Printed in the United States of America

Table of Contents

Introduction

Gordon A. Babst

Moral Argument, Religion, and Same-Sex Marriage: Advancing the Public Good deploys ethical argumentation with respect to gay rights broadly speaking, and with reference to the right to marry in particular. The arguments advanced in each chapter are presented in moral terms and in terms of the nation's foundational political principles. Each chapter advances a morals discourse, including sometimes even in religious terms, within the framework of the American constitutional regime's promise of meaningful equal liberty and citizenship across the board, regardless of whether one is, or is regarded as being a member of a sexual minority, or in an atypical family situation. The authors contest the perceived, if not actual, heteronormative establishment in the law and public policy that continues to work against sexual minorities, and is usually and improperly couched in the language of American values, thus misunderstanding the nation's political principles, or willfully miscasting them as inapplicable to sexual minorities.

This unique approach is further enhanced through the diversity of its chapter authors, building on the published scholarship of each coeditor, and extending ethical argumentation to a variety of important public policy areas such as marriage and the rearing of children.[1] While most of the chapters reference liberal-democratic theory in one way or another, my Introduction to this volume is by way of a review of recent history a bit closer to home, because it illustrates the overall public comprehension of the issues that we believe is compelling, and animates the entire work. One novelty of our approach is that we consciously do not engage the old, arguably tired questions of the past, such as whether gays are normal, whether homosexuality is natural or sinful, whether the traditional husband-wife family is best for children, and so on. The new territory we stake is not predicated any other assumption than that the Constitution, properly understood, offers nothing less than full and equal citizenship before the law, and after, and that its protections are sincere, not facetious.

On May 15, 2008, the California State Supreme Court ruled to allow same-sex marriages in the state, a historic decision that made California only the second state that legally recognizes a same-sex marriage.[2] Of great significance also in this case is its application of the judicial standard of strict scrutiny, establishing that any California law that turns on the basis of sexual orientation is constitutionally suspect. In the wake of the court ruling, Proposition 8, an initiative for the 2008 November ballot to amend the state's constitution to ban same-sex marriage, picked up steam and was eventually passed by the voters.[3] Back in 2000 a majority of Californians had passed Proposition 22, a ballot initiative similar to those in many other states to ban same-sex marriage.[4] Naturally, citizens of California and elsewhere are riveted by the juxtaposition of the court's 2008 decision and the earlier proposition, and, on top of that, the political whirlwind, if not state constitutional crisis should the court strike down Proposition 8. Results from the 2008 election in California indicate that Proposition 8 passed by about a 53 percent to 47 percent margin, rather less than the earlier Proposition 22.

In the wake of the 2008 court decision with Proposition 22 remaining on the books, the *Los Angeles Times* teamed with local television station KTLA to commission a poll to gauge popular opinion in California, to see whether Californians were likely to revalidate Proposition 22 through the new initiative, Proposition 8, or whether over the intervening years they have changed their minds on the issue of same-sex marriage and so would side with the ruling of the court.[5] While the poll's chief result is informative, that 54 percent of registered California voters would back the initiative to amend the state constitution, one of the poll's five questions stands out because it probably would not occur on any poll regarding the marriage or family practices of any other sub-group of the population.[6] This is poll question number four: "Do you believe that same-sex relationships between consenting adults are morally wrong?"[7] Of all respondents, 39 percent replied that such relationships are morally wrong, 54 percent replied that they are not, and 7 percent replied "don't know."[8]

While it is gratifying to see yet another indicator of a majority of people refraining from expressing moral disapproval of same-sex relationships, that this sort of question was brought into play at all marks the persistence of this one frame, a morals frame with deep religious roots. The poll did not ask, and it would even sound odd if it did, whether respondents thought same-sex relationships would help stabilize neighborhoods, contribute to the social or economic good of a community, or produce the same beneficial or costly effects that other sanctioned relationships often entail, such as divorce. Indeed, all of those more empirically-oriented public policy concerns seem always secondary to the morals question that many people still take to be fundamental to any discussion of sexual minorities. In no other area of law or public policy does serious discussion flounder as soon on the shoals of moral and religious concerns. This has been the distinguishing feature of gay rights in the public square, and so is the bar advocates for America's sexual minorities must meet if they hope for lasting success in the public arena.

Frequently in the past opponents of equal rights for American citizens who fall into one or other sexual minority have deployed moral arguments, oftentimes playing an explicitly religious card.[9] And, also frequently in the past, advocates for equal rights have attempted to deflect the thrust of their opponents' arguments and assertions, and have expressed qualms among themselves about how best to respond without having to engage moral questions or social concerns expressed in moral terms.[10] Since about the 1950s, advocates for gay rights and their supporters have often turned to science, or deployed social-science-based arguments in the hopes that an empirically-based approach to the challenges they face would appeal to the all but hardened in their views as regards sexual propriety. Or, advocates would utilize the language of rights and individualism, the American public philosophy of live and let live so long as you don't harm anyone else or disturb the peace, in the hopes that a secular public philosophy approach would win the favor of their fellow Americans who are not particularly religious, or, though religious, have a strong faith or stake in our public philosophy.[11] To their constituents' repeated disappointment over several decades, the many who argued for gay rights almost invariably declined to address the central moral components of the opposition, or sought to evade recognizing or engaging with the deeply held religious convictions of the opposition, and they kept losing out, or continually faced the same roadblocks anew, eking out a victory here and there, but never being in a position to rest on their accomplishments.

This volume takes an explicitly different tack, and engages directly the moral questions and concerns that before were usually shied away from. The authors of the present volume do not attempt to belittle or rule out of bounds the moral concerns and religious beliefs of their opponents, even where the most modest of separation anxieties would be rankled, or where sympathetic religious believers might curtail discussion owing to their fellow believers' intolerance or lack of familiarity with their own religious history.[12] In the United States overlapping social, political, and legal arenas have been the sites of formal contestation and popular struggle to configure public and private forms of domination and discrimination, despite rule of law guarantees to all Americans such as equal citizenship. We believe that current advocates for gay rights are not really engaging their opponents unless they are engaged with the moral nature of their opponents' views and arguments. Such moral argumentation is a necessary intervention into the unfolding power struggles, regardless of however happenstance or constructed opposing arguments may be. The continued, though somewhat dwindling resonance of traditional gay rights opponents' arguments have nonetheless so far successfully anchored the inequality of sexual minorities, if not their political oppression. Hence, at least in the realm of our present research, that of moral, legal, and political-philosophical argument, we feel that both the debate and the public good need to be advanced anew.

Unlike many of our predecessors, the authors of the present volume believe that moral argument in terms of the public good is on our side, and not on the side of those who would deny equal rights, or do worse, to members of America's sexual minorities.[13] As a variety of moral perspectives are in evidence among our authors, we leave it to the reader to decide whether there is an overarching moral argument, or strategic deployments of morals discourse to unseat the heteronormative bias still present in our law and politics—despite the American civic discourse of equality, liberty, and the rule of law, itself a morals discourse or at least reflecting the Constitution's moral commitments.[14]

On the morning of March 5, 2009, the California Supreme Court heard the arguments for and against invalidating Proposition 8. One source of particular consternation among opponents of Proposition 8 is the out-of-state financial support it received from the Church of Jesus Christ of Latter-day Saints—the Mormons—and individual members to the tune of at least $20 million, by far the largest single contribution in the most expensive ballot race ever in our nation's history, exceeded in the 2008 election cycle only by the amount spent on the race to the White House.[15] While a variety of political voices such as Governor Arnold Schwarzenegger, Senator Dianne Feinstein, and both candidates for president, as well as major business leaders lent their support in opposition to Proposition 8, its supporters were mainly religious groups or family groups with a religious affiliation headquartered out-of-state. The legal questions raised by Proposition 8's passage include whether it should ever have been on the ballot in the first place, as it was a mere ballot initiative requiring passage by a bare majority of the voters, yet sought to rescind a fundamental right for one class of Californians, and thus apparently would infringe on the state constitution's equality provisions, which the May 15 ruling, discussed earlier, strengthened with respect to sexual orientation by making it a suspect classification in the State of California.[16]

If the reasoning in the chapters that follow is sound, then the issue before the California Supreme Court should have been seen as one of legal, moral, and political principle, and should have been decided on that basis, rather than on the basis of deference to the democratic process, to popular majority vote.[17] One idea in play is that the rights of one part of the citizenry were improperly subject to a popular vote, in the face of what the same Court had asserted barely a year ago—the principle of equality in the fundamental right to marry. Given that the State of California provides for civil unions for same-sex couples, the separate-but-equal doctrine appears also to be at play, evincing a principle long rejected as incompatible with American liberal constitutionalism. The victory of Proposition 8 shows that the separation of one group of American citizens from the rest in terms of their rights and liberties is still permitted if not encouraged by a majority of the voting public, regardless of previous legislative and judicial outcomes in favor of same-sex marriage in the State of California.[18]

Proposition 8 was an assertion of the people, but not in the name of the people as constituted under law with its embedded moral, political principles, such as republicanism, equality of citizenship, equality under the law, and the rule of equal laws. While the passion and traditional religious persuasion in favor of Proposition 8 are real, even these must demur before being allowed to sanction impermissible inequality in the law.

In *Moral Argument, Religion, and Same-Sex Marriage: Advancing the Public Good* we engage not only the moral questions that often arise in connection with gay rights and specific issues such as same-sex marriage, but argue that the moral case for equal rights and recognizing fully all the other lawful incidents of American citizenship is on our side, that the moral argument is eminently winnable, and that a significant public good is to be had by the full inclusion of American citizens who happen to be in a sexual minority. Contributors to this volume have all published, presented papers, or been active in public discussions of the issues, and so bring to this volume considerable professional and personal reflection. We, the editors, hope that this book fills a niche in the literature and points both theorists and practitioners towards a deeper understanding of the public good and to new avenues for research and policymaking, and helps to move our nation forward in fulfilling its promises to all American citizens, especially those who for reason of their sexual minority status have been relegated to less than equal.

NOTES

1. A special mention should be made of one of our contributors, Carlos Ball, whose 2002 book *The Morality of Gay Rights: An Exploration in Political Philosophy*, inspired our approach.

2. *In re Marriage Cases* (2008) 43 Cal.4th 757 [76 Cal.Rptr.3d 683, 183 P.3d 384]. The other state, Massachusetts, has allowed same-sex marriages since May 17, 2004, owing to the earlier Supreme Judicial Court of Massachusetts' landmark ruling in *Goodridge v. Department of Public Health* (798 N.E.2d 941 [Mass. 2003]). Among the first California couples to marry were pioneers of the gay rights movement, Del Martin, 87, and Phyllis Lyon, 84, who had then been partners for over forty years. See Lisa Leff, "And now, June weddings for all," *Orange County Register* June 17, 2008, News p. 9.

3. The 2008 election was also a national election, and so saw a huge voter turnout, resulting in the election of a new president. Many have speculated that in the past such propositions were placed on the ballot to stimulate a good turnout among conservative Christian voters, who have been the most likely to vote republican. Interestingly, the California Supreme Court Chief Justice who shepherded the 121-page, 4–3 decision in *In re Marriage Cases*, Ronald George, is a lifelong republican. See Howard Mintz, "Taking the tough Road," *Orange County Register* June 2, 2008, News p. 3. It turns out that California Republicans have been at the forefront of the activism that exists within Republican party circles on behalf of sexual minorities, and same-sex marriage in particular. See James Kirchick, "Golden Opportunity," *The Advocate*, no. 1012 (August 12, 2008): 30–31. Even the *Orange County Register*'s Senior Editorial Writer and Columnist, Steven Greenhut, weighed in on the side of allowing same-sex marriage. See his Sunday edition essay "Gay marriage foes: Let it go," *Orange County Register* August 3, 2008, Commentary pp. 1, 5.

4. Proposition 22 passed by a 61 percent margin of victory. Proposition 8, a re-invigoration of the earlier one, garnered a similar cast of supporters, most prominent being evangelicals, Mormons, and Catholics. For example, the pastor of a large San Diego church attempted to organize about 1,000 other ministers representing congregations of about one million Californians to work in support of Proposition 8, an effort to "include a 40-day fasting period leading up to election day, along with 100 days of prayer," and to fill San Diego's Qualcomm Stadium "with people praying for a ban on gay marriage" just before the election. See Jessica Garrison, "Pastor rallies clergy against gay marriage," *Los Angeles Times* June 26, 2008, pp. A-1, A-17. Such church participation in the political arena raises questions of church-state separation and the meaning and practice of neutrality, topics discussed at length by several of our contributors.

5. See Cathleen Decker, "Californians barely reject gay marriage," *Los Angeles Times* May 23, 2008, pp. A-1, A-27.

6. The marriage and family practices of members of the Church of Jesus Christ of Latter-day Saints might garner such a poll question as well, given their historical association with the practice of polygamous marriage. A subsequent Field Poll found that 51 percent of California voters oppose Proposition 8, and back same-sex marriage. See Jessica Garrison and Dan Morain, "Voters warm to gay marriage," *Los Angeles Times* July 19, 2008, p. B-4. Alas, the actual election returns proved quite the opposite.

7. See Decker, "Californians barely reject gay marriage," p. A-1.

8. See Decker, "Californians barely reject gay marriage," p. A-1.

9. A tradition that continues to this day. See Marc D. Stern, "Will gay rights trample religious freedom?" *Los Angeles Times* June 17, 2008, p. A-15, who argues with great displeasure that the court's ruling in *In re Marriage Cases* is a typical outcome when religious freedom and the equal protection interests of a group come into conflict. Also see Brittany Levine, "Churches dissent," *Orange County Register* July 12, 2008, News p. 3, reporting on the Family Research Council's view that same-sex marriage hurts religious liberties.

10. This is not to say that there have not been several fine, critical excavations into and examinations of religion, particularly Christianity and homosexuality, for example, though these have tended to advocate for sympathy or understanding by way of arguing that the Bible is not nearly as ethically cramped as the traditional take on its teachings has lead many to believe.

11. After all, neither Christianity nor religion in general are monolithic as regards same-sex marriage, and the California court's decision has renewed interfaith dialogue over biblical passages and the nature of God's love. See Duke Helfand, "Doctrine disputes grow as gays wed," *Los Angeles Times* June 19, 2008, pp. A-1, A–B-8.

12. The arguments and concerns of religious believers are taken at face value, even though sometimes one may well wonder if they are seriously meant. Ron Steiner addresses some such arguments in his contribution to this volume, such as whether acknowledging gay rights would bring about the end of western civilization.

13. Our concluding chapter, by Chai Feldblum, introduces the reader to the "Moral Values Project," which provides a resource and base for moral advocacy on behalf of sexual minorities.

14. "Morality" is, of course, an essentially contested concept, especially when invoked in politics or made into a politics. Nonetheless, we believe that there is enough of a sense of morality in our constitutional law and practice to count as a sufficient resource for morals discourse to work with as we engage in politics, even in the face of the older, more religiously-determined morals discourse that arguably has been notoriously unamenable to political persuasion, though it has been frequently relied on by the traditional opposition to gay rights and sexual minorities in general.

15. Supporters and opponents of Proposition 8 spent a total of about $80 million in support of, or against its passage. See Maura Dolan, "Court looks unlikely to kill Prop. 8," *Los Angeles Times* March 6, 2009, p. A-14. The Mormon Church directly donated about $190,000 in support of Proposition 8, and spent about $96,849.31 worth of compensated church employees' staff time, in addition to the approximately $20 million donated by Mormon church members to the Yes on 8 campaign. See McClatchy Newspapers, "Mormon spending on Prop. 8 detailed," *Orange County Register* February 2, 2009, News p. 9. The Colorado Springs-based Evangelical organization Focus on the Family donated about $657,000 "in cash and services" to promote Prop. 8. See Lisa Leff, "Last-minute spending rush," *Orange County Register* February 3, 2009, News p. 9.

16. A proposal to alter the state constitution requires a supermajority vote, rather than a bare, or 50 percent plus one majority, which is all a measure to amend the existing state constitution requires.

17. There were at least two fundamental questions before the Court. First, whether Proposition 8 as a ballot initiative provided for an impermissible revision, rather than amendment to the state constitution. Secondly, there is the issue of whether the approximately 18,000 same-sex couples married by the State of California between when the Court's May 15, 2008 decision went into effect in June, and the certification of the election results in November, 2008, will remain married. Attached to this question is the further issue of whether the state will recognize same-sex marriages performed in other states during this same time period and then, if it continues to recognize those same-sex marriages performed under California law and also recognizes those performed elsewhere in the United States, whether it will indeed be obligated to recognize all duly solemnized same-sex marriages performed elsewhere. See Dolan, "Court looks unlikely to kill Prop. 8," p. A-1.

18. As of this writing the lower houses in both the State of New Hampshire and the State of Vermont have passed legislation to allow same-sex marriage, in the latter case even in the face of its pioneering civil union statute, which detractors view as a contemporary instance of the unconstitutional doctrine "separate but equal." See Editorials, "The gay-marriage march," *Los Angeles Times* March 28, 2009, p. A-28.

I

SAME-SEX MARRIAGE AND PARTNERSHIPS

Introduction

Jason Pierceson

Debates over gay and lesbian rights are framed significantly by majoritarian moralistic and religious arguments against equality for sexual minorities. Unlike other contemporary movements for inclusion and equality, the lesbian and gay rights movement faces an automatic and pervasive barrier to its claims. In the United States, this is particularly pronounced because of the institutional entrenchment of secular and religious conservatism. Churches, think tanks, litigation groups, and other institutions are constantly at the ready to employ fairly standard and predictable objections to a broad range of gay rights claims from antidiscrimination laws to same-sex marriage.

These arguments can be placed into three categories. The first, and perhaps the oldest, is a moral and religious condemnation of homosexuality from a particular strain of theological dogma. This view asserts that homosexuality is sinful and "unnatural." However, as this argument has become more marginalized, the second argument is increasingly invoked: The assertion that religious freedom is threatened by laws protecting and promoting the equality of sexual minorities. The Obama inauguration invocater, Reverend Rick Warren, articulated a version of this argument when he pointed to critics of his position on the legal status of sexual minorities as antireligious hate speech and "Christophobia." This, of course, cleverly turns the tables on sexual minorities. A small minority whose oppression is intimately tied to religious dogma on sex and sexuality is labeled the oppressor for pointing out this ongoing and powerful connection. Apparently, according to this perspective, certain religious views are to drive policy and be protected from competing views under the rubric of religious freedom. The third category is a neoconservative social policy argument against relationship equality for sexual minorities. This perspective views the heterosexual, two-parent family as the essential building block of society and asserts that decline of society is imminent with the sanctioning and support of same-sex relationships. According to this view, there is an inverse relationship between societal stability and support of relationship equality. Judges have used this argument as a way to deflect challenges to the unequal treatment of same-sex couples. While most judges are reluctant to argue that preserving a moral or religious viewpoint is a valid function of the law, many have been willing to defer to legislative judgments that preserving the heterosexual nature of marriage out of a concern over procreation. The authors in this section directly examine and reject these arguments in favor of positions that support a full range of gay rights claims.

Ronald Steiner takes direct aim at the "decline of civilization" argument, first noting the persistence of cultural expressions of same-sex attraction and gender role challenges throughout history. Rather, he argues that liberal democracies strengthen "civilization" by living up to fundamental principles of freedom and equality through the extension of policies that affirm and protect sexual minorities.

Karen Streuning examines how judges apply fundamental rights and substantive due process analysis to same-sex marriage cases and argues that there is nothing fundamental about this. Rather, liberals and conservatives on the courts view fundamental rights very differently, especially the fundamental right to marriage. This is a judicial manifestation of the political and philosophical debates surrounding the issue. Struening notes that many judges are still accepting the majoritarian views of sexuality and the "natural" family reflected in *Bowers v. Hardwick* while ignoring the substantial shift in doctrine in *Lawrence v. Texas* that affirms the personhood of gay and lesbian individuals and their intimate choices. While persuasively demonstrating that this approach is flawed, Streuning argues that this appears to be a pervasive approach that does not bode well for future same-sex marriage claims in court. It seems that majoritarianism is difficult to escape, even in the courts.

Rather than opposing religious freedom and same-sex marriage, Emily Gill argues that support for the free exercise of religion requires state-sanctioned same-sex marriage. As a starting point, Gill argues that both religious and sexual identity are central to modern human identity. To value one form of identity (religious) over another (sexual) creates an illiberal situation, because one will be privileged in the law and the other will not. After all, many same-sex couples desire to marry for religious reasons, a point often missed in this debate. Gill corrects this myopia by elevating religious and sexual identity to the same plane. In addition, while criticizing the deep majoritarianism of religion scholars like Michael McConnell as always finding a way in their seemingly fair analysis to favor majoritarian religious views, Gill notes that "We are not two communities, one of insiders and one of outsiders, but one United States with one rule of law and one type of citizen."[1]

Carlos Ball rejects the conservative arguments but also convincingly argues that liberals need to abandon their fear of inserting moral judgments into policy and legal questions. He argues that it is inevitable and necessary for the state to make a moral judgment about the goodness of same-sex relationships in order to recognize them—there is no "easy way out" with appeals to formal equality. Ball argues that the liberal principle of pluralism, applied to human relationships, is a moral judgment that liberals and progressives ought to be comfortable promoting. Legislating political, rather than theological, morality can be a good thing, and it is required to achieve full equality for sexual minorities.

All of these authors point a clear way out of philosophical and legal conservatism and argue for the full protections in law and policy for sexual minorities, particularly the protection and affirmation that comes with state-recognized marriage. All authors present a corrective to the surprising recent trend toward a vigorous majoritarianism in political and legal thought, surprising because of the clear ignoring of "liberal" in liberal democracy. Finally, all authors in this section strongly support, and persuasively move forward, the larger project of this volume: to make a strong and clear case for placing the rights of sexual minorities at the center of contemporary debates about political morality and to affirm the dignity of individuals of all sexualities through law and policy.

NOTE

1. Emily R. Gill, "The Religion Clauses and Same-Sex Marriage," 68.

A Commentary on the Old Saw that Same-Sex Marriage Threatens Civilization

Ronald L. Steiner

Discussions of same-sex marriage frequently entertain the notion that civilization is somehow at stake were a society to award legal sanction to it, and to gay rights more generally. Typically, those who express concern for negative civilizational consequences have in mind Western civilization, and more specifically Christian civilization. This civilizational concern will often be amplified by the implication that opposite-sex, or opposite-sex monogamous marriage is a timeless human universal. Any other marital regime is presumed to be an aberration, most likely the result of grave moral depravity of a sort supposedly facilitated by the modern rights-based society.

Sometimes this line of denunciation of same-sex marriage and gay rights more generally is coupled with the suggestion that an overly "liberal" United States is out of step with, or must maintain a moral distinction from, other similar political regimes. Hence, extending legal recognition and attendant benefits to same-sex couples is to depart from the true nature of our political values and our democratic-republican regime. In sum, same-sex marriage and gay rights generally are held to be inconsistent with pretty much everything worthy: humanity-at-large as people and human communities supposedly have existed throughout history, modern liberal democracy, and even civilization itself.

The purpose of this chapter is to cast serious doubt on these critiques of same-sex marriage. It challenges the assumption that the current Western conception of "traditional" marriage is a human universal and thus a constant across time and place, and that erosion of the primacy of place of "traditional" marriage will have very serious negative consequences to society and civilization. It is not our purpose here to cast doubt on the self-understandings of the detractors of same-sex marriage, or gay rights more generally; to the contrary, we accept their concerns at their face value, and accept their contributions to the world's plurality. But one might well ask; if tolerance of same-sex relationships is a sign of civilizational decline, then is the reverse also true? Is intolerance of same-sex relationships a sign of concern for a civilization's health? Would anyone really argue that those six or seven countries where gay persons face execution for homosexual behavior are those where civilizational concerns are held most paramount?

We also do not take a position on the desirability of same-sex marriage for any couple. Each couple, and even each set of intimates outside the pair-bond paradigm, must decide for themselves whether to obtain legal recognition or formalizing of their relationship, and thus make their own contribution to the conversation regarding the many benefits and burdens of same-sex marriage, whether these be economic, political, legal, or social.

We also assume, however, that these civilizational concerns are empirically testable in the context of the debate over same-sex marriage, and so in this chapter provide counter examples to any claims regarding hegemonic and universal norms against same-sex relationships and homosexuality more generally. In light of that empirical survey, the subsequent discussion suggests that western civilization, and modern liberal-democracies in particular, are realizing their core moral and political values of equality and respect for the dignity of each individual human being when they extend legal recognition to same-sex couples, rather than reject or denounce their claims to full inclusion.

While serious public advocacy of "same-sex marriage" became a subject of great controversy in Western countries in the late twentieth and early twenty-first centuries, love and intimacy have always existed between persons of the same sex and/or gender. Such relationships sometimes have even been validated by cultural recognition and, less frequently, by institutional and legal formalities. Some societies have socially sanctioned and even culturally or religiously solemnized same-sex intimate partnerships. A very large number of societies, probably the majority across time, have socially recognized multiple partner, usually polygynous, relationships, including the ancestral societies of the Judeo-Christian tradition. Marriage as limited to "one man and one woman," far from being traditional, is actually a less common pattern than its modern defenders acknowledge. Of course, most societies with an institution of legally licensed civil marriage, a more recent cultural development, have limited it to heterosexual pairs, though many also have been accepting of polygamy.

NON-WESTERN TRADITIONS OF "TWO-SPIRITEDNESS" AND OTHER SAME-SEX RELATIONS

As far back as the mid-twentieth-century studies by Ford and Beach, anthropologists examining cross-cultural data have confirmed that same-sex relationships of intimacy and family have existed throughout history and across cultures.[1] Such studies acknowledge that same-sex intimate behavior has never been shown to the predominant sexual activity among adults in any society. However, in about two-thirds of societies, same-sex relations were socially acceptable and not considered deviant, at least for certain members of the society.[2]

Numerous cultures believe some people have the "spirit" of both male and female, thus taking on a gender-role different from that conventionally assigned to their biological sex or adopting a "third gender" altogether. Modern anthropology suggests that "gender diversity," often labeled "berdache," while never a dominant form, was a conventional behavioral pattern among many tribal peoples.[3] In almost all instances where a two-spirit person would have intimate relations with a conventionally-gendered person, the partner of two-spirit person was not perceived to be "homosexual" or in any way gender-diverse themselves.[4]

Many Native American peoples have recognized, sometimes venerated, and sometimes even feared the power of "two-spirit" persons. Such individuals might have special cultural roles, serving as traditional healers or tellers of fortunes, handling and burying the deceased, conducting certain sexual rites, and preserving traditions, songs, and artisanship. Biologically male two-spirit people might engage in male activities such as sweat lodges and warfare, but they also might take on traditional female roles such as gardening, cooking, clothes making, and child rearing.

With some variation between tribal groups, two-spirits might form romantic bonds and engage in intimate relations with partners of either sex, sometimes solemnized as marriages. Some tribes saw an advantage in having a biologically male two-spirit person marrying a widower, which provided a nurturing new mother without any chance of creating new children whom the new step-mother might favor. In another variation, Lakota *koskalaka* women, loosely and colloquially translated as "dyke" by Paula Gunn Allen, could be joined in a socially validated union via "rope baby" ceremony.[5]

Native Hawaiians and numerous other Polynesian groups also have exhibited a richer and more complex tradition of romance, sex, and intimacy than that tolerated by Western conventions by the early twentieth century. Two-spirit individuals living gender roles opposite to their biological sex is reflected in the *mahu* of Hawaii and elsewhere, along with the Samoan *faʻafafine* (a male who lives "like a woman") and *faʻatama* (a female "like a man") and the Tongan categories of *fakaleiti* and *fakatangata* (again, woman-like males and male-like females). The *mahu* and related forms included biological males living as females, often from a very young age, and who generally entered into romantic and sexual relationships exclusively with males. Thus, the *mahu* themselves reflected gender-diversity, but their relationships with others reaffirmed a gendered, heterosexual norm of intimacy.[6]

However, some Pacific island cultures also included the *aikane* relationship, which denoted an intense bond between two men, sometimes between a person of chiefly status and a commoner. The *aikane* role differed from that of the *mahu* in that there was no gender-diversity, since the *aikane* otherwise manifested the gender congruous with their biological sex, and even married opposite-sex spouses with whom they reared children.

Though there is no doubt that many if not most *aikane* relationships included sexual relations, the culture was indifferent to whether or not sexual contact was involved and the fact that the traditional Hawaiian culture did not bother to take account of that issue further illustrates the difficulty of drawing parallels to Western cultural terms such as "gay" or "homosexual."[7]

South Asian *hijra* also do not fit the cultural norms of either gender. Hijra were formerly but somewhat erroneously equated with the European concept of "eunuch," though only a few hijra undergo castration or other genital surgery. Most hijra are biologically male (or hermaphroditic), but they consider themselves to be of a third gender. Their dress and linguistic forms follow female gendered patterns, often with conscious exaggeration. Hijra may live together in intimate family groups, but they also may be involved with men who are considered heterosexual. Some hijras may even "marry" a male intimate partner, though such marriages have not usually been formally recognized.[8]

In traditional China, same-sex relationships were never treated illegal or "sinful," though some Confucians argued that men should adhere to gender-assigned public social roles. Some Taoists argued that exclusive homosexuality was an "unbalanced" pairing of yang and yang, while others argued that every person contains some mix of yin and yang, so individual same-sex relationships might still be "balanced." During the millennial span from the Song to the Qing dynasties, same-sex relations, especially those between men, were publicly practiced and expressed in art and literature without significant censure or even much concern. A Chinese practice of "sworn sisterhoods" continued into the twentieth century, in which two women would contract legal binding agreements of mutual intimacy and support, perhaps even including an agreement to provide joint support of children. The Golden Orchid movement of marriage resisters in the late nineteenth- and early-twentieth century was considered even in its day to be associated with lesbian sexuality, sometimes in pairs and occasionally in intimate relations not limited to couples.[9]

In several parts of Africa, a practice of "woman marriage" existed into the early twentieth century, whereby a successful older childless woman contracted with a younger woman to have children. The older woman might be married to a man or might not. Among the Nuer of Sudan, for example, the "woman-husband" married her wife in exactly the same way as a man marries a woman. A male kinsman or neighbor would be engaged to conceive children with the wife, and perhaps to offer ongoing assistance to the couple and child. He may be rewarded for his service with a "cow of the begetting" at the time of the child's eventual marriage. A wealthy woman might have several wives and enjoy most privileges of a male head-of-household. Like any other husband, she could demand damages if a wife had relations with men without her consent. As the father of the children, she received "the cattle of the father," and her siblings would receive the other cattle, which go to the father's side in the distribution of bridewealth. The practice of "boy-wives" has also been noted among some African cultures, where an older male formally pairs with younger male via all the essential cultural protocols of marriage. Same-sex partnerships of these kinds became less acceptable by mid-twentieth century, particularly under pressure from Western missionaries and colonial governments.[10]

All these various traditional forms are a function of cultural tolerance for a degree of gender variety that only recently is beginning to reemerge in modern Western society. In most if not all societies, some children are found to exhibit a misalignment as to expected gender behavior and biological sex, often at a very young age. This misalignment is reflected through such things as clothing preferences and interests in forms of play and work associated with the opposite gender. The West generally has sought to redirect such children to the gendered behavior conventionally congruent with their biological sex. In other traditional societies, with a tolerant and a more capacious understanding of gender and personal identity, such children could grow into adulthood being accepted into a socially validated role reflecting their preferred personal identity not constrained by their biological sex.

In the period of Western colonial expansion and cultural imperialism, the more "modern" Americans and Europeans viewed both two-spirited individuals and their same-sex intimates as deviant and homosexual. Modern Westerners also were more rigid in demanding congruence between biological sex and gender behavior, and generally intolerant of males or females who do not adhere to gender norms. "Indeed, it has been argued that extreme homophobia is a distinctly Anglo-American trait."[11] Not surprisingly, contemporary indigenous and traditional peoples have been influenced by Western cultural patterns, and have become conflicted, if not overtly hostile, in their attitudes toward personal relationships between persons of the same-sex. For example, despite traditional recognition of "two-spirit" persons, a number of Native American tribes recently acted to limit legal marriage to one man and one woman. And, though the postapartheid South African Supreme Court has mandated equal rights to same-sex couples based on the country's new constitution which prohibits discrimination on the basis of sexual orientation, a significant faction within the governing African National Congress has labeled homosexuality un-African and criticized the movement to legalize same-sex marriages.

THE WEST'S OSCILLATING ATTITUDES TOWARDS GENDER DIVERSITY AND SAME-SEX RELATIONSHIPS

The story of the West's early acceptance of same-sex relationships is generally well-known; no one with even passing familiarity with the Greeks can ignore the fact that tolerance, even celebration, of same-sex intimacy is a Hellenic "traditional value" lurking beneath the surface of Western Judeo-Christian society. Christianity increasingly marginalized and persecuted such relationships, though they clearly continued to exist. As Rictor Norton, Dirk Jaap Noordam, and others have indicated, such relationships, sometimes denominated "marriages" by those involved, were known in most parts of early modern Europe.[12] The more controversial works of John Boswell on same-sex unions in premodern Europe makes the same point.[13]

Into the early twentieth century, many Western societies also had traditional arrangements in which intimate relationships of people of the same-sex were socially accepted, even if not formally recognized. With its "Molly houses" of the eighteenth century and its Victorian reputation as "Sodom on the Thames," London was well-established as a place that wrestled with conflicting impulses about same-sex intimacy. The phenomenon of "Boston marriages" or "Wellesley marriages" involving intense intimate relationships between two women, allowed such couples to live together, travel and socialize together, and generally provide mutual support as domestic partners. Sometimes these relationships included a degree of formal legal recognition through contract, joint property ownership, and trusts or wills. Though their relationships were treated as acceptable under the pretense that they were non-sexual (though some, even many, were lesbian relationships), such "women-identified women" existed outside the scope of conventional heterosexuality in a bond that functionally paralleled marriage. Early twentieth century Paris, for example, provided a haven for an outstanding community of same-sex couples, both French and expatriate. Gertrude Stein and Alice B. Toklas established a renowned literary and artistic salon, while nearby American journalist, Janet Flanner lived with her French girlfriend, Georgette LeBlanc, and American heiress, Natalie Barney and the poet, Renée Vivien also held court. Sylvia Beach and her lover, Adrienne Monnier were the proprietors of the Shakespeare & Company bookshop, legendary in the 1920s and 1930s as a home for the likes of James Joyce and Ezra Pound.

By the 1950s, urban enclaves in America and elsewhere were opening wherein same-sex couples could live relatively unmolested, if not completely freely. In San Francisco in 1955, Del Martin and Phyllis Lyon, a lesbian couple, joined with other lesbians to form the Daughters of Bilitis, a social club and activist organization that eventually spread to San Diego and Los Angeles, to Denver, Chicago, New Orleans, Detroit, and Cleveland, and to Philadelphia and New York. The Bilitis publication, *The Ladder*, first edited by Lyons, continued in circulation until 1970, and provided advocacy, advice, and community for lesbian and gay individuals and their families and supporters. As first president of the organization, Martin called for lesbian women to step out into the open and confront "the evils of ignorance, superstition, prejudice, and bigotry." As she wrote in the first edition of *The Ladder*, "Nothing was ever accomplished by hiding in a dark corner. Why not discard the hermitage for the heritage that awaits any red-blooded American woman who dares to claim it?"[14]

An important historical footnote: After living in a committed relationship for fifty-five years, Del Martin and Phyllis Lyon were married in June 2008, the first same-sex couple married in San Francisco in the aftermath of the California Supreme Court's decision mandating the recognition of equal marriage rights. In a sign of how far things had changed, San Francisco Mayor Gavin Newsome officiated. In August 2008, Del Martin died at the age of eighty-seven.[15]

RECOGNITION OF EQUAL MARRIAGE RIGHTS

The eventual recognition of equal marriage rights by several national governments, and by the American states of Massachusetts, Vermont, Iowa, New Hampshire, and Connecticut (and the contested recognition by California), was made inevitable given that the debate over same-sex marriage is taking place at a time in which the very nature of marriage has been undergoing dramatic changes in the West, and, to some extent, elsewhere in the world. The changes in the lived experience of marriage, concomitant changes in legal institutions of marriage and family law, and the broader pressure toward equality in civil and political rights made it increasingly difficult throughout Western society to deny the logic of equal marriage rights.

The twentieth century saw a series of profound changes in the social norms that define the roles and behavior of married couples. Andrew Cherlin and others have noted that the traditional "institutional marriage," which gave priority to the social and even economic interests of the family and the community, gave way to the notion of "companionate marriage," which prioritized the emotional interests of the couple, and then to the "individualized marriage," which emphasized personal choice and self-development. This was reflected in the rise of divorce and its rapid social acceptance, and in the increase in the number and variety of cohabiting relationship, ultimately including same-sex relationships.[16] Given such fundamental changes in the very nature of marriage, the impulse toward same-sex marriage has become increasingly hard to resist. However, with superficial irony but perfect predictability, these fundamental changes in the practical realities of heterosexual marriage have been accompanied by a backlash against same-sex relationships and an increasing conviction as to the symbolic significance of the traditional vision of marriage.

As William Eskridge argues in *The Case for Same-Sex Marriage*, once the focus of marriage is on interpersonal commitment, denying same-sex couples the right to marriage cannot be seen as anything other than denying gays and lesbians the same rights that heterosexuals enjoy. Interestingly, some critics of same-sex marriage actually agree with this point, and explicitly argue for a return to an institutional conception of marriage. For example, conservative California Assembly Member Tim Leslie has argued that "if the central purpose of marriage is the spouses' happiness . . . then heterosexual-only wedlock is indeed discrimination." But, he goes on, the belief that "the overriding purpose of marriage is the spouses' mutual pleasure," the belief that "companionship and sexual pleasure are matrimony's preeminent ends," seems to him a deviation "from what every culture in history has recognized as the heart of marriage: the begetting and education of children." Though this might be disappointing to his constituents, Leslie insists that individual "'happiness' produces no definitive benefit for society, whereas the rearing of children clearly does," so that "it makes sense for society to support traditional marriage alone," and "allowing same-sex spousal unions makes no sense."[17]

In addition to changes in the social purpose of marriage, the stigma against same-sex relationships is slowly eroding in the face of the modern gay rights movement, as well as experience and research that demonstrates that same-sex couples are not inferior to, or even much different from, heterosexual couples.[18] "Overall, research paints a positive picture of gay and lesbian couples and indicates that they tend to be more similar to than different from heterosexual couples."[19] There are few differences in terms of the various factors indicative of relationship health, and, where differences do exist, they more often reflect better functioning within same-sex couples. That is, compared to married heterosexual couples, gay and lesbian couples tend to share household chores more fairly and resolve conflict more constructively. This seems to be true even when couples move into parenting. That is, the relationships of gay and lesbian couples change to accommodate the presence of children in essentially the same ways as those of heterosexual couples. Similarly, research in developmental psychology has consistently shown there are no significant differences between children raised by lesbian and gay couples and those raised by heterosexuals. Such empirical research served to confirm the general public's increasing experience with (if not comfort with) neighbors, friends, and coworkers in same-sex relationships. This eventually helped smooth the path toward changes in laws relating to sodomy statutes, discrimination in the workplace, and hate crimes, and these inevitably led to further demands for equality and full civil rights.[20]

Many jurisdictions proceeded in a somewhat piecemeal fashion to extend legal benefits to those in same-sex relationships. Several jurisdictions graduated to offering more complete recognition in the form of so-called "civil unions" or other domestic partnership alternatives. Many have complained that such alternatives were not a legal victory for same-sex couples. Instead, such alternative arrangements cannot help but cement an imbalance between same-sex and heterosexual couples. For example, a close examination of the rhetoric of those touting such alternatives often betrays a sense of apprehension and even fear as the ultimate, underlying rationale for refusing to put same-sex relationships on the same grounds as officially sanctioned marriages. Rather than prepare the ground for the eventual acceptance of equal marriage rights, such inferior arrangements validate the dominant society's fears of gay and lesbian identity, and continue to trumpeting heterosexual primacy.[21] Eskridge and other advocates, on the other hand, argued that societies may need to get comfortable with some sort of intermediate institution (like registered partnerships or civil unions) before they can become tolerant of same-sex marriage.[22]

Marriage equality continued as an important goal, even in places like California and Connecticut, where alternative legal arrangements offered same-sex couples virtually all benefits the state offered via legal marriage. Indeed, while the research confirms that gay men and lesbians form committed relationships and parent successfully, it also indicates that the very denial of marriage rights does disadvantage same-sex couples. After all, legally and socially sanctioned marriage does provide significant tangible and intangible benefits in terms of social, cultural, legal, economic, and political advantages. Obviously, many same-sex couples feel the same emotional need that heterosexual couples do to have society recognize their commitment to each other. They also seek the security and financial benefits provided through the hundreds of legal advantages automatically available through heterosexual marriage. Even through complex and expensive alternative legal arrangements under contract and property law, same-sex couples may not be fully able to share health and retirement benefits, take bereavement leave after a death in the family, file joint tax returns, benefit under property and inheritance laws, or visit loved ones in medical facilities. In addition, many same-sex families include children, whether the biological offspring of one of the partners or adopted, and require the protections and obligations of marriage under family law.

Same-sex marriage advocates parallel their cause with the earlier struggle to permit interracial marriage. Eventually, societies rejected the putative equality of antimiscegenation laws that prohibited the marriage of a white to a person of color. Same-sex couples similarly seek the freedom to choose equally between male and female partners. The so-called "equal application" argument accepted in many cases permitting bans on same-sex marriage parallels an argument rejected in the U.S. Supreme Court decision in *Loving v. Virginia* (1967), (e.g., that a race-based ban that applies equally to blacks and whites is not a denial of equal protection because it applies to everyone.) Thus, some have argued, a ban on same-sex marriage applies to all persons equally, both straight and gay. To follow this line of argument, however, is to accept that social and legal discrimination is unobjectionable so long as it is equal, rather than to reject discrimination as wrongful in and of itself without significant justification. The context of racism, as the Court in *Loving* to its credit found, casts a shadow over the virtue of equality in marriage discrimination, tarnishing it; similarly, so too does the context of heterosexism or heteronormativity cast a shadow over any positive valence equality likewise brings to the denial of same-sex marriage to both gay persons and nongay persons.

An opposite approach, initially most common among libertarians, but recently including centrists like legal scholar Douglas Laycock[23] and religious scholar Tony Campolo,[24] argues that the state should get out of the business linking legal benefits to any religious sacrament. Instead, the state should offer only civil recognition to all relationships, including those of heterosexual couples, leaving religious consecration a private affair. Some American states, such as New Jersey and Vermont, as well as foreign jurisdictions such as Denmark, have established a legal status (often labeled "civil union") for same-sex couples (and sometimes heterosexual unmarried partners) that have essentially all the legal attributes of marriage without the word. However, no such jurisdiction has eliminated legal "marriage" for heterosexual couples so as to put same-sex couples on an equal footing with opposite sex couples.

Some gay rights activists and scholars such as Michael Warner and Jeff Redding have cautioned that the fight for same-sex marriage may leave those who do not want to subject their intimate personal relationships to regulation by the state without a basis for claiming social respect or legal protection. Furthermore, they and others note, even where there has been relative tolerance for or recognition of same-sex relationships, this did not mean an acceptance of all varieties of intimate relations. Often, tolerance extends only to those relationships that parallel stereotypical heterosexual monogamous pairs.

Critics such as Warner argue the priority should be on making certain legal benefits now connected with marriage available to those in nontraditional relationships, whatever their orientation, or in no conventionally recognizable relationship form at all. He complains that a "sexual shaming" lurks behind the quest for same-sex marriage, making it consistent with efforts to close down bathhouses, stigmatize nonmonogamous sexuality, and in some cases, impede safe-sex education by foreclosing discussion about healthy forms of nonmonogamous relationships.[25]

Redding has argued, in a related fashion, that while many involved in same-sex intimacies want to identify as "gay," some do not, and that this is especially common in the non-Western world. Many such persons do not necessarily understand same-sex attraction as first and foremost a sexual identity, such that "their gayness or homosexuality is deeply interwoven with personal experiences" and understandings of religion and culture.[26] Redding argues that this means, among other things, that a hegemonic personal law which privileges couples who at least aspire to permanence in a state-sanctioned marriage may well be inconsistent with the very dignity for all that so many see as the central value in the pursuit of marriage equality.[27]

THE BACKLASH AGAINST MARRIAGE EQUALITY

Fundamentalist religious movements have largely spearheaded the traditionalist backlash against legal benefits for same-sex relationships.[28] Some claim religious law only permits heterosexual marriage. Others insist that the government's interest in marriage is solely in promoting (and regulating) procreation, which they argue justifies refusing marriage to same-sex partners. This backlash has resulted in legislation and constitutional provisions prohibiting a jurisdiction from giving marriage benefits to same-sex couples. Several American states and the U.S. federal government have enacted prohibitions or severe limits on extending marriage beyond heterosexual pairs,

and sometimes, as in the cases of Virginia and Wisconsin, even banned civil
unions and domestic partnerships. This is not unique to the United States.
Other countries, including Latvia, Poland, and Lithuania, also have recent
enactments limiting benefits available to those other than heterosexual pairs,
and most countries allow for neither civil unions nor same-sex marriages.

The arguments have some impact in the popular debates, but tend to fair
less well in legal and academic realms. This is in part because religious traditionalists and other so-called conservatives (Andrew Sullivan and Dale Carpenter would challenge the label) who would exclude same-sex couples from
marriage have to maintain a rather untenable set of propositions. They argue
that marriage is (1) good for the people who are married in myriad ways, and
(2) good for society because it sustains personal relationships and supports
healthy child rearing, but (3) becomes bad for society when same-sex couples
and their families are involved. The obvious question is how sustaining some
relationships and supporting some families produces a social good, while
sustaining other relationships and other families produces a social harm.[29]

Some "anti" social observers and political activists analogize same-sex
families to heterosexual adoptive or stepparent families. They suggest that
there is some research and some reason to believe that such families are less
stable and less successful in terms of child development, and that same-sex
couples may exhibit similar patterns. Even if true, the analogy begs the question of what justifies extending marriage to heterosexual blended and stepparent families but denying it to same-sex families. This is especially problematic given that blended and stepparent families of heterosexual couples
will always vastly outnumber those of same-sex couples. Similarly, assisted
reproduction is a practice dominated by infertile heterosexual couples.[30] If
two parent biological bonds are to be preferred by law, the greatest brunt of
such a ban must fall on heterosexual couples — but, of course, there is essentially no one pushing for that.

The "anti" argument also needs to confront the fact that same-sex families
have always existed, and exist even more openly in modern society, and there
is no reason to expect that genie is going back in the bottle. An estimated
1.5 million adults live as same-sex couples, and approximately one million
children currently live in families with same-sex parents. The "anti" proponents face a high hurdle in trying to prove why the benefits of married family
life must be denied to these adults and their children. How great a showing
of benefit to the children of heterosexual couples would be required to justify denying the benefits of married family life to the children of same-sex
couples? Indeed, could such an argument even be morally entertained? The
"anti" argument is at best a form of "malign neglect," argues Dale Carpenter:
"I really suspect that many traditionalists do not give much thought at all to

the needs of gay families. If they think about these things at all, they wish it would simply go away. But it is not going away."[31]

Furthermore, as Carpenter, Andrew Sullivan, and others have noted, extending the right to marriage to same-sex couples is much more likely to change those couples than to change the behavior of heterosexual couples. As Carpenter has stated: "Marriage is not a reward for good behavior, but an inducement to it."[32] The customs and laws of marriage function as a set of carrots and sticks and are designed to induce spouses to be more committed, and all the evidence is that these inducements work. There is every reason to believe, and increasing empirical evidence which proves, that these inducements work on same-sex couples just as they work on heterosexual couples.

And how serious is the prospect, central to the opposition's case, that the existence of same-sex marriage will materially harm the marriages of heterosexual couples? Is there any reason to think that heterosexual couples will think less of their own relationships, will have less affection for their spouses and children, or take less seriously their legal and customary obligations, simply because same-sex couples are offered the same opportunity for legal marriage? Again, the increasing empirical evidence shows no such impact, and logic alone suggests that the inevitably small fraction of families formed by same-sex couples makes the prospects of these alleged threats even less plausible.

THE CURRENT EVOLVING LANDSCAPE

Beginning with Denmark's recognition of civil unions in 1989, countries and jurisdictions throughout the world, especially in the advanced industrial democracies, have begun to establish legal recognition for relationships between same-sex couples. Full marriage rights were extended to same-sex couples in the Netherlands, in 2001, and shortly thereafter in Belgium, Spain, Canada, and South Africa. The Supreme Courts of Massachusetts, California, Iowa, and Connecticut, and the legislatures in Vermont, Maine, and New Hampshire concluded that same-sex marriage could not be denied under their respective state constitutions—after prolonged controversy and debate.

Other forms of civil recognition, some nearly identical to marriage without the name and some with substantially less benefits, have been established. By the first decade of the twenty-first century, civil recognition of same-sex relationships was available in Andorra, Argentina, Brazil, Columbia, Croatia, Czech Republic, Denmark, Finland, France, Germany, Iceland, Israel, Luxembourg, Mexico, New Zealand, Norway, Portugal, Slovenia, Sweden, Switzerland, and the United Kingdom; the Australian state of Tasmania, and the states of Hawaii, Maine, Oregon, Washington, Nevada, New Jersey, and Vermont; and the city of Washington, D.C., California, and Connecticut had also extended such recognition, which played a significant role in the state courts' conclusion that denying the word "marriage" to same-sex relationships was discriminatory. The European Parliament and European Courts of Human Rights have extended principles of nondiscrimination to same-sex couples and their families, which might lead to further extensions of rights and benefits within the European Union in future years.

Thus, by the final years of the twentieth century, the West had lost much of its hostility toward same-sex relationships. Same-sex couples seemed less alien and threatening as they became more familiar—in pop culture if not in terms of personal experience. Criminal prosecutions were firmly interred, and benefits under civil law were increasingly well-established. By the early years of this century, substantial and significant domestic partnership benefits in both public law and private law was unremarkable, and "civil unions" or some other marriage-like legal recognition was increasingly acceptable. Full marriage equality, though still legally uncommon, had become something of a social commonplace, and the subject of common and largely sympathetic and supportive presentation in Western popular culture. When American television talk-show darling Ellen Degeneres could ask then President Bush's daughter if she could use the First Family's ranch for her upcoming same-sex nuptuals, to the roaring applause of a delighted audience, there would appear to be no turning back.

However, despite all the celebrations of same-sex nuptials, some caution is in order. As noted above, global generalizations about cultural patterns and traditions regarding same-sex relationships are a difficult business. Yet the treatment of same-sex relationships in the modern world does illustrate an ironic truth: respect for those in same-sex relationships not only does not threaten civilization, the reality is that intolerance for such relationships is a marker of those places where uncivilized behavior is most institutionalized. For example, that modern Iran and Afghanistan, the homelands of traditional Persian mystical *ghazals* celebrating same-sex eroticism, are now one of the few places where gay men risk execution. Europe and America, which once had exported their relatively modern antipathy toward gender diversity and hostility toward same-sex relations through a century of colonialism and cultural imperialism, now offer extensive legal recognition and benefits, if not outright marriage equality, to same-sex couples. Without getting into causes, and at the risk of ethnocentrism, the places in the world today where "civilization" flourishes—where the arts and sciences are most productive and innovative, where representative democracy and republican values are most secure, where the rule of law is most often respected—are the very places where same-sex relationships are most tolerated. And the reverse also obtains; where the highest values of human civilization are most imperiled and human development least secure, intolerance of same-sex relationships is at a peak. Same-sex relationships are a sort of modern "miner's canary"; where the right to secure and celebrate family and intimate partnership are not equally available, it is there that civilization is truly at risk.

NOTES

1. Ford, Clellan S. and Frank A. Beach. 1951. *Patterns of Sexual Behavior*. New York: Harper.

2. Davis, D. L. and R. G. Whitten. 1987. "The Cross-Cultural Study of Human Sexuality." *Annual Review of Anthropology* 16: 69–89.

3. Though the term "berdache" is a generic term, still commonly used by anthropologists, it is increasingly rejected by Native Americans and other tribal peoples, who object to the term's etymological roots as a reference to a "kept" prisoner or boy forced into sexual service. It has widely been replaced with "two-spirit." Jacobs, Sue-Ellen, et al. 1997. *Two-spirit People: Native American Gender Identity, Sexuality, and Spirituality*, Champaign, Ill.: University of Illinois Press.

4. Jacobs, 1997.

5. Allen, Pamela Gunn. 1992. *The Sacred Hoop: Recovering the Feminine in American Indian Traditions*. Boston: Beacon Press.

6. Morris, Robert. 1990. "Aikane: Accounts of Hawaiian Same-sex Relationships in the Journals of Captain Cook's Third Voyage (1776–80)." *Journal of Homosexuality* 19(4): 21–54; Davis and Whitten, 1987.

7. The traditional relative tolerance of same-sex relationships among Native Hawaiians renders somewhat ironic the public backlash against the Hawaiian Supreme Court's 1989 decision in *Baehr v. Lewin*, which held that equal protection guarantees extended to same-sex couples. The decision was "overruled" in 1997 by a public referendum amending the state constitution.

8. Nanda, Serena. 1998. *Neither Man Nor Woman: The Hijras of India*. Belmont, Calif.: Wadsworth Publishing.; Davis and Whitten, 1987.

9. Lau, M. P. and M. L. Ng. 1989. "Homosexuality in Chinese Culture." *Culture, Medicine, and Psychiatry* 13(4): 465–88.; Ng, Vivien. 1989. "Homosexuality and the State in Late Imperial China," in *Hidden from History: Reclaiming the Gay and Lesbian Past*, eds. Martin Duberman, et al. New York: New American Library, 76–89. Ng, Vivien. 1997. "Looking for Lesbians in Chinese History," in *A Queer World, the Center for Lesbian and Gay Studies Reader*, ed. Martin Duberman. New York: New York University Press, 199–204.

10. Evans-Pritchard, E. E. 1951. *Kinship and Marriage among the Nuer*. Oxford: Clarendon Press.; Davis and Whitten, 1987.

11. Davis & Whitten, 1987, 80.

12. Norton, Rictor. 2006. *Mother Clap's Molly House: The Gay Subculture in England* 1700-1830. 2nd ed., London: The History Press Ltd.; Noordam, Dirk Jaap.

1989. "Sodomy in the Dutch Republic, 1600–1725" in *The Pursuit of Sodomy: Male Homosexuality in Renaissance and Enlightenment Europe*, eds. Kent Gerard and Gert Hekma. New York: Harington Park, 207–28. See also Kaplan, Morris. 2005. *Sodom on the Thames: Sex, Love, and Scandal in Wilde Times*. Ithaca, N.Y.: Cornell University Press.

13. Boswell, John. 1981. *Christianity, Social Tolerance, and Homosexuality: Gay People in Western Europe from the Beginning of the Christian Era to the Fourteenth Century*. Chicago: University of Chicago Press. Boswell, John. 1994. *Same-Sex Unions in Premodern Europe*. New York: Villard Books.

14. Gallo, Marcia M. 2006. *Different Daughters: A History of the Daughters of Bilitis and the Rise of the Lesbian Rights Movement*. Philadelphia: Seal Press.

15. *Id.*

16. Cherlin, Andrew J. 2004 "The Deinstitutionalization of American Marriage," *Journal of Marriage and Family* 66 (4): 848–61.

17. Leslie, Tim. 2004. "The Case Against Same-Sex Marriage," *Crisis: Politics Culture and the Church* (January 8, 2004); available at www.crisismagazine.com/january2004/leslie.htm.

18. See, for example, Herdt, Gilbert and Robert Kertzner. 2006. "I Do, but I Can't: The Impact of Marriage Denial on the Mental Health and Sexual Citizenship of Lesbians and Gay Men in the United States," Sexuality Research and Social Policy 3(1): 33–49; Herek, Gregory M. 2006. "Legal Recognition of Same-Sex Relationships in the United States: A Social Science Perspective." American Psychologist 61(6): 607–21; Kurdek, Lawrence A. 2006. "Differences Between Partners From Heterosexual, Gay, and Lesbian Cohabiting Couples." Journal of Marriage and Family 68(2): 509–28; Kurdek, Lawrence A. 2004. "Are Gay and Lesbian cohabiting couples really different from heterosexual married couples?" Journal of Marriage and Family 66(4), 880–900; Mathy, Robin M., Shelly K. Kerr, and Barbara A. Lehmann. 2004. "Mental Health Implications of Same-Sex Marriage: Influences of Sexual Orientation and Relationship Status in Canada and the United States." Journal of Psychology & Human Sexuality 15(2/3): 117–41.

19. Kurdek, Lawrence A. 2005. "What Do We Know About Gay and Lesbian Couples?" *Current Directions in Psychological Science* 14(5): 251–54.

20. The impact, or nonimpact, of recognizing same-sex relationships in Scandinavia has been thoroughly studied. See M. V. Lee Badgett, "Will Providing Marriage Rights to Same-Sex Couples Undermine Heterosexual Marriages? Evidence From Scandinavia and the Netherlands," Council on Contemporary Families and Institute for Gay and Lesbian Studies, July 2004, and William N. Eskridge, Darren R. Spedale, and Hans Ytterberg, "Nordic Bliss? Scandinavian Registered Partnerships and the Same-Sex Marriage Debate," *Issues in Legal Scholarship*, available at www.bepress.com/ils/iss5/art4/ Cf. Stanley Kurtz, "No Nordic Bliss," *National Review Online*, February 28, 2006, available at article.nationalreview.com/?q=NmNlNWYxNmZjMjVjNjEzYjdhODAwYmFiYTUwMWQyMTM

21. Thomas, Susan L. 2005. "In Search of a More Perfect Heteroarchy: Vermont, Civil Unions and the Harm of 'Separate-but-Equal,'" *Journal of Homosexuality* 50 (1), 27–51.

22. Eskridge Jr., William and Darren Spedale. 2006. *Gay Marriage: For Better or For Worse?* New York: Oxford University Press; see also the extensive discussions of this by Andrew Sullivan in various works, beginning with Sullivan, Andrew. 1995. *Virtually Normal: An Argument about Homosexuality*. New York: Knopf.

23. Laycock, Douglas. 2008. "Afterword," in Douglas Laycock, Anthony M. Picarello, and Robin Fretwell Wilson, eds., *Same-Sex Marriage and Religious Liberty*, Lanham, Md.: Rowman & Littlefield.

24. Campolo, Tony. 2008. *Red Letter Christians: A Citizen's Guide to Faith and Politics*, Ventura, Calif: Regal Books.

25. Warner, Michael, 1999. *The Trouble with Normal: Sex, Politics, and the Ethics of Queer Life*. New York: The Free Press.

26. Redding, Jeff. 2006. "Human Rights and Homo-Sectuals: The International Politics of Sexuality, Religion, and Law," *Northwestern Journal of International Human Rights*, 4(3), 436–92.

27. Redding, Jeff. 2008. "Slicing the American Pie: Federalism and Personal Law" *New York University Journal of International Law and Politics*, 40(4): 941–1018.

28. Cox, Cece. 2005. "To Have and To Hold—Or Not: The Influence of the Christian Right on Gay Marriage Laws in the Netherlands, Canada, and the United States." *Law & Sexuality* 14: 1–50.

29. Carpenter, Dale, Robert Nagel, Andrew Koppelman, and Amy Wax. 2008. *The Federalist Society Online Debate Series: Same-sex Marriage*, (August 6, 2008, available at www.fed-soc.org/debates/dbtid.24/default.asp); see also Carpenter, Dale. 2005. "Bad Arguments Against Gay Marriage," *Florida Coastal L. Rev.* 7: 181.

30. As Andrew Koppelman has argued, "Such families are being formed, in states with and states without same-sex marriage, and mostly by heterosexuals. All that denying same-sex marriage does is prevent some (not all, or even most) children begotten by assisted reproduction from having married parents." He suspects that those opposed to same-sex marriage must "have some causal scenario in mind about how denying same-sex marriage will make this situation better," but concedes, "since I can't tell what that scenario is, I can't respond to it." Carpenter, et al., 2008.

31. Carpenter, 2008.

32. Carpenter, 2008.

2

Looking for Liberty and Defining Marriage in Three Same-Sex Marriage Cases

Karen Struening[1]

The legal debate over same-sex marriage reveals a judiciary deeply divided over both constitutional interpretation and definitions of family.[2] This chapter examines how state supreme court justices look for liberty and define marriage in three same-sex marriage cases: *Goodridge v. Public Health,*[3] *Hernandez v. Robles,*[4] and *Andersen v. King County.*[5] I argue that divisions between justices on substantive due process methodology are mirrored by their disagreements over the meaning of marriage. This is because how justices conduct substantive due process analysis and define the institution of marriage is largely based on the value they ascribe to personal autonomy—or to the ability of individuals to think independently and to express and define themselves. Justices who favor expanding constitutional protections so that same-sex couples can marry understand marriage as a choice-based, identity-shaping association.[6] In contrast, justices who support exclusive marriage laws define marriage as a legal mechanism for regulating procreation and promoting a biological model of family.[7] In the former case, justices stress the importance of individuals making their own choices regarding intimate associations, including marriage. In the latter case, justices place greater value on the state's power to uphold traditional social institutions and to express the moral beliefs of the majority.

The best way to unravel how state court justices look for liberty is to examine how they respond to two Supreme Court cases, *Washington v. Glucksberg,*[8] a 1997 decision that upheld a Washington state statute outlawing physician-assisted suicide, and *Lawrence v. Texas,*[9] a 2003 decision that struck down a Texas law criminalizing same-sex sodomy. These two cases lay out contrasting methods for conducting substantive due process analysis.

Glucksberg adopts a strict two-tier system of review that makes it quite difficult to expand constitutional protections for liberty.[10] *Lawrence* rejects much of *Glucksberg* and inaugurates what Nan Hunter has called a "new approach to substantive due process."[11] Justices who want to avoid expanding constitutional recognition of liberty interests follow *Glucksberg*'s methodology very closely.[12] How liberal justices look for liberty is a bit harder to pin down but owes a great deal to Justice Kennedy's iconoclastic substantive due process analysis in *Lawrence*. While *Glucksberg* makes expanding protection for formally unrecognized liberties all but impossible,[13] *Lawrence* allows for restrictive statutes to be struck down without requiring the finding of a fundamental right.[14]

Reliance on the substantive due process analysis of *Glucksberg* in same-sex marriage cases has allowed *Bowers v. Hardwick*, the infamous 1986 decision which upheld a Georgia antisodomy law, to rear its ugly head.[15] While *Lawrence* sternly warns that private same-sex sexual activity is as worthy of respect as different-sex sexual activity,[16] *Bowers* describes the liberty interests in same-sex sexual activity as entirely foreign to those protected in cases such as *Griswold v. Connecticut* and *Roe v. Wade*.[17] While *Lawrence* holds that the state's interest in perpetuating the morality of the majority cannot serve as a legitimate reason for upholding Texas's antisodomy statute,[18] *Bowers* holds that it can.[19] By following *Glucksberg* in the same-sex marriage cases, conservative state supreme court justices return us to the logic of *Bowers* and reject the strong emphasis that *Lawrence* places on personal autonomy in intimate relationships. Moreover, by adopting *Bowers'* position that the state has the authority to promote a particular family form, conservative state court justices disregard current family law which has expanded legal protection for nontraditional families.[20]

From the early 1990s through 2008, nine state courts of highest jurisdiction ruled on whether exclusive marriage laws are constitutional. In 1993, the Supreme Court of Hawaii ruled that a Hawaii statute excluding same-sex couples from marriage violated the equal protection clause of the Hawaii constitution on grounds of sex.[21] This decision was nullified in 1998 by a state constitutional amendment that gave the legislature the power to restrict marriage to different-sex couples.[22] In 1999 the Vermont Supreme Court ruled that same-sex couples cannot be deprived of the statutory benefits and protections afforded to different-sex couples who choose to marry.[23] Vermont now provides same-sex couples with civil unions, which include all state-level rights and benefits attached to marriage.[24] In 2003, ten years after the Hawaii ruling, the Massachusetts Supreme Judicial Court determined that the state of Massachusetts cannot deny same-sex couples the right to marry.[25] In the same year, courts of highest jurisdiction in the states of New York and

Washington found that restricting marriage to different-sex couples does not violate their respective constitutions. In *Hernandez v. Robles*, the New York Court of Appeals affirmed a lower court decision that denied same-sex couples the right to marry.[26] In *Andersen v. King*, the Washington Supreme Court reversed trial court decisions that found Washington's 1998 Defense of Marriage Act (DOMA) unconstitutional.[27] In 2006, the New Jersey Supreme Court essentially went the way of Vermont, holding that same-sex couples are entitled to all of the rights and benefits attached to marriage.[28] The New Jersey Court left it up to the legislature to decide if the remedy would be to expand marriage to include same-sex couples or to implement a form of civil union; the legislature took the latter option.[29] In 2007, the Maryland Court of Appeals determined that restricting marriage to a man and a woman did not violate the Maryland state constitution.[30] On May 15, 2008, California became the second state to find exclusive marriage laws unconstitutional.[31] On October 10, 2008, the Connecticut Supreme Court ruled that gay and lesbian couples are entitled to full marriage rights.[32] However, on November 4, 2008, a closely decided ballot measure in California excluded same-sex couples from the right to marry by revising the California Constitution.

This paper will focus on *Goodridge*, *Andersen* and *Hernandez*. These three cases aptly illustrate the distinctions I wish to explore between justices who favor and oppose marriage equality. Plaintiffs in all three cases argue that state marriage statutes violate their fundamental rights to equal protection and due process of the law under their respective state constitutions. In *Hernandez* and *Washington*, the New York Court of Appeals[33] and the Supreme Court of Washington State employed *Glucksberg's* two-tier system of review to determine how their state marriage statutes would be evaluated. According to this doctrine, if the Court finds that the plaintiffs' fundamental rights have been violated under either the Equal Protection Clause or the Due Process Clause, it will apply strict scrutiny to the statute in question. The majorities in *Hernandez* and *Andersen* held that: (1) same-sex couples do not qualify as a suspect class on the basis of sex or sexual orientation and (2) the constitutionally recognized right to marriage does not include a right to same-sex marriage. They therefore declined to use strict scrutiny and instead invoked a conventional version of the rational basis test. Prior to *Romer v. Evans*[34] and *Lawrence*, which together initiated a much tougher form of rational basis review, statutes not subject to strict scrutiny were typically upheld. According to the more conventional rational basis review, exemplified by *Glucksberg*, the Court need only find a rational relationship between a state interest and the statute in question. *Hernandez* and *Andersen* determined that state marriage laws that exclude same-sex couples serve the legitimate state purposes of regulating procreation and protecting the welfare of children.

Consequently, limiting marriage to different-sex couples does not violate their respective state constitutions.

In contrast, the majority in *Goodridge* found that limiting marriage to different-sex couples violates the Massachusetts Constitution.[35] The Massachusetts Supreme Judicial Court determined that the constitutionally protected right to marry includes the right to marry the person of one's own choice.[36] However, while the Court recognized that a fundamental right had been violated, it declined to make its ruling on the basis of strict scrutiny. Instead, influenced by *Lawrence*, the Goodridge Court held that applying heightened scrutiny was unnecessary because even under the far less stringent rational basis review, Massachusetts' marriage law could not be upheld.[37] The Court determined that excluding same-sex couples from marriage did not serve a legitimate state purpose.

This paper proceeds in the following way: In part I, Looking for Liberty: *Glucksberg* and *Lawrence*, I describe two very different models of substantive due process analysis and the consequences that follow from adopting one over the other. In part II, Looking for Liberty: *Goodridge, Hernandez,* and *Washington*, I argue that justices writing against marriage equality closely follow the substantive due process doctrine laid out in *Glucksberg*. In contrast, those writing in favor of marriage equality depart from *Glucksberg* in significant ways, and adopt important elements of *Lawrence*. In part III, Marriage's Meanings, I discuss how justices on both sides of the same-sex marriage issue define marriage and link these strikingly different conceptions of marriage to how justices look for liberty.

PART ONE

Looking for Liberty I: Substantive Due Process Analysis in *Glucksberg* and *Lawrence*

Justice Rehnquist, writing for the majority in *Glucksberg*, and Justice Kennedy, writing for the majority in *Lawrence*, both hold that the Due Process Clause of the Fourteenth Amendment protects procedural as well as substantive liberties.[38] This means that individuals are accorded the rights necessary to ensuring a fair judicial process. However, it also means that specific liberties, some of which have a textual basis in the Bill of Rights and others of which do not, are recognized as deserving constitutional protection. In both *Glucksberg* and *Lawrence*, the majority opinion recognizes a line of cases, stretching from *Meyer v. Nebraska*[39] to *Planned Parenthood v. Casey*[40] that protect substantive liberties or as Kennedy puts it the "substantive dimensions" of liberty.[41] What the two justices, who frequently find themselves on the same side of a judicial decision, disagree about is how to identify which liberties are protected by the Fourteenth Amendment.

In *Glucksberg*, the Court was asked to determine whether a Washington statute banning physician-assisted suicide violates the Due Process Clause. To answer this question, the Court had first to identify the liberty interests at stake in the case. Justice Rehnquist, writing for the majority, rejects characterizations of the right in question offered by respondents ("liberty to choose how to die," a right to "control one's final days," "the liberty to choose a humane, dignified death" and "the liberty to shape death").[42] He also objects to the way justices writing concurring opinions framed the liberty interests in question.[43] Justice O'Connor suggests the right question to ask is "whether a mentally competent person who is experiencing great suffering has a constitutionally cognizable interest in controlling the circumstances of his or her imminent death."[44] Justice Stevens asserts that individuals have a liberty interest in "[a]voiding intolerable pain and the indignity of living one's final days incapacitated and in agony."[45] Rehnquist opts for a considerably more narrow definition: "a right to commit suicide which itself includes a right to assistance in doing so."[46]

The conflict over whether rights should be defined narrowly or broadly is part of a larger debate over the Court's role in protecting individual rights. Rehnquist's substantive due process analysis in *Glucksberg* begins with the assumption that identifying "new rights" is something to be avoided.[47] According to Rehnquist, the due process clause presents justices with a temptation that some cannot resist—the opportunity to provide the liberties they personally value with constitutional protection.[48] To avoid this temptation, Rehnquist advises describing liberty interests in a manner that closely resembles the conduct that is forbidden by the statute being examined.[49] Once a "careful description" of the liberty interest in question has been formulated, the task of the Court is to determine whether it qualifies as a fundamental right.[50] Rehnquist explains: "we have regularly observed that the Due Process Clause specially protects those fundamental rights and liberties which are, objectively, 'deeply rooted in this Nation's history and traditions' and 'implicit in the concept of ordered liberty such that neither liberty nor justice would exist if they were sacrificed.'"[51] If a liberty interest passes the "deeply rooted" test the statute in question will be subject to strict scrutiny and only a statute based on a compelling state interest that is narrowly tailored to fit its purpose can be allowed to stand.[52] If, on the contrary, a survey of U.S. history and tradition finds little reason to think the liberty interest in question has been recognized as a fundamental right in the past, the statute will be subject to rational basis review. Here the question is whether the statute bears a rational relationship to a legitimate state interest.[53] According to standard

due process doctrine, rational basis review implies a high level of deference
to the state and as a result statutes subject to rational basis review are almost
always upheld.

   Rehnquist explicitly rejects the idea that claims brought on the basis of personal autonomy are worthy of constitutional protection. He denies that there
is common ground between the privacy cases and *Glucksberg*. Commenting
on plaintiffs' efforts to identify the liberty interests at issue in *Glucksberg*
with those in *Casey*, Rehnquist warns: "That many of the rights and liberties
protected by the Due Process Clause sound in personal autonomy does not
warrant the sweeping conclusion that any and all important, intimate, and
personal decisions are so protected, and *Casey* did not suggest otherwise."[54]
Defining rights narrowly makes it difficult to identify a continuum of liberty
interests grounded in the importance of personal autonomy.

   Justice Souter, while concurring with the majority's holding in *Glucksberg*,
provides an extensive critique of Rehnquist's substantive due process analysis.
Souter's opinion features Justice Harlan's advice on how to conduct substantive
due process analysis in *Poe v. Ullman*.[55] In his famous dissent, Harlan asserts
that looking for liberty cannot be reduced to a formula or code.[56] He argues
instead for balancing "the liberty of the individual" and the "demands of an
ordered society," adding that the "balance of which I speak is the balance struck
by this country, having regard to what history teaches are the traditions from
which it developed as well as the traditions from which it broke."[57] Harlan's
call for examining traditions "from which it broke," warns justices that not all
important liberty interests will have a historical pedigree. Because history is full
of examples in which specific classes of people have been denied their rights,
expanding constitutional protection for liberty will involve recognizing rights
that are not "deeply rooted" in American traditions.

   Justice Souter recommends that liberty interests be described broadly so
that their relationship to constitutionally protected principles can be determined.[58] He also shifts the emphasis of substantive due process analysis from
whether a right can be declared fundamental to whether the state has placed
arbitrary constraints on liberty.[59] By diminishing the importance of whether a
right is "deeply rooted in our Nation's history and traditions" and increasing
the importance of whether the state has acted reasonably, Souter undermines
the distinction between strict scrutiny and rational basis review. He claims
that without the finding of a fundamental right, legislation that arbitrarily and
irrationally constrains an important liberty interest can be struck down.

   Nan Hunter suggests we view *Lawrence* as Kennedy's attempt in collusion
with Souter (and Stevens) to rework standard substantive due process doctrine so that it does not place an intractable barrier in the way of expanding
our understandings of liberty. According to Hunter, in *Lawrence*, Kennedy

engages in the Harlan-inspired arbitrariness review recommended by Souter in his dissent to *Glucksberg*. She writes:

> The *Lawrence* opinion marks a new majority for Harlan's arbitrariness review, in substance if not in name. Justice Kennedy (who had joined Chief Justice Rehnquist's opinion in *Glucksberg*) extended substantive due process protection without declaring that the right at issue was fundamental, although the opinion details at great length the ambiguity surrounding the legal history associated with sodomy laws. The logic of the analysis in *Lawrence* largely tracks that of Justice Souter's concurring opinion in *Glucksberg*, combining the inquiry into whether the government's justification was reasonable with consideration of the nature and the weight of the individual interests asserted.[60]

Hunter claims that Kennedy's adoption of a "new approach to substantive due process analysis" stems from his realization "that the conservative wing of the party has fought to enshrine the category of fundamental rights as a containment device."[61] According to Hunter, decisions such as *Glucksberg* show that the language of fundamental rights, the deeply rooted test and the distinction between strict scrutiny and rational basis review are being deployed to avoid the expansion of substantive rights. In addition, noting the absence of privacy language in *Lawrence*, Hunter and others suggest that the three justices may be in search of a substantive due process analysis that replaces the right to privacy with a new emphasis on liberty.[62]

Like Souter, Kennedy rejects narrow characterizations of liberty interests. Comparing *Lawrence* with the 1986 decision upholding the criminalization of same-sex sodomy, Kennedy condemns Justice White's description of the liberty interest in *Bowers* as "the right to engage in homosexual sodomy."[63] Kennedy explicitly overrules *Bowers* in *Lawrence* and accuses Justice White of failing to understand the "extent of the liberty at stake"[64] in the case. Kennedy also downplays the conventional distinction between strict scrutiny and rational basis review. While recognizing that plaintiffs have a "right to liberty under the Due Process Clause" that "gives them the full right to engage in their conduct without intervention of the government," Kennedy never uses the term fundamental right.[65] Instead, Kennedy identifies the kinds of liberty interests that are at stake when a law prohibits certain kinds of sexual conduct between consenting adults in the privacy of the home.[66] Kennedy argues that sex acts can not be separated from meaningful relationships and that while not all sex acts involve or evolve into relationships, the two are necessarily intertwined.[67] A narrow characterization of the liberty interests at stake in sexual activity blinds us to the true impact of sodomy laws. According to Kennedy, the liberty interest at stake in *Bowers* and *Lawrence* is not the right to engage in homosexual sodomy but the right to exercise autonomy in intimate relationships.[68]

Kennedy's description of the liberty interests at stake in *Lawrence* is similar to Justice Blackmun's in *Bowers*.[69] In his dissenting opinion, Blackmun states, "all individuals have a liberty interest in controlling the nature of their intimate associations."[70] Blackmun's definition universalizes the right at issue, and makes clear that all individuals, regardless of sexual orientation, have a liberty interest in making their own decisions about their personal lives and intimate relationships. This definition of the liberty interests at issue in *Bowers* allows comparisons to be drawn between *Bowers* and earlier cases, such as *Griswold* and *Roe*, which emphasized the individual's ability to make life-shaping personal decisions about intimate relationships.[71] In contrast, Justice White's majority opinion in *Bowers* explicitly rejects any connection between *Bowers* and other privacy cases by insisting that *Griswold* and *Roe* were about marriage, family, and procreation, and that there can be no connection between these socially sanctioned and legally protected institutions and homosexual sexual activity.[72] White essentially defines gay men and lesbians as "family outlaws," foreshadowing the distinctions between same-sex and different-sex couples that will be drawn by the *Andersen* and *Hernandez* majorities.[73]

Kennedy establishes a strong connection between the liberty interests at stake in *Lawrence* and those that are central to the right to privacy cases. He states that the series of cases stretching from *Griswold* to *Casey* guarantee "constitutional protection for personal decisions relating to marriage, procreation, contraception, family relationships, child rearing, and education."[74] Kennedy tells us that in all of these cases, the question is one of "the respect the Constitution demands for the autonomy of the person in making these choices."[75] Kennedy dwells on the important passage in *Casey* where O'Connor bases the right to terminate a pregnancy on the necessity of protecting individuals' ability to think freely and arrive at their own conceptions of life's meaning. By emphasizing the importance of independent self-expression and self-definition, Kennedy draws out the positive, affirmative dimensions of the right to privacy. As Nancy Marcus has noted, *Lawrence* highlights "not only a negative right to be let alone but an affirmative right to equal respect and autonomy in intimate relationships that transcends the spatial spheres of the home."[76] *Lawrence* builds on, while going beyond, the privacy cases by suggesting that government owes individuals more than a pledge not to interfere in their private lives; it also owes them equal respect for the acts of self-definition involved in forming intimate relationships.

In identifying common ground between *Lawrence* and the privacy cases, Kennedy jettisons the privilege accorded to heterosexual marriage and heterosexuality in *Bowers* and stresses the similarity between different-sex and same-sex relationships. In essence, Kennedy looks beyond the form to the function that intimate relationships play in the lives of individuals. He admonishes us to value relationships not because they conform to history, tradition, or the majoritarian morality but because of the role they play in our lives. Because they benefit individuals in the same essential ways, the state should treat all intimate relationships that are consensual and do not involve harm with equal respect.[77]

In the opening sentences of *Lawrence*, Kennedy suggests that substantive liberty cannot be reduced to a list of acts deserving of constitutional protection.[78] This reductionism, which Lawrence Tribe has called a "naming game,"[79] would violate Justice Harlan's warning that the liberty guaranteed by the Due Process Clause cannot be found in or limited by the precise terms of the specific guarantees elsewhere provided in the Constitution. "This 'liberty' is not a series of isolated points picked out in terms of the taking of property; the freedom of speech, press, and religion; the right to keep and bear arms; the freedom from unreasonable searches and seizures; and so on. It is a rational continuum which, broadly speaking, includes freedom from all substantial arbitrary impositions and purposeless restraints. . . ."[80]

Kennedy suggests that liberty must be viewed as a unitary concept based on the value we ascribe to autonomy: "Liberty presumes an autonomy of self that includes freedom of thought, belief, expression, and certain intimate conduct."[81] In some cases, we may be concerned with speech and in others, we may be concerned with sexual conduct, but at base what we are protecting is "autonomy of self" in activities or areas of life that are essential to identity and happiness.

After identifying the liberty interest at the heart of *Lawrence* as the right to exercise autonomy in intimate relationships, Kennedy turns to the question of whether the state can proscribe consensual and private sexual activity between same-sex couples. He finds the Texas statute unconstitutional because it "furthers no legitimate state interest which can justify its intrusion into the personal and private life of the individual."[82] In doing so, Kennedy sidesteps the more standard substantive due process analysis affirmed in *Glucksberg*, which would require the finding of a fundamental right and the application of strict scrutiny in order to strike down a state law. Instead he follows Souter's call to strike down laws that arbitrarily restrict individual liberty.[83]

Kennedy also rejects the claim that history, tradition, or the promotion of the morality of the majority supply Texas with a legitimate interest in regulating same-sex sexual conduct. He does this by reviewing Justice White and Justice Burger's use of history and Judeo-Christian values to uphold Georgia's

anti-sodomy law in *Bowers*. After providing a brief history of the criminalization of sodomy in the United States, in which he shows that antisodomy laws
targeted all non-procreative sexual conduct and not just same-sex conduct,
Kennedy concludes that "the historical grounds relied upon in *Bowers* are
more complex than the majority opinion and the concurring opinion by Chief
Justice Burger indicate."[84] He goes on to assert that "History and tradition are
the starting point but not in all cases the ending point of the substantive due
process inquiry."[85] Most relevant to the present inquiry, Kennedy explains, is
the past half century, during which we can see "an emerging awareness that
liberty gives substantial protection to adult persons in deciding how to conduct
their private lives in matters pertaining to sex."[86] Kennedy echoes Harlan's
injunction that we look not only to our nation's traditions but also to the traditions we have broken from by stating: "times can blind us to certain truths and
later generations can see that laws once thought necessary and proper in fact
serve only to oppress."[87]

Taking history as our guideposts, as Rehnquist advises us to do in
Glucksberg,[88] frequently means allowing majoritarian values and norms to
determine which liberties are recognized and constitutionally protected. The
deeply rooted test essentially assumes that before a new right can be protected
under the Due Process Clause it must be recognized as an old right. But when
rights are defined narrowly finding historical precursors can be difficult. That
is why expanding constitutional protection for liberty requires defining rights
broadly as Kennedy does in *Lawrence*. The description of rights in which
Kennedy engages highlights the interest in autonomy of self that lies behind
specific acts, and establishes connections between specific liberty interests
and constitutionally protected values.

My aim in contrasting substantive due process analysis in *Glucksberg* and
Lawrence has been to show that while following the former makes it difficult
to expand constitutional protection for liberty, *Lawrence* provides a new and
more expansive approach to substantive due process analysis. A review of
these two decisions also demonstrates that while Rehnquist rejects personal
autonomy as a constitutionally protected value, Kennedy embraces it. Kennedy identifies a liberty continuum based on the principle that individuals
are entitled to respect by their government for the choices they make regarding their intimate relationships. In addition, while Kennedy is eager to draw
on connections between *Lawrence* and earlier cases involving autonomy in
intimate life, Justice White in *Glucksberg*'s predecessor, *Bowers*, rejects any
connection between same-sex sexual conduct and "marriage, family, and
procreation." In the next section, I will look at how justices deciding marriage equality cases have responded to the contrasting ways *Glucksberg* and
Lawrence look for liberty.

PART TWO

Looking for Liberty: *Goodridge, Hernandez,* and *Washington*

The majority opinions in *Andersen* and *Hernandez*, as well as the dissent in *Goodridge*, closely follow the method of due process review conducted by Rehnquist in *Glucksberg*. They first reduce the right in question to an act involving a specific class of people—marriage between same-sex couples—and then look to history and tradition to see if it has been protected in the past. By defining the right in question in relationship to a group that has been despised and discriminated against, these justices guarantee that it will not meet the deeply rooted test. In addition, justices writing against the constitutionality of same-sex marriage avoid exploring the liberty interests at issue in the right to marry. They deny that there is any link between the interests at stake in cases such as *Griswold, Roe, Casey* and *Lawrence* and the liberty interests of individuals in same-sex relationships who desire to marry.

At first glance, it might seem as if justices writing in favor of the constitutionality of same-sex marriage hew fairly close to the *Glucksberg* decision as well. Unlike Justice Kennedy in *Lawrence*, the majority in *Goodridge* and the dissenting justices in *Hernandez* and *Andersen* employ the language of two tier review and fundamental rights and are explicit about whether they are using a strict scrutiny or rational basis test. But they follow *Lawrence* by (1) defining rights broadly, (2) replacing the deeply rooted test with the criterion of arbitrary state action, and (3) emphasizing personal autonomy in intimate relationships. Thus, while appearing to adopt *Glucksberg's* substantive due process methodology, *Goodridge* and the dissents in *Hernandez* and *Andersen* depart from it in important ways.

The Right to Marry

Substantive due process analysis in same-sex marriage cases generally begins with the acknowledgement that marriage is a fundamental right recognized by the Supreme Court in several twentieth-century precedents such as *Turner v. Safley*,[89] *Skinner v. Oklahoma*,[90] *Zablocki v. Redhail*,[91] *Loving v. Virginia*,[92] and *Griswold v. Connecticut*.[93] In *Goodridge* and in dissents to *Andersen* and *Hernandez*, justices writing in favor of same-sex marriage claim that the constitutionally protected right to marry includes "the right to marry the person of one's own choice." This formulation is drawn from the California antimiscegenation case, *Perez v. Sharpe*, in which the California Supreme Court found that "the essence of the right to marry is freedom to join in marriage with the person of lone choice."[94] By analogy to *Perez* and the 1967 Supreme Court case *Loving v. Virginia*,[95] which struck down all state antimiscegenation laws, justices writing in favor of the constitutionality of same-sex marriage argue that the right to marry includes the right to marry the person of one's choice and that just as race cannot be used to prevent an individual from marrying the person he or she chooses, neither can sexual orientation.[96]

The majority opinions in *Hernandez* and *Andersen*, as well as the dissent in *Goodridge*, recognize the constitutionally protected right to marry. However, they argue that there is no relationship between this well-established right and the entirely new one that plaintiffs wish to have protected. According to the majority opinions in *Hernandez* and *Andersen*, as well as the dissent in *Goodridge*, the right at the center of their cases is not the right to marry the person of one's choice but the right to same-sex marriage. These justices view this right as distinct from the right to marry, which they understand to be derivative of or based on the right to procreation.[97] The right to marry does not, on their reading, include a right to marry the person of one's choice, regardless of gender or sexual orientation. Indeed, they claim that far from being embedded in the right to marry, the right to marry someone of the same-sex is an entirely new right.

The difference between defining the right at the center of these cases as the right to same-sex marriage or the right to marry the person of one's choice may at first glance appear to be mere semantics. But given that *Hernandez*, *Andersen*, and the dissent in *Goodridge* follow the method of due process analysis used in *Glucksberg*, how the right at the center of a case is formulated makes all the difference. After defining the right in question narrowly and in reference to a specific class of persons, the New York and Washington courts ask if this right is "deeply rooted in our Nation's history and traditions?" The New York court arrived at the following answer: "The right to marry is unquestionably a fundamental right. The right to marry someone of the same sex, however, is not 'deeply rooted'; it has not even been asserted until relatively recent times."[98] The Washington court found that only the right to marry someone of the opposite sex has been recognized as fundamental in the past: "The vast majority of states historically and traditionally have contemplated marriage only as opposite-sex marriage, and the majority of states, including Washington, have recently reaffirmed this understanding and tradition. Federal decisions have found the fundamental right to marry at issue only where opposite-sex marriage was involved."[99] Determining that the right to same-sex marriage is not fundamental or constitutionally protected allows the *Andersen* and *Hernandez* majority and the dissent in *Goodridge* to apply rational basis review to the marriage statutes of their respective states. According to *Glucksberg*, justices are obligated to defer to the legislature when it comes to determining whether there is a rational relationship between a state interest and the state statute in question.[100] The majorities in *Andersen* and *Hernandez* and the dissent in *Goodridge* held that limiting marriage to different-sex couples is consistent with the state interests in regulating procreation and fostering child well-being.[101]

Justice Fairhurst, dissenting in *Andersen*, objects to both how the majority defines the right in question and the majority's assertion that plaintiffs are asking for recognition of an entirely new right. Justice Fairhurst accuses the plurality and concurrence in Andersen of "artificially limiting" the inquiry into what liberty interests are at stake in the case by defining the right in question as the "fundamental right to same-sex marriage."[102] Referencing *Lawrence's* critique of Bowers, Justice Fairhurst states: "United States Supreme Court precedent has taught us again and again that framing the inquiry into a constitutional right in such a narrow way misunderstands and undermines the value of the right at stake."[103] Justice Fairhurst argues that past Supreme Court cases took care to define rights in the broadest possible manner in order to protect the liberty interests in question:

> In *Meyer v. Nebraska* and *Pierce v. Society of Sisters*, the Court considered whether there was a fundamental right to decisions in educating one's children, not whether there was a fundamental right to have your children learn German or attend a private school. Likewise, in *Skinner v. Oklahoma ex rel. Williamson*, the Court asked whether there was a fundamental right to be free from unwarranted government intrusion into decisions whether to have children, not whether a convicted criminal had a fundamental right to reproduce. In *Zablocki* and *Turner*, the Court considered whether there was a fundamental right to be free from unwarranted governmental intrusion in decisions to marry, not whether delinquent fathers or inmates had a fundamental right to marry. Perhaps most relevant and important here, in *Loving* the Court asked whether there was a fundamental right to marry, not whether there was a fundamental right to interracial marriage.[104]

Justice Fairhurst's analysis of past cases shows that when rights are narrowly defined, it is difficult to appreciate the extent and importance of the liberty that is being lost. At first glance, it may not be immediately apparent what is at stake when the state prohibits the teaching of German. Is there a fundamental right to teach one child German? Is it a right that is deeply rooted in our Nation's history and traditions? In contrast, *Meyer's* formulation of the liberty interests at stake highlights the relationship between parent and child and the parents' interest in making choices about their child's education. It is not a singular act—the learning of a particular language—that is at stake, but the parents' interest in transferring their cultures and values to their child.

Chief Justice Kaye, dissenting in *Hernandez*, also references *Lawrence* and its criticism of *Bowers*. Kaye writes: "Indeed, in recasting plaintiffs' invocation of their fundamental right to marry as a request for recognition of a 'new' right to same-sex marriage, the Court misapprehends the nature of the liberty interest at stake."[105] Justice Kaye goes on to explain that by describing the right to marry in terms of a class of people who historically have been treated as family outcasts the justices guarantee that no support for it will be found. She writes: "The Court concludes, however, that same-sex marriage is not deeply rooted in tradition, and thus cannot implicate any fundamental liberty. But fundamental rights, once recognized, cannot be denied to particular groups on the ground that these groups have historically been denied those rights."[106] Justice Kaye argues that a decision in favor of the constitutionality of same-sex marriage would not create a new right. Instead, it would create universal access to a right already recognized as fundamental. Kaye sees a clear analogy between laws denying the right to marry on the basis of race and those that deny it on the basis of sexual orientation. She argues against the deeply rooted test by pointing out that if it had played the same central role in the antimiscegenation cases as it was allowed to play in *Hernandez*, *Loving* would have upheld the prohibition on interracial marriage.[107]

Both Fairhurst and Kaye argue that rights should not be defined in relationship to a specific class of people. Doing so suggests that the group's liberty interests are particular as opposed to universal and that the group is seeking a special right as opposed to one that other groups already enjoy.[108] For example, as we have seen, in *Bowers*, the majority defined the right at stake as the right to commit homosexual sodomy. In contrast, Blackmun's dissent defined it as an interest in controlling one's intimate associations, an interest that is shared by all people. Justice White's definition stressed the particularity of same-sex sexual activity, while Blackmun's emphasized what same-sex and different-sex couples have in common. Defining the right at the center of the same-sex marriage cases as "the right to marry the person of one's own choice" identifies what straight and gay people have in common: within each group there are many people who hope to find a soul mate, make a commitment to him or her and create a future together.

Goodridge **and** *Arbitrariness Review*

Goodridge follows many aspects of *Lawrence* while retaining some of the language of *Glucksberg*. The majority distinguishes between rational basis and strict scrutiny review, but after declaring that the fundamental right to marry includes the right to marry the person of one's choice, declines to employ strict scrutiny. The Massachusetts Court explains: "Because the statute does not survive rational basis review, we do not consider the plaintiffs' arguments that this case merits strict judicial scrutiny."[109] Like *Lawrence*,

Goodridge asks whether the state has gone too far in restricting an important liberty interest: "The liberty interest in choosing whether and whom to marry would be hollow if the Commonwealth could, without sufficient justification, foreclose an individual from freely choosing the person with whom to share an exclusive commitment in the unique institution of civil marriage."[110] *Goodridge* conducts a careful review of all the reasons the state forwards for exclusive marriage laws and rejects each one in turn.

According to *Goodridge*, the state's interest in regulating procreation is not rationally related to the exclusion of same-sex couples from marriage. Expanding marriage law to include same-sex couples will not decrease the number of different-sex couples that marry and have children.[111] *Goodridge* also argues that marriage cannot be reduced to an institution for regulating procreation. Marriage should be understood as a committed relationship between two people.[112] Hence, as I will explore more thoroughly in part III, the Massachusetts Court rejects the argument, employed by New York and Washington, that only those couples who can procreate biologically (and without assistance) should be allowed to marry.[113]

In addition, *Goodridge* finds that the state's interest in protecting the welfare of children is not advanced by prohibiting same-sex couples from marrying. According to *Goodridge*, excluding same-sex couples from marriage conflicts with state law and policy that protects the parenting rights of gay men and lesbians.[114] It makes little sense to bar same-sex couples from marriage on the grounds that it is preferable to raise children in households headed by heterosexual parents in a state that facilitates gay and lesbian parenthood. Indeed, the *Goodridge* Court concludes that the exclusion of same-sex couples from marriage is due to animosity toward gay men and lesbians.

The absence of any reasonable relationship between, on the one hand, an absolute disqualification of same-sex couples who wish to enter into civil marriage and, on the other, protection of public health, safety, or general welfare, suggests that the marriage restriction is rooted in persistent prejudices against persons who are (or who are believed to be) homosexual.[115]

After concluding its review of the state's reasons for limiting the right to marry to different-sex couples, *Goodridge* simply declares that exclusive marriage laws violate the state constitution.[116] Following *Lawrence*, *Goodridge* uses rational basis review to strike down state laws that arbitrarily restrict important liberty interests.

Personal Autonomy in Intimate Relationships

Goodridge and the dissents in *Andersen* and *Hernandez* also follow *Lawrence* by recognizing personal autonomy in intimate relationships as a key theme in

late twentieth and twenty-first century constitutional law. In much the same
way that Blackmun's dissent characterized the liberty interest in *Bowers* as
"the fundamental interest all individuals have in controlling the nature of their
intimate associations with others,"[117] Justice Fairhurst claims that her case is
about "the fundamental liberty interest in making one's own personal decisions relating to intimate partners."[118] Referencing *Griswold, Roe, Lawrence,*
and *Cruzan*, Fairhurst argues that "No choice could be more private, and
indeed fundamental, than the choice of marital partner."[119]

The *Goodridge* Court recognizes that individuals have a strong liberty
interest in decisions about relationships that transform identity: "the decision
whether and whom to marry is among life's momentous acts of self-definition."[120] By focusing on identity, the *Goodridge* Court links its case to both
Blackmun's dissenting opinion in *Bowers* and O'Connor's majority opinion
in *Casey*. Blackmun argues in *Bowers* that we form our identities through
our relationships with others, including our sexual relationships.[121] When we
are unable to freely choose our sexual partners, part of our ability to define
ourselves is lost. In *Casey*, O'Connor explains that the right to terminate a
pregnancy is ultimately rooted in personal autonomy. If the state were to ban
abortion based on one interpretation of when life begins, individuals would
not be at liberty to arrive at their own understanding of life's meaning. Their
identities would be formed "under compulsion of the State."[122]

In contrast, state supreme court justices writing against the constitutionality
of same-sex marriage frequently distinguish their cases from both *Lawrence*
and the privacy cases. They follow Rehnquist, who declared in *Glucksberg*
that due process analysis should not be reduced to granting protected status
to all decisions of a deeply personal nature.[123] For example, the *Goodridge*
dissent claims that the Supreme Court granted constitutional protection to
certain liberties in the privacy cases because they are "deeply rooted in our
nation's history and tradition"[124] and not because they involved personal autonomy in life-shaping relationships.

The majority in *Hernandez* uses the distinction between privacy's negative
and positive dimensions to distance *Hernandez* from *Lawrence*. According
to *Hernandez*, the liberty interest at stake in *Lawrence* should be defined as
the "right to privacy in intimate relationships."[125] The New York court denies
that this liberty interest has any relevance to those at stake in *Hernandez*. According to *Hernandez*, the plaintiffs in *Lawrence* sought "protection against
state intrusion on intimate, private activity," while those in *Hernandez* seek
"access to a state-conferred benefit that the Legislature has rationally limited
to opposite-sex couples."[126] The majority separates *Hernandez* from *Lawrence* and the entire line of privacy cases by severing the negative, "right to
be left alone" dimension of the right to privacy from its affirmative, "right

to autonomy and equal respect" dimension. The *Hernandez* majority fails to see how *Lawrence* and the privacy cases (in particular, *Casey*) go beyond a right against state intrusion. They require the state to respect the ability of individuals to think independently and to make their own choices regarding intimate relationships. *Lawrence* goes further still by consistently stating that same-sex and different-sex couples are owed equal respect for their decisions about intimate relationships. While it is true that *Lawrence* tries to set up a line between respecting choices and recognizing relationships, that line is hard to maintain given Kennedy's emphasis on government's obligation to provide equal respect to same-sex and different-sex couples.[127] The logic of *Lawrence* suggests that if the state extends the right to marry the person of one's choice to different-sex couples it must extend the same right to same-sex couples. As several commentators have mentioned, Kennedy's coupling of the equal protection clause with the due process clause makes *Lawrence* a much stronger decision.[128]

In part II, I have shown that while *Goodridge* and the dissents in *Andersen* and *Hernandez* do not completely reject substantive due process analysis as it is practiced in *Glucksberg*, they are much closer in spirit to *Lawrence*. Following *Lawrence*, these justices argue for expanding constitutional protection for personal autonomy in intimate relationships. In contrast, following *Glucksberg*, the majorities in *Hernandez* and *Andersen* provide judicial outcomes that are consistent with majoritarian norms and values. In part III, I explore how these different ways of looking for liberty map onto conceptions of marriage.

PART THREE

Marriage's Meanings

State supreme court justices discuss the meaning of marriage in two different sections of their opinions: The first is when they are conducting substantive due process analysis or looking for liberty. The second is when they are conducting rational basis analysis and reviewing the reasons the state has provided for excluding same-sex couples from marriage. Whether they are considering marriage from the state's or the individual's perspective, justices opposed to marriage equality consistently define marriage in terms of procreation. When conducting due process analysis, they argue that the right to marriage is based on a more foundational right to procreate; when conducting rational basis review they argue that exclusive marriage laws serve the legitimate state purposes of regulating procreation and promoting the welfare of children. This emphasis on procreation reveals a preference for a model of family consisting of two different-sex parents who have conceived their own children biologically without the use of fertility technologies or gestational contracts. I therefore use the term "biological approach" to capture how justices who favor exclusive marriage laws conceive of marriage.

When looking at marriage from the individual's perspective, justices who favor marriage equality define it as a choice-based association, emphasizing the individual's intention to create a shared way of life with another person. When conducting rational basis review, these justices reject the state's assertion that exclusive marriage laws are rationally related to the regulation of marriage. They accept the state's claim that it has a legitimate interest in creating stable homes in order to benefit children but reject its assertion that this interest justifies limiting the rights and benefits of marriage to different-sex couples. Instead, *Goodridge* and the dissents in *Hernandez* and *Andersen* hold that the welfare of children will best be met by expanding marriage to include same-sex couples. I refer to this approach to marriage as choice-based because it emphasizes the individual's interest in personal autonomy in intimate relationships.

The Biological Approach to Marriage

As we saw in part II, justices writing for and against marriage equality recognize a constitutionally protected right to marry. However, those who are opposed to expanding this right to include same-sex couples assert that marriage is a fundamental right because it protects collective and/or individual interests in procreation. For example, the *Andersen* Court states: "*Loving*, *Zablocki*, and *Skinner* tie the right [to marry] to procreation and survival of the race."[129] Justice Graffeo, concurring in *Hernandez*, argues that Supreme Court decisions highlight "the link between marriage and procreation" and that "to ignore the meaning ascribed to the right to marry in these cases and substitute another meaning in its place is to redefine the right in question and to tear the resulting new right away from the very roots that caused the U.S. Supreme Court and this Court to recognize marriage as a fundamental right in the first place."[130]

According to Cordy, dissenting in *Goodridge*, "Supreme Court cases that have described marriage or the right to marry as 'fundamental' have focused primarily on the underlying interest of every individual in procreation, which, historically, could only legally occur within the construct of marriage because sexual intercourse outside of marriage was a criminal act."[131] For these justices, once we scratch the right to marry, we find the right to procreate.

The question of whether the interest being protected by the right to marry is that of the human race or of the individual is an important one because a matter of general welfare, such as the survival of the human race, cannot serve as the basis for an individual right. The survival of the human race is the sort of collective good that the state is mandated to protect. In contrast, rights protect individuals from the possibility that a majority might define the collective good in such a way that the dignity and freedom of a class of individuals might be sacrificed.[132] If it is the survival of the race that is being protected as opposed to the individual's interest in bearing his or her own children, procreative interests cannot serve as the basis for the right to marry. Thus there is a basic flaw in how many of the justices writing against marriage equality define the right to marry. They confuse the individual's liberty interest in procreating with the state's interest in regulating and promoting procreation.

When discussing state interests and whether they justify exclusive marriage laws, the majority and the concurrence in *Hernandez* both adopt the "responsible procreation" argument first offered by an Indiana Appeals Court in *Morrison v. Standhal*.[133] According to the Indiana court, the primary purpose of the legal institution of marriage is to encourage natural procreators (e.g., fertile, different-sex couples) to conceive and raise children within a stable, state-sanctioned relationship. Different-sex and same-sex couples are not similarly situated in regards to procreation because the former conceives spontaneously and sometimes without much thought for the consequences, while the latter must employ in vitro fertilization or artificial insemination, adopt, or seek out a gestational surrogate. The Indiana Court reasons that since same-sex couples cannot have children without carefully planning for their conception or adoption, the state does not need to provide them with the same sort of incentives to marry as it does to natural procreators. While the state needs a mechanism for prodding different-sex couples into stable parenting partnerships, it need not worry about same-sex parents. They have had to invest a great deal of time, energy, and money into becoming parents and are likely to have carefully thought out this joint project.

Hernandez follows *Morrison's* argument for distinguishing between different and same-sex couples. Writing about same-sex couples, the majority states: "These couples can become parents by adoption, or by artificial insemination or other *technological marvels*, but they do not become parents as a result of accident or impulse."[134] Like the Indiana Court of Appeals, the New York court reasons that given what the state hopes to achieve with its marriage laws, it is unnecessary to allow same-sex couples to marry. While this may appear to be a backhanded compliment—same-sex couples are already responsible, we don't have to provide incentives to make them so—its effect is to privilege a biological conception of marriage and family.

This implicit preference for the biologically-based family is made more explicit in Justice Graffeo's concurring opinion in *Hernandez* and by the

Andersen majority. Justice Graffeo reduces the legal institution of marriage to the biological activity of procreation. He writes: "The binary nature of marriage—its inclusion of one woman and one man—reflects the biological fact that human procreation cannot be accomplished without the genetic contribution of both a male and a female."[135] Same-sex couples, who do not procreate naturally or without assistance, can be excluded from the legal institution of marriage because it mirrors a biological process in which they are unable to take part.

Graffeo's argument no longer holds true in an age that has seen considerable progress in the development of new fertility technologies. Unassisted, natural procreation is no longer the only way (indeed, never was the only way) to become a parent. Artificial insemination, in vitro fertilization, gestational contracts, and adoption have created forms of legal parenthood that are not based on a genetic tie. Graffeo's remarks assume that since human procreation requires genetic material from a male and a female, all children will necessarily have two, different-sex legal parents. However, courts in the United States do not accord parenting rights to anonymous sperm donors.[136] Children born to unmarried women who became pregnant using the services of a fertility clinic do not have legally recognized fathers. In addition, while Graffeo posits a seamless connection between genetic contribution, gestation, and parenthood, gestational contracts disrupt such a scenario. The existence of a growing and largely unregulated market in genetic material in the United States undermines Justice Graffeo's conception of procreation.

Andersen does not employ the responsible procreation argument. Instead, it simply accepts the state of Washington's preference for a biologically-based family.[137] Explaining why the state may exclude same-sex couples from marriage, the court explains: "The State reasons that no other relationship has the potential to create, without third-party involvement, a child biologically related to both parents, and the legislature rationally could decide to limit legal rights and obligations of marriage to opposite-sex couples." The Washington court adds: "But as *Skinner, Loving,* and *Zablocki* indicate, marriage is traditionally linked to procreation and survival of the human race. Heterosexual couples are the only couples who can produce biological offspring of the couple." However, these statements beg the question, why is a family that includes biological offspring more deserving of the state's protection than those who are not? Why should families created without "third-party involvement" be privileged over those that required the aid of fertility clinics, gestational surrogates or adoption agencies?

The language adopted by justices who employ the biological approach and the distinctions they make between different-sex and same-sex couples often suggest that the latter are somehow unnatural or abnormal. Different-sex couples are said to procreate "on their own," while same-sex couples require "third-party involvement;" different-sex couples are said to conceive naturally, while same-sex couples require "technological marvels;" different-sex couples conceive spontaneously and impulsively, same-sex couples are only able to reproduce with careful planning. This series of contrasts serves to uphold the historical and ontological primacy of the biologically-based family. Heterosexual families are historically primary because it is only recently that the general public has become aware that same-sex couples have and raise children together. They are ontologically primary because of their connection with the natural. While never explicitly stated, the implication is that since opposite-sex couples have children naturally and without the aid of technology, they are *meant* to have children. Same-sex couples, who are unable to conceive "on their own" are clearly not meant to procreate and form families. Those who do are derivative of the natural family, aping its form but incapable of creating families without legal (adoption, surrogacy) and medical (artificial insemination) help.

A legal definition of marriage that privileges the biological model of family assumes that the only basis of parenthood is genetic. This conflicts with general trends in family law that are moving away from biological and genetic understandings of family and toward more social and functional ones.[138] In cases involving the dissolution of same-sex relationships, courts are using doctrines such as *de facto* parenthood and parenthood by estoppel to recognize the rights of nonbiological parents.[139] In addition, more than half of states allow the nonbiological or second parent in a same-sex relationship to adopt his or her partner's child without requiring the biological parent (or primary adoptive parent) to give up his or her rights. Moreover, California courts have begun to employ the concept of intentional parenthood in some court cases. In a contested surrogacy case, the court reasoned that since it was the commissioning couple's intention to have a child that gave rise to the child's birth, they were entitled to be the child's legal parents.[140]

The development of fertility technologies and their use by different-sex and same-sex couples disrupts the assumptions on which the biological model of family is based. Parenthood is no longer strictly based on a genetic tie. The market in genetic material has allowed same-sex couples to reproduce and the state has recognized individuals as parents who have no marital connections to their partner (the biological parent) and no biological connections to their children. Given this general trend, it is striking that several state supreme courts have decided to place so great an emphasis on biology and the distinction between aided and unaided forms of procreation.

Choice-Based Marriage

As we saw above, justices writing against marriage equality argue that the Supreme Court has recognized the right to marry as fundamental because of collective and individual interests in procreation. However, there are several Supreme Court cases that provide non-procreative conceptions of marriage. For example, in *Griswold*, the Supreme Court held that married couples have a right to marital privacy that protects their freedom to use birth control. Far from basing the right to marriage on a fundamental right to procreation, this decision effectively separated marriage from procreation. Indeed, *Griswold* held that marriage is an expressive and identity-forming act of association. In Justice Douglas' famous words: "It is an association that promotes a way of life, not causes; a harmony in living, not political faiths; a bilateral loyalty, not commercial or social projects."[141] By describing marriage as an act of association, the *Griswold* Court emphasizes its foundation in the choice two people make to form a life together.

In *Turner v. Safley*,[142] a 1987 Supreme Court decision that struck down a Louisiana law prohibiting the marriage of inmates at a state prison, the Court acknowledged that during the inmate's confinement her marriage would not be consummated. However, it stressed that marriage has multiple meanings and identified emotional intimacy and the making of a public commitment as core attributes of marriage: "inmate marriages, like others, are expressions of emotional support and public commitment. These elements are an important and significant aspect of the marital relationship."[143] Once again, the Court stressed the idea that marriage is a commitment between two people to create an enduring bond as a couple, and not solely an institutional arrangement designed to secure "the survival of the race." *Turner* makes clear that we are guaranteed a right to marry not solely because of the benefits marriage secures for society but also because of those it brings to the individual.

State and federal antimiscegenation rulings identify the freedom to choose one's spouse as essential to the right to marry. In a 1948 California ruling, *Perez v. California*, the Court stated: "the essence of the right to marry is freedom to join in marriage with the person of one's choice."[144] In *Loving v. Virginia*, decided almost twenty years after *Perez*, the Supreme Court held that the liberty to choose one's marital partner is essential to personal happiness: "The freedom to marry has long been recognized as one of the vital personal rights essential to the orderly pursuit of happiness by free men."[145] In these decisions, it is the individual's ability to find happiness through affiliation with another person that defines marriage.

Like the Supreme Court's decision in *Griswold* thirty-eight years earlier, *Goodridge* defines marriage as a committed partnership or bilateral association. It explicitly rejects the argument that marriage is about procreation: "While it is certainly true that many, perhaps most, married couples have children together (assisted or unassisted), it is the exclusive and permanent commitment of the marriage partners to one another, not the begetting of children, that is the sine qua non of civil marriage."[146] Moreover, rather than understanding marriage in terms of the state's interest in regulating impulsive sexual behavior, *Goodridge* sees marriage as an act of affiliation and association that is self-transformative: "the decision whether and whom to marry is among life's momentous acts of self-definition."[147] Here, as in *Griswold*, *Turner* and the miscegenation cases, marriage is understood as a life-shaping choice of immense value to the individual. By harking back to *Griswold*, a case that was decided thirty-eight years ago and was then affirmed by *Eisenstandt*, *Roe*, *Casey*, and *Lawrence*, the choice-based approach anchors the right to marry the person of one's choice in established precedent. Defining marriage as an identity-shaping choice reveals what the same-sex marriage cases have in common with past cases that protect personal autonomy in intimate relationships.

Justices who employ the choice-based approach to marriage accept that the state has an interest in ensuring that children are raised in stable homes with parents who are committed to each other and that marriage is the main mechanism the state employs to create such homes. But they object to the claim that the rights and benefits of marriage should be given only to those couples who are able to procreate without assistance. Basing exclusive marriage laws on the distinction between assisted and unassisted procreation is arbitrary and irrational if the purpose of marriage laws is to create stable homes for children. Establishing a rational relationship between state interests and marriage laws requires expanding the right to marry to include same-sex couples.

Defining Marriage, Looking for Liberty

Justices writing in favor of marriage equality assume that choice—the choice to form a lifelong partnership—as opposed to "accidents and impulses"—is the true basis of marriage. This understanding of marriage is consistent with the way that these justices define the right at stake in their cases: the right to marry the person of one's choice. How they define marriage and how they define the liberty interests at stake in their cases have a common basis: respect for personal autonomy in intimate relationships.

Defining marriage in terms of choosing a life partner allows us to understand that gay and straight individuals have the same liberty interests in marriage. They both seek to find a person with whom they can create a shared way of life. The choice-based approach allows us to recognize that when marriage is defined as establishing a common way of life it has no intrinsic relationship to its traditional form: the union of one man and one woman. And once we see the commonality between same and different sex couples, it is difficult to think of the right to marry the person of one's choices as a radical redefinition of marriage or the creation of a brand new right.

Justices who adhere to the biological approach to marriage are unable to see that same-sex and different-sex couples have the same liberty interests in marriage. By defining marriage in terms of procreation and privileging the biological model of family, they erase what same-sex and different-sex couples have in common. As we have seen, they employ the distinction between unassisted and assisted conception to suggest that same-sex families are distant cousins of the real, biological family. Aping its form, they nonetheless cannot quite replicate the biological family in which both parents are genetically connected to their own children. Because their definition of marriage obscures what same-sex and different-sex couples have in common, justices who employ the biological approach define the right at stake in their cases in a narrow and particularistic way. It comes as no surprise to anyone that "the right to same-sex marriage" is not deeply rooted in our Nation's history and traditions.

CONCLUSION

The three state supreme court decisions I have examined reveal a judiciary starkly divided over substantive due process analysis and conceptions of marriage and family. Liberal justices see marriage as a choice-based association and define rights broadly, following the method of substantive due process analysis outlined in *Lawrence*. In contrast, conservative justices see marriage as a legal mechanism for regulating procreation and promoting the biological family. They define rights narrowly and adopt the substantive due process analysis of *Glucksberg*. While this chapter establishes a connection between how justices conduct substantive due process analysis and define marriage, I have purposively not argued that there is a casual relationship between the two. Divisions over how to look for liberty and define marriage are derivative of a larger philosophical difference over the extent to which individuals should exercise autonomy in their intimate relationships. Justices who value personal autonomy in intimate relationships are likely to employ a method of substantive due process analysis that allows for the expansion of constitutional protections for liberty. Those that place greater weight on maintaining traditional social institutions will follow a method that makes such an expansion unlikely.

What are the consequences of this split over recognizing personal autonomy in intimate relationships? Justices in favor of marriage equality have kept alive Kennedy's emphasis in *Lawrence* on "autonomy of self" in intimate relationships despite what legal commentators see as a trend in state and federal cases of ignoring *Lawrence*.[148] To the extent that *Goodridge* follows *Lawrence*, and I have tried to show that it does in significant ways, *Lawrence's* definition of liberty as a continuum that must be protected against arbitrary state action is strengthened. The vigorous dissents to *Andersen* and *Hernandez*, while having no value as precedent, nonetheless provide stirring calls for greater freedom in personal life and greater respect for lesbian, gay, bisexual, and transgendered (LGBT) families.

These cases also show that the use of *Glucksberg's* methodology in the same-sex marriage cases has revived *Bowers* and that despite Kennedy's heroic attempt in *Lawrence*, *Bowers* is far from dead. Indeed, justices writing against marriage equality employ the same reasoning that Justice White did in *Bowers*. Like White, they adopt traditional assumptions about what constitutes family life, and thereby allow majoritarian norms to determine judicial outcomes. What is perhaps somewhat surprising is the extent to which decisions like *Andersen* and *Hernandez* depend on a biological conception of family given widespread acceptance of fertility technologies. In order to deny lesbians and gay men recognition of their family relationships, conservative state supreme court justices have degraded all families conceived through the use of artificial insemination, in vitro fertilization, and surrogacy contracts. Their adoption of this model of family in the face of expanding legal recognition for nontraditional families indicates that interest groups that advocate government promotion of traditional family forms have the ear of the judiciary and will continue to be a political force. It also suggests that the question of whether individuals should be free to determine the form and meaning of their intimate relationships will remain one of the most contested questions of our time.

NOTES

1. I would like to thank my research assistant, Derek Wikstrom for his excellent work on this project.

2. In, *Hernandez v. Robles*, 855 N.E.2d 1 (N.Y. 2006) three justices formed the majority, Justice Graffeo wrote a concurring opinion but did not join in the majority opinion, two justices dissented, and one justice abstained. In *Andersen v. King County*, 158 Wn.2d 1 (Wash. 2006), the court was divided 5–4 in the judgment and the controlling opinion was written by a three judge plurality. In *Goodridge*, the court was divided 4–3 in the judgment and the controlling opinion was written by a three judge plurality.

3. *Goodridge v. Dep't of Pub. Health*, 798 N.E.2d 941 (Mass. 2003).

4. *Hernandez v. Robles*, 855 N.E.2d 1 (N.Y. 2006).

5. *Andersen v. King County*, 158 Wn.2d 1(Wash. 2006).

6. *Goodridge v. Dep't of Pub. Health*, 798 N.E.2d at 954 (Mass. 2003).

7. *Hernandez v. Robles*, 855 N.E.2d 1, 3–6 (N.Y. 2006).

8. *Washington v. Glucksberg*, 521 U.S. 702 (1997).

9. *Lawrence v. Texas*, 539 U.S. 558 (2003).

10. See, Lawrence H. Tribe, Lawrence v. Texas: The "Fundamental Right" that Dare Not Speak Its Name, 117 *Harv. L. Rev.* 1893, 1923–1925 (2004); Brian Hawkins, The Glucksberg Renaissance: Substantive Due Process Since Lawrence v. Texas, 105 *Mich. L. Rev.* 409 (2006).

11. Nan D. Hunter, Living with Lawrence, 88 *Minn. L. Rev.* 1103, 1105 (May 2004). (According to Nan Hunter, Kennedy's opinion can best be understood as "the convergence of various strands of a new approach to substantive due process, not yet a full-blown theory, but one which gels in his opinion more fully than it has before.").

12. Brian Hawkins, The Glucksberg Renaissance: Substantive Due Process Since Lawrence v. Texas, 105 *Mich. L. Rev.* 409 (2006). (Based on a survey of 102 cases, Hawkins claims the vast majority of appellate courts have followed Glucksberg and ignored Lawrence.).

13. *Id.* Nan D. Hunter, Living with Lawrence, 88 *Minn. L. Rev.* 1103, 1105 (May 2004).

14. Nan D. Hunter, Living with Lawrence, 88 *Minn. L. Rev.* 1103; Nancy C. Marcus, Beyond Romer and Lawrence: the Right to Privacy Comes Out of the Closet, 15 *Colum. J. Gender & L.* 355.

15. *Bowers v. Hardwick*, 478 U.S. 186 (1986).

16. *Lawrence v. Texas*, 539 U.S. 558, 567 & 578 (2003).

17. *Bowers v. Hardwick*, 478 U.S. 186, 191 (1986).

18. *Lawrence v. Texas*, 539 U.S. 558, 577-78 (2003).

19. *Bowers v. Hardwick*, 478 U.S. 186, 197 (1986).

20. Karen Struening, "Families 'In Law' and Families 'In Practice': Does the Law Recognize Families As They Really Are?" in ed., Barbara Risman, *Families As They Really Are* (New York: Norton, forthcoming); David D. Meyer, Parenthood in a Time of Transition: Tensions Between Legal, Biological, and Social Conceptions of Parenthood, *Am. J. Comp. L.* 125.

21. *Baehr v. Lewin*, 852 P.2d 44 (Hawaii 1993).

22. Hawaii Constitution, Article I, Section 23.

23. *Baker v. State*, 744 A.2d 885 (Vt. 1999).

24. 2000 Vt. Acts and Resolves 91.

25. *Goodridge v. Dep't of Pub. Health*, 798 N.E. 2d 941, 948 (Mass., 2003).

26. *Hernandez v. Robles*, 855 N.E.2d 1 (N.Y. 2006).

27. *Andersen v. King County*, 158 Wn.2d 1 (Wash. 2006).

28. *Lewis v. Harris*, 908 A.2d 196 (N.J. 2006).

29. *Id.* at 221.

30. *Conaway v. Deane*, 932 A.2d 571 (Md. 2007).

31. *In re Marriage cases,* S147999 (Calif. 2008).

32. *Kerrigan and Mock v. Department of Public Health* SC 17716 (Conn. 2008).

33. The New York State Court of Appeals is the name of the Supreme Court of the State of New York.

34. Romer V. Evans, 517 U.S. 620 (1996).

35. *Goodridge* 798 N.E.2d at 948.

36. *Goodridge* 798 N.E.2d at 958.

37. *Goodridge* 798 N.E.2d at 961.

38. *Washington v. Glucksberg*, 521 U.S. at 719-721 (1997) ("In a long line of cases, we have held that, in addition to the specific freedoms protected by the Bill of rights, the 'liberty' specially protected by the Due Process Clause includes the right to marry . . . "); *Lawrence v. Texas,* 539 U.S. 558, 565 (2003) ("Roe recognized the right of a woman to make certain fundamental decisions affecting her destiny and conformed once more that the protection of liberty under the Due Process Clause has a substantive dimension of fundamental significance in defining the rights of the person.").

39. *Meyer v. Nebraska*, 262 U.S. 390 (1923).

40. *Planned Parenthood of Southeastern Pennsylvania v. Casey,* 505 U.S. 833 (1992).

41. *Lawrence v. Texas*, 539 U.S. 558, 565 (2003).

42. *Washington v. Glucksberg*, 521 U.S. at 722-723 (1997).

43. *Id.* at 721–723.

44. *Id.* at 736 (O'Connor, J., concurring).

45. *Id.* at 745 (Stevens, J., concurring).

46. *Id.* at 723.

47. *Id.* at 720 ("But we 'have always been reluctant to expand the concept of substantive due process because guideposts for responsible decision making in this uncharted area are scarce and open-ended.' Collins, 503 U.S. at 125.")

48. *Id.*

49. *Id.* at 723.

50. *Id.* at 721.

51. *Id.* at 720–721, quoting *Moore v. City of East Cleveland*, 431 U.S. at 503 (1977).

52. *Id.* at 721.

53. *Id.* at 722.

54. *Id.* at 792.

55. *Id.* at 762-763 (Justice Souter, concurring).

56. *Poe v. Ullman,* 367 U.S. 497, 542 (1961) (Harlan, J., dissenting).

57. *Id.* at 542.

58. *Washington v. Glucksberg*, 521 U.S. at 765 (Justice Souter, concurring).

59. *Id.* at 761 (Justice Souter, concurring). ("the more durable precursors of modern substantive due process were reaffirming this Court's obligation to conduct arbitrariness review . . . ").

60. Nan D. Hunter, Living with Lawrence, 88 *Minn. L. Rev.* 1103, 1122 (May 2004).

61. *Id.* at 1119.

62. Lisa K. Parshall, Redefining Due Process Analysis: Justice Anthony M. Kennedy and the Concept of Emergent Rights, 69 *Alb. L. Review*. 237, 247 (2005) ("But whereas Griswold and its progeny centered on the constitutional right of privacy, Justice Kennedy's opinion in Lawrence revolved around the concept of liberty for which he had expressed a consistent preference.").

63. *Bowers v. Hardwick*, 478 U.S. 186, 190 (1986).

64. *Lawrence v. Texas*, 539 U.S. 558, 567 (2003).

65. *Id.* at 577.

66. *Id.* at 567.

67. *Id.* ("When sexuality finds overt expression in intimate conduct with another person, the conduct can be but one element in a personal bond that is more enduring. The liberty protected by the Constitution allows homosexual persons the right to make this choice.").

68. *Id.* at 573.

69. Kennedy quotes Stevens' dissent in Bowers, but not Blackmun's. This may be because Blackmun adopts the language of privacy.

70. *Bowers v. Hardwick*, 478 U.S. at 205 (1986).

71. *Griswold v. Connecticut*, 381 U.S. 479 (1965); *Roe v. Wade* 410 U.S. 438 (1973).

72. *Bowers v. Hardwick*, 478 U.S. at 191(1986).

73. See, Cheshire Calhoun, "Family Outlaws: Rethinking the Connections Between Feminism, Lesbianism and the Family," in *Feminism and Families*, ed. Hilde Lindeman Nelson (N.Y.: Routledge, 1997), 131–50.

74. *Lawrence v. Texas*, 539 U.S. at 574 (2003).

75. *Id.*

76. Nancy C. Marcus, Beyond Romer and Lawrence: the Right to Privacy Comes Out of the Closet, 15 *Colum. J. Gender & L.* 355–56 (2006).

77. *Lawrence v. Texas*, 539 U.S. at 578 (2003) ("The case does involve two adults who, with full and mutual consent from each other, engaged in sexual practices common to a homosexual lifestyle. The petitioners are entitled to respect for their private lives. The State cannot demean their existence or control their destiny by making their private sexual conduct a crime).

78. Lawrence Tribe, "Lawrence v. Texas: The 'Fundamental Right' that Dare Not Speak Its Name, 117 *Harv. L. Rev.* 1893, 1924–1925 (2004) ("The Glucksberg opinion does indeed put forth an effort to collapse claims of liberty into the unidimensional and binary business of determining which personal activities belong to the historically venerated catalog of privileged acts and which do not . . . "); Nan D. Hunter, Living with Lawrence, 88 *Minn. L. Rev.* 1103, 1118 ("Under the Glucksberg approach, fundamental rights constitute a frozen category and a limiting principle that operated to bar any meaningful protection for interests that could not meet its eligibility criteria."); Lisa K. Parshall, Redefining Due Process Analysis: Justice Anthony M. Kennedy and the Concept of Emergent Rights, 69 *Alb. L. Review*. ("Under Glucksberg's specific test, the discovery of new rights was virtually foreclosed; fundamental status was preserved for only those rights firmly embedded in the nation's history and tradition.").

79. Lawrence Tribe, "Lawrence v. Texas: The 'Fundamental Right' that Dare Not Speak Its Name, 117 *Harv. L. Rev.* 1893, 1922 (2004).

80. *Poe v. Ullman,* 367 U.S. 497, 542–43 (1961) (Harlan, J., dissenting).

81. *Lawrence v. Texas*, 539 U.S. at 562 (2003).

82. *Id.* at 578.

83. Lawrence Tribe, "Lawrence v. Texas: The 'Fundamental Right' that Dare Not Speak Its Name, 117 Harv. L. Rev. 1893, 1922 (Tribe argues that the fundamental claim in Lawrence is that "intimate relations may not be micromanaged or overtaken by the state.").

84. *Lawrence v. Texas*, 539 U.S. at 571 (2003).

85. *Id.* at 572, citing *County of Sacramento v. Lewis*, 523 U.S. 833, 857 (1998) (Kennedy, J., concurring).

86. *Id.*

87. *Id.* at 579.

88. *Washington v. Glucksberg*, 521 U.S. at 721 (1997).

89. 482 U.S. 78 (1987).

90. 316 U.S. 535 (1942).

91. 434 U.S. 374 (1978).

92. 388 U.S. 1 (1967).

93. 381 U.S. 479 (1965).

94. *Perez v. Sharp*, 198 P.2d 17 (Calif. 1948).

95. *Loving v. Virginia*, 388 U.S. 1 (1967).

96. *Goodridge v. Dep't of Pub. Health*, 798 N.E.2d 941, 958 (Mass. 2003); In her dissent to *Hernandez*, New York Court of Appeals Chief Judge Kaye (*Hernandez v. Robles*, 885 N.E.2d 1, 23 (N.Y. 2006) discusses *Loving* and arbitrary restrictions on the right to marry: "Under our Constitution, discriminatory views about proper marriage partners can no more prevent same-sex couples from marrying than they could different-race couples."

97. See part III.

98. *Hernandez v. Robles*, 855 N.E.2d 1, 9 (N.Y. 2006).

99. *Andersen v. King County*, 158 Wn.2d 1, 30 (WA 2006).

100. *Washington v. Glucksberg*, 521 U.S. 702, 721 (1997).

101. *Hernandez v. Robles*, 855 N.E.2d 1, 4-6 (N.Y. 2006), *Andersen v. King County*, 158 Wn.2d 1, 30 (Wash. 2006).

102. *Andersen v. King County*, 158 Wn.2d 1, 129 (Fairhurst, J., *dissenting*).

103. *Id.,* n.97.

104. *Id.* at 144–145 (citations omitted).

105. *Hernandez* 855 N.E.2d at 23 (Kaye, C.J., *dissenting*).

106. *Id.* at 23.

107. *Id.* at 24.

108. Chief Justice Alexander of the Supreme Court of Washington, concurring in *Andersen*, argues that special interests espousing political correctness are behind the call for expanding marriage to include same-sex couples: "The weighty record of history, overwhelming societal consensus, and the strong force of legal authorities from Washington courts and its legislature, as well as from the United States Supreme

Court, do not allow such a cavalier and arbitrary redefinition of marriage by a court. Though advanced with fervor and supported by special interests loudly advocating the latest political correctness, the arguments (and the dissenters) cannot overcome the plain legal and constitutional principles supporting Washington's definition of marriage." *Andersen v. King County*, 158 Wn.2d 1, 58 (Wash. 2006) (Alexander, C. J., *concurring*).

109. *Goodridge* 798 N.E.2d at 961.

110. *Id.* at 959.

111. *Id.* at 961–63.

112. *Id.* at 961.

113. *Id.* at 961–92.

114. *Id.* at 963.

115. *Id.* at 968.

116. *Id.* at 968.

117. *Bowers v. Hardwick*, 478 U.S. 186, 206 (1986).

118. *Andersen* 158 Wn.2d at 150 (Fairhurst, J., *dissenting*).

119. *Id.* at 151.

120. *Goodridge* 798 N.E.2d at 955.

121. *Bowers v. Hardwick*, 478 U.S. 186, 205 (1986).

122. *Planned Parenthood of Southeastern Pa. V. Casey*, 505 U.S. 833, 851 (1992).

123. *Washington v. Glucksberg*, 521 U.S. 702, 792 (1997).

124. *Goodridge* 798 N.E.2d at 987 (Cordy, J., *dissenting*).

125. *Hernandez v. Robles*, 855 N.E.2d, 10 (2006).

126. *Id.*

127. *Lawrence v. Texas*, 539 U.S. 558, 578 (2003).

128. Lawrence Tribe, "Lawrence v. Texas: The 'Fundamental Right' that Dare Not Speak Its Name, 117 *Harv. L. Rev.* 1893, 1898 ("Lawrence, more than any other decision in the Supreme Court's history, both presupposed and advanced an explicitly equality-based and relationally situated theory of substantive liberty. The 'liberty' of which the Court spoke was as much about equal dignity and respect as it was about freedom of action—more so in fact."); Nan D. Hunter, Living with Lawrence, 88 *Minn. L. Rev.* 1103, 1134.

129. *Andersen v. King County*, 138 P.3d 963, 979 (Wash. 2006).

130. *Hernandez v. Robles*, 855 N.E.2d 1, 10 (Graffeo, J. *concurring*).

131. *Goodridge* 798 N.E.2d at 985 (Cordy, J., *dissenting*).

132. Ronald Dworkin, *Taking Rights Seriously* (Cambridge, Mass.: Harvard University Press, 1977).

133. Morrison v. Sadler, 821 N.E.2d 15; 2005 Ind. App. LEXIS 75. I would like to thank Scott Barkley for pointing this out to me.

134. *Hernandez* 855 N.E.2d at 7.

135. *Hernandez* 855 N.E.2d at 15 (Graffeo, J., *concurring*).

136. Walter Wadlington and Raymond C. O'Brien, *Family Law In Perspective* (New York: Foundation Press, 2007), p. 113.

137. The Court states no fewer that three times that the rational basis test is highly deferential.

138. Karen Struening, "Families 'In Law' and Families 'In Practice': Does the Law Recognize Families As They Really Are?" in (ed.) Barbara Risman, *Families As They Really Are* (N.Y.: Norton, 2009); David D. Meyer, Parenthood in a Time of Transition: Tensions Between Legal, Biological, and Social Conceptions of Parenthood, *Am. J. Comp. L.* 125.

139. Nancy D. Polikoff, "This Child Does Have Two Mothers: Redefining Parenthood to Meet the Needs of Children in Lesbian Mother and Other Nontraditional Households," 78 *Geo L. R.* (1990); *In re Custody of H.S. H.-K.*, 533 N.W. 2d 419 (Wis. 1995); *V.C. v. M.J.B.*, 748 A.2d 539, 550 (N.J. 2000); *Elisa B. v. Superior Court* 117 P. 3d 660 (Calif. 2005).

140. *Johnson v. Calvert* (1993) 5 C.4th 84, 19 C.R.2d 494, 851 P.2d 776.

141. *Griswold v. Connecticut*, 381 U.S. 479, 486 (1965).

142. *Turner v. Safley*, 482 U.S. 78 (1987).

143. *Id.* at 95–96.

144. *Perez v. Sharp*, 198 P.2d 17, 21 (Cal. 1948).

145. *Loving v. Virginia*, 388 U.S. 1, 12 (1967).

146. *Goodridge v. Dep't of Pub. Health*, 798 N.E.2d 941, 961 (Mass. 2003).

147. *Id.* at 955.

148. Brian Hawkins, The Glucksberg Renaissance: Substantive Due Process Since Lawrence v. Texas, 105 *Mich. L. Rev.* 409 (2006).

3

The Religion Clauses and Same-Sex Marriages

Emily R. Gill

Although a great deal has been written about same-sex marriage from vary-ing standpoints, relatively little has focused on possible comparisons and contrasts between religious freedom and sexual freedom. Opposition both to same-sex relationships and to same-sex marriage is frequently defended for religious reasons. Religion and sexual orientation, however, share an affinity that often goes unnoticed. In theory, both are regarded as private matters. In practice, on the other hand, the dominant consensus enshrines majoritarian views in ways that marginalize dissenters from that consensus. Despite the lack of a formal establishment of religion and the constitutional guarantee of the free exercise of religion, "Christianity, and often conservative Christian-ity, functions as the yardstick and measure of what counts as 'religion' and 'morality' in America."[1] Ethical views that do not fit within or at least overlap this consensus often go unrecognized as moral values. In the realm of sexual orientation, the role of Christianity is occupied by heteronormativity, which "describes the moral and conceptual centrality of heterosexuality in contem-porary American life."[2] That is, heterosexuality represents the norm, and the idea that alternative sexual practices could possess ethical significance is unconsciously overlooked or ignored.

In the case of both religion and sexual orientation, privacy does not protect those whose beliefs, identities, and practices diverge from the norm, but in-stead marginalizes them, preventing them from participating fully in the public sphere while being open about their beliefs and identities. Regarding religion, even under a more protective standard than is now in force, the "Supreme Court could not see its way clear to ruling in favor of a free exercise exemption that would support a non-Christian religious practice."[3] Public authority also takes notice of sexuality, of course, both by the exclusion of known gays and lesbians from military service, and also in most states by confining civil marriage to contracts between men and women. Both religious and sexual freedom may require not only noninterference, as in the Religious Freedom Restoration Act or the 2003 deconstitutionalization of antisodomy laws, but also positive action through public policy, as in removing barriers to same-sex couples whose conscientious beliefs impel them to commit to civil marriage.

Public attitudes toward sexual orientation provide an interesting contrast with attitudes toward religious belief. Despite the public hegemony of Christianity, most people as individuals would accord equal consideration and respect to all who engage in religious practices considered acceptable in the polity. They would agree that religious practice is a matter of personal obligation, desire, or choice, but that the expression of religious belief is open to all. They would not argue that respect for diversity requires that the convictions of those who dislike certain manifestations of religious belief be treated in public policy as if on a par with the convictions of those who simply wish to engage in their own religious practices without loss of respect or civic standing. Yet on issues of sexuality, many people move in the opposite direction. They suggest that although individuals with to-them-distasteful sexual practices should be accorded grudging toleration, they should adopt a low profile and need not receive respect equal to that accorded to those pursuing other practices. They argue that although sexuality is a personal matter, its public expression, as in civil marriage, may be regulated to the detriment of those who simply desire equal access to a public institution freely available to other couples. Moreover, the very conception of marriage as the public expression of sexuality assumes that individuals are essentially defined by this feature of their identities. Finally, they argue that liberal hospitality to diversity means that persons who dislike certain sexual practices possess an equal entitlement to shape public policy that governs them as do those individuals whose practices they abhor.

Same-sex attraction, then, is currently an area in which freely according equal consideration and respect to divergent practices is particularly controversial, especially when this requires not simply refraining from interference, but also positive action through public policy. In this essay, I shall first consider Michael McConnell's interesting attempt to apply the First Amendment's religion clauses to the subject of sexual orientation and same-sex marriage and explain why I believe it to be inadequate. Second, I shall argue that the free exercise of conscientious belief requires the inclusion of same-sex couples in the institution of civil marriage. Finally, I shall suggest that because the institution of marriage is a civil establishment, the exclusion of same-sex couples from that institution constitutes a public expression of civic inequality that should have no place in a liberal polity. Overall, I agree with Janet Jakobsen and Ann Pellegrini that more religious freedom need not mean more government support for religion in the public square. "We want the freedom not to be religious and the freedom to be religious differently. And we want both these positions to count as the possible basis for moral claims and public policy."[4] In my view, this means greater attention to conscientious belief and its manifestation in practice through the inclusion of same-sex couples in civil marriage.

McCONNELL'S "FIRST AMENDMENT" APPROACH

Both religion and sexuality, suggests McConnell, involve choice but also go beyond it, encompass both opinion and conduct, possess both public and private aspects, and, in short, "are central aspects of personal identity."[5] If the pluralist solution to religious difference has been to avoid a public position on the merits of contending religious views, might the solution to deep divisions about the morality of same-sex relationships be refusal to take a public position on this topic as well? A "First Amendment" position would treat both conflicting views "as conscientious positions, worthy of respect, much as we treat both atheism and faith as worthy of respect."[6] Sketching the jurisprudence of the religion clauses, McConnell distinguishes between the privatization approach, often associated with the "wall of separation" as it consigns religion-sensitive issues to the private sphere, and the equal access approach, often associated with neutrality between religion and nonreligion because it allows "competing groups to participate in the public sphere on equal terms." In the context of sexuality, privatization "would insist that all activities directly related to the formation of opinion about homosexuality be confined to private institutions, where there should be no interference with either beliefs (orientation) or conduct." Equal access would call for equal treatment in the public domain for all private views, but would "be careful not to convey the impression that the government is expressing a view."[7] Applying these jurisprudential categories to sexual orientation and practice, McConnell's test is whether governmental stances in various areas convey moral approval or disapproval, on the one hand, or whether they merely allow those endorsing or disapproving various types of sexual expression to participate on equal terms in the public sphere like those of diverse religious beliefs, on the other.

Although McConnell applies this formulation in interesting ways to a wide variety of issue areas,[8] my focus is the institution of marriage. To McConnell, the case for same-sex marriage as a free exercise or equal access claim is weak, because "most combinations of human beings are ineligible for matrimony." In *Reynolds v. United States*, [9] Reynolds was seeking neither benefits nor the recognition of polygamous marriage, but only to be left alone. "In other words, Reynolds unsuccessfully sought what homosexuals already have: the right to live with the person(s) of their choice, as if married, without hindrance from the state. . . . It is one thing to say that the government may not interfere with a religious (or sexual) practice in the privacy of the home, and quite a different thing to say that the government must adjust the definition of a public institution to conform to the doctrines or desires of a minority." [10] As a majoritarian, McConnell apparently dismisses the need for judicial assistance when a minority cannot pursue a rights claim through the ordinary political process.

As a disestablishment claim, on the other hand, the recognition of same-sex marriage would not solve the "establishment" problem for McConnell, but only broaden the "establishment" to give favored status to two "churches." [11] Because the civil institution of marriage accords respect and benefits to those pursuing a specific sort of choice and conception of the good, true disestablishment would require eliminating marriage as a public institution. Unions would be privately formed and celebrated, just as like-minded individuals associate to form religious groups and institutionalize them. In a persuasive account, Gordon Babst argues that the ban on same-sex marriage can be attributed to a *de facto* shadow establishment that has enshrined a sectarian definition of marriage. Similarly to McConnell, he suggests that apart from simply recognizing same-sex marriages, another alternative "would be to let individual couples decide for themselves within their communities of faith, or otherwise, what marriage signifies for them and their communities, rather than have a definition imposed on them by the State." [12] This solution would not preclude the expression of a secular public interest through law on divorce, adoption, inheritance, and other worldly interests.

McConnell is himself suggesting that there is no neutral position regarding same-sex marriage. Although it could be justified on the argument that same-sex couples are "sufficiently similar to heterosexual couples—sharing in the same goods of love and commitment, reinforced by a similar bond of sexual intimacy—that they should be treated the same way by law," [13] this is not a neutral stance. "Limitation of marriage to heterosexual unions necessarily implies that homosexual unions lack the qualities for which marriage is legally recognized and favored, while extending marriage to homosexual unions would necessarily imply that homosexual unions have those socially favored qualities." [14] Equating same-sex unions with traditional marriage will appear to many, for better or for worse, as a promotion or upgrade, and hence a moral endorsement of these unions. As a further complicating factor, some experiencing same-sex attraction may already feel marginalized, and those who cannot or will not enter long-term commitments may feel demoted by comparison with those who can and do. On all sides, the presumption is that when the state sanctions an institution or practice, this constitutes a moral endorsement.

McConnell suggests that a defense of same-sex marriage is best grounded on its ability to "publicly reaffirm the values of faithfulness and monogamy, while subordinating the more contentious moral question of homosexuality per se."[15] He implies, then, that same-sex marriage would be an endorsement of the values that traditional marriage represents to many people, rather than an endorsement of same-sex relationships in and of themselves. Overall, he suggests that if same-sex rights supporters' concern is with the real effects of discrimination rather than ideological victories, they should not attempt to make antidiscrimination laws into moral statements. Otherwise, "it will be apparent that their real purpose is . . . to impose their beliefs through the power of the state."[16] This conclusion ignores the fact that the majority has been imposing its beliefs all along by excluding same-sex couples from marriage.

Although McConnell's attempt to provide a "First Amendment" solution to moral disagreements on the value of same-sex relationships is ingenious in its conceptualization, I do not believe that it works. First, including same-sex couples in the institution of marriage would indeed "reaffirm the values of faithfulness and monogamy," but, as McConnell himself recognizes, it would not end contention over the moral status of such relationships. The institution of marriage itself carries a normative status. As put by Jyl Josephson, "Marriage posits a specific desirable form for intimacy and family life—despite contemporary reality—and reinforces that form through legal, economic, political, and social privileges."[17] In other words, the contours of the institution of marriage itself are not neutral, but instead represent an endorsement of a particular and preferred view of how citizens should, ideally, conduct their lives. This view applies not only to couples, but also to single heterosexual individuals.

Matrimonial law thus conditions people's ideas and expectations concerning the proper ordering of their personal relationships. To traditionalist opponents, the inclusion of same-sex couples in marriage detracts, to say the least, from the value of a bedrock human institution by subjecting its definition to the vagaries of popular culture. To skeptics about marriage itself, however, this inclusion bolsters the sway of a rigid social institution at the expense of non-participants. To put this differently, while traditionalist opponents fear that the inclusion of same-sex couples will devalue marriage, skeptics fear that it will add *too much* value, increase the institution's hegemony, and devalue *them* by comparison. Even the disestablishment of marriage as a public institution and the relegation of its spiritual or ethical meaning to the private sphere would not instantiate neutrality. Both traditionalist opponents and proponents in this dispute want marriage to remain a public institution: traditionalist opponents want to maintain the status quo, while same-sex couples seeking to marry and their allies seek no change in the substance of marriage, but want only to be included on the same terms as opposite-sex couples. Neither traditionalists nor same-sex marriage advocates, then, wish to engage in the merely private pursuit of what they understand as the value of marriage; both want the endorsement that accompanies only a public institution.

Second and more important, there is an asymmetry in McConnell's "First Amendment" solution to conflicts regarding same-sex attraction. He is correct, of course, that the pluralist solution to religious difference has been to avoid a public position on the merits of contending religious views. When the government avoids a public position on the merits of contending religious views and avoids endorsing one or some over others, however, it is attempting to be neutral as to the *substance* of the competing views in question. McConnell's solution, on the other hand, is like an attempt at neutrality between the idea that a particular religion should be accorded recognition equal to that accorded to other religions, and the idea that a particular religion, because it offends many people, need not be thus recognized or respected. Although his solution is supposed to be neutral regarding sexual orientation, when we apply it to religious belief we can see that it is not. When neutrality is defined as noninterference, too often the dominant consensus is in the driver's seat.

David A. J. Richards suggests that same-sex attraction is a form of conscience central to ethical identity, but that it has traditionally been silenced, "condemned as a kind of ultimate heresy or treason against essential moral values."[18] Advocates of this identity "should be compelled to abandon their claims to personal and ethical legitimacy and either convert to the true view or return to the silence of their traditional unspeakability."[19] From this perspective, opposition to identity claims as a form of conscience suggests that this identity "is as unworthy of respect as a traditionally despised religion like Judaism; the practice of that form of heresy may thus be abridged, and certainly persons may be encouraged to convert from its demands or, at least, be supinely and ashamedly silent."[20] If we apply McConnell's solution to Richards's analogy, it is as if those on one side were to argue that Judaism be recognized as on a par with other religious beliefs, while those on the other side argued that Judaism is an offensive belief system that need not be respected. Moreover, the government could then be neutral and avoid a moral position in the face of this dispute. Yes, Jews would be protected against private violence and possibly against employment discrimination, but there would be many conscience-based exemptions. Finally, the government would have to ensure that its efforts were not intended to effect a cultural education and transformation of attitudes towards Judaism in general and Jews in particular. It would not be surprising if, over time, people became desensitized to instances of discrimination that would immediately be recognized as such in an alternative context. Political correctness would impel a nominal respect for Judaism, but cultural reality would convey heavy-handed reminders that such respect emanated not from conviction but from grace.

What McConnell is suggesting, then, is not neutrality among religious positions, but neutrality among *attitudes* that citizens might take *toward* religious positions. He implicitly admits this point when he mentions the massive educational effort that would be needed to discipline "aggressive, undercivilized" military troops to accept openly gay comrades, concluding that the government would have to go beyond mere civil toleration to inculcate full acceptance of their moral legitimacy.[21] This point also suggests that when a dominant consensus exists, whether represented by those offended by a religion or by same-sex relationships, governmental neutrality between that consensus and the minority position has the effect, regardless of intention, of endorsing the status quo. To put this differently, those who may hate and those who are hated are often portrayed as two extremes, equidistant from a "tolerant middle" that holds the balance of public opinion. "In a situation framed by the rhetoric of tolerance," suggest Jakobsen and Pellegrini, "the public is not expected to take a stand against injustice, but merely to tolerate both sides of a conflict."[22] Finally, where religious groups may consider their own beliefs and practices superior to those of other religious groups and may even criticize others, their own beliefs and practices generally possess an objective status or reality for them, apart from their opinions of other groups. For individuals or groups who believe that acting on same-sex attraction is immoral, however, expression of these attitudes is often central, rather than incidental, to their own "religious practice."

Overall, then, McConnell's "First Amendment" approach does not instantiate a neutral public stance regarding controversy over same-sex attraction in general or same-sex marriage in particular. As long as civil marriage exists as a public institution, it is tantamount to an establishment and thus functions as a gatekeeper. Public institutions and policies, or their absence, will always shape social attitudes. Therefore, we need a different formulation of the analogy between religion and sexual orientation. First, same-sex couples who wish to marry are entitled to the same respect accorded to others protected in the free exercise of practices flowing from their conscientious convictions. Second, when public policy institutionalizes such practices in ways that favor some adherents over others, public authority is maintaining an establishment that distinguishes between insiders and outsiders by privileging some over others. It is to these issues that I now turn.

RELIGIOUS COMMITMENT AND SAME-SEX MARRIAGE

In Richards's view, the true evil of any kind of discrimination, whether grounded in race, sex, religion, or sexual orientation, is in its cultural dehumanization of individuals, a status that he terms moral slavery. "This structural injustice is marked by two features: first, abridgment of basic human rights in a group of persons, and second, the unjust rationalization of such abridgment on the inadequate grounds of dehumanizing stereotypes that reflect a history and culture of such abridgment."[23] That is, the dominant culture devalues some human beings as bearers of rights, and then justifies this devaluation on the basis of history and experience that both bear the marks of this original dehumanization. These individuals thus lose the ability to define their own identities because they are culturally constructed by the dominant culture, a form of intolerance that Richards describes as a violation of "the inalienable right to conscience, which I identify as the free exercise of the moral powers of rationality and reasonableness in terms of which persons define personal and ethical meaning in living."[24] For Richards, the fundamental right to an intimate life, like the right to conscience, "protects intimately personal moral resources . . . and the way of life that expresses and sustains them in facing and meeting rationally and reasonably the challenge of a life worth living."[25]

In essence, Richards is arguing that the experience of same-sex attraction is a core feature of one's personal identity, just as religious allegiance may be for believers. The living out of these features propels one to engage in particular practices. Denial of the ability to do so openly, or in some cases even to admit to such an allegiance, amounts to a denial of values that are central to one's ethical identity. For Richards, in the American constitutional tradition "the right to intimate life is as much a basic human right as the right to conscience; conscience is so personally engaged with the issues of intimate sexual life because both involve the resources of thought, conviction, feeling, and emotion at the heart of the ultimate concerns of moral personality."[26]

Rights of conscience may admittedly be abridged under some circumstances: we would not allow human sacrifice even if its proponents argued its practice fulfilled their conscientious beliefs. Richards, however, suggests that such abridgment must be "justified on compelling secular grounds of protecting public goods reasonably acknowledged as such by all persons"[27] or "a compelling public reason, not on grounds of reasons that are today sectarian (internal to a moral tradition not based on reasons available and accessible to all)."[28] He does not believe that these grounds exist. First, the procreational model of sexuality is "a sectarian ideal lacking adequate secular basis in the general good that can alone reasonably justify state power,"[29] a point that the Supreme Court supported in striking down anticontraception and antiabortion laws. Maintaining a close link between sex and procreation may be a legitimate public aim, but it does not command universal allegiance and should not be enforced at the expense of those who do not define their lives in this manner. Second, the traditional condemnation of homosexuality, argues Richards, has been rooted in its perceived "degradation of a man to the passive status of woman," a stigma that was itself premised on ancient assumptions about the degraded nature of women.[30] Although some may still maintain the superiority of maleness, just as some do of whiteness, this is, again, a sectarian view. This "embattled sectarian perspective on gender orthodoxy" is responsible, he suggests, for the demonization of same-sex marriage as a threat to marriage as a social institution.[31]

Overall, religious or particularistic secular grounds should not count as grounds of abridgment. If they did count, weighing your religious objections, for example, against my practice of my conscientious beliefs implies that your beliefs somehow trump my own. On the other hand, the individual right to conscience as a basis for same-sex marriage can indeed comprise not only religious grounds, but secular ones as well. If the claiming of same-sex attraction is a form of conscience, it should be protected, Richards argues, as our tradition of religious liberty has traditionally protected all forms of conscience, both theistic and nontheistic.[32] In sum, "Liberal political culture . . . must extend to all persons the cultural resources that enable them critically to explore, define, express, and revise the identifications central to free moral personality."[33]

I believe that Richards is persuasive in equating sexual orientation with conscientious belief. Because the government does not interfere with the activity of religious communities that endorse and are willing to celebrate same-sex unions on a religious basis, however, some commentators hold that these unions do not directly implicate the free exercise of religion under the First Amendment. The religious significance of marriage, however, implicitly including civil marriage, has been recognized by the Supreme Court, which has noted that because "many religions recognize marriage as having spiritual significance to some. . . , therefore, the commitment of marriage may be an exercise of religious faith as well as an expression of personal dedication."[34] The institution's religious significance is certainly endorsed by opponents of same-sex marriage.[35] For same-sex couples who are religiously inclined, the ability to participate in the institution of marriage is a desire for the free exercise of their religious beliefs, which they view as being denied by those who wish to maintain traditional marriage as an exclusive institution. But even same-sex couples who are nonreligious may be thwarted in the exercise of their broader conscientious beliefs by their inability to marry.

First, sexual freedom, like religious freedom, implies not only identity and belief, but also practice. Although the polity may hold some instances of religious practice, such as human sacrifice, as contrary to public policy, practices that are not curtailed should be freely available to practitioners of all religious beliefs. Similarly, the public commitment represented by civil marriage available to traditional couples should be available to same-sex couples as well, who want only to participate in this institution on the same terms as others.[36] We should not expect some citizens to convert to a different religion to gain access to the material benefits and public respect accorded to other citizens; in the same way, citizens should not be denied these goods because they are of the "wrong" sexual orientation.

Second, a broad interpretation of religion helps to unite the First Amendment's religion clauses, which are often seen as irreconcilable. As Jakobsen and Pellegrini note, "The secularists often talk about the separation of church and state, but they rarely talk about religious freedom; the religionists talk about religious freedom, but rarely do they talk about the separation of church and state."[37] That is, emphasis on the disestablishment of religion is often equated with minimizing and even denigrating the importance of religious practice, while emphasis on the free exercise of religion is associated with support for religious dominance, especially by those for whom religion and morality require a Christian interpretation. For Jakobsen and Pellegrini, however, disestablishment is a precondition of free exercise. "Without disestablishment, free exercise will confuse public space with government support."[38] Disestablishment of religion allows the space for people to be traditionally religious, differently or nontraditionally religious, or nonreligious.

In the area of sexual orientation and practice, the "disestablishment" of heteronormativity, or of the assumption that heterosexuality is the norm and measure of sexuality, does not mean that asexuality is the norm. Rather, disestablishment opens up the space for people to be heterosexual, gay, lesbian, bisexual, or asexual if that is their orientation, without being disadvantaged in the context of the dominant consensus. Unlike those such as McConnell, who think the state should be neutral as to whether same-sex attraction is bad or good, Jakobsen and Pellegrini suggest that true disestablishment means neutrality between same-sex attraction and opposite-sex attraction.[39] This sort of neutrality is analogous to religious neutrality: religious disestablishment means that the state is neutral as to the comparative merits of Roman Catholicism and Judaism, not on whether Judaism, for example, is bad or good.

On the view of Andrew Murphy, however, the equation of sexual orientation and its expression with religious allegiance and its practice lacks precision. Richards's view equates conscience with personal autonomy, requiring a much broader conception of the private sphere than did traditional interpretations of toleration, which simply focused on the negative liberty of noncoercion and state neutrality.[40] Where the conscience paradigm requires equal treatment before the law and the removal of barriers, identity politics "instead argues for a positive commitment to equal respect between social groups and even the affirmation and celebration of difference *per se*."[41] The conscience paradigm does not valorize self-respect, "but instead the promotion of a pacific public space in which citizens can live out their deepest beliefs."[42] Murphy admits, nonetheless, that because beliefs about ultimate truth, religious or not, are foundational in one's sense of self, "conscience contains within it at least a latent notion of identity,"[43] despite their distinct sociopolitical agendas. That is, "conscience-based politics boils down to the claim that states must recognize individuals' beliefs and values about truth and the good . . . as sacrosanct. . . . Within the parameters of civil peace and social order, government must grant the liberty to act upon such values, as a necessary corollary to the free workings of the human mind."[44] In typical conscience-based politics, dissenters wish to practice in accordance with religious beliefs that are different from those enshrined in and endorsed by the dominant consensus. In the same-sex marriage controversy, however, the "dissenters" wish to practice their beliefs in exactly the same way that the majority does. If, as Murphy suggests, the conscience paradigm promotes "a pacific public space in which citizens can live out their deepest beliefs," the quest for same-sex marriage, I would argue, qualifies as conscience-based politics.

Although the debate surrounding same-sex marriage is often portrayed as one in which secularly-based opinions are arrayed against religiously-based ones, Mark Strasser notes, "[r]ather, the most that can be claimed is that the state position supports the religious dictates of *some* but not all religions."[45] Even if no religious tradition recognized same-sex marriages, for Strasser this alone would not justify state refusal to do so also. In Richards's terms, opposition to same-sex marriage would still be, as it is now, a sectarian viewpoint. Additionally, traditionalists fear that the recognition of same-sex marriage would open the floodgates to the claims of any and every type of union, including polygamous ones. Although detailed discussion of this issue is beyond the scope of this essay, I would agree with Evan Gerstmann that vague speculation "about the potential evils of nontraditional families is exactly the sort of attack that has so often been used against same-sex couples."[46] The point is not to defend polygamy, but to suggest that the legitimacy of any type of relationship should be determined on its own merits. "Polygamists have the same right as same-sex couples to go to court and demand that the state give real reasons—not just stereotypes and unsupported generalizations—for banning their marriage."[47] Moreover, polygamists have the same right to a public response couched in nonsectarian terms, or those not implicitly grounded in religious principles.

If, as Richards does, we may equate intimate life with conscience in that the right to both protects "personal moral resources and the way of life that expresses and sustains them in facing and meeting . . . the challenge of a life worth living,"[48] both may also require protection in the form of positive action by the state to enable individuals to live in accordance with their conscientiously chosen or affirmed convictions about how they should live their lives. The protection of core features of moral identity should be directed both against laws that unreasonably burden the free exercise of conscientious conviction, as the free exercise clause directs, and also against laws that encourage conversion to some form of sectarian orthodoxy, as the antiestablishment clause suggests.[49]

Although I have argued that the institution of marriage, including civil marriage, carries religious significance, the free exercise of conscientious belief may also be defended on grounds that are not conventionally religious in nature. For example, the cumulative weight of court cases recognizing the rights of conscientious objectors to exemptions from military service or from making weapons of war is to recognize nonreligious ethical and moral beliefs as equivalent to religious ones in their eligibility to count as conscientious beliefs. In 1965 in *United States v. Seeger*, the Supreme Court broadly interpreted Congress's provision that unconventional belief in a relationship to a Supreme Being could ground conscientious objection, suggesting that "[a] sincere and meaningful belief which occupies in the life of its possessor a place parallel to that filled by God" also fulfilled the statutory definition.[50] Five years later in *Welsh v. United States*, the Court found that Welsh's convictions as a conscientious objector were religious in a broad, ethical sense despite their inclusion of political and economic objections to war.[51]

More central for our purposes, in a concurring opinion in *Welsh*, Justice John Marshall Harlan declared that once Congress chose to offer exemptions from military service to conscientious objectors, "It cannot draw the line between theistic and nontheistic religious beliefs, on the one hand, and secular beliefs on the other."[52] That is, if the policy allows both theistic and nontheistic but religious views to qualify as bases for conscientious objection, to be neutral it must also allow exemptions for all conscientious objections, including those emanating from purely moral, ethical, and philosophical sources. If we apply these cases to the issue of same-sex marriage, *Seeger* would suggest that for same-sex couples, the desire to marry occupies the same place that it does for traditional couples. They wish to participate in a universally recognized institution for the same reason that traditional couples do, publicly and as citizens to affirm their long-term commitments. As per Harlan in *Welsh*, we can argue, along with Richards, that morally and ethically based desires to marry are on an equal footing with religiously based ones.

Also pertinent to the free exercise of conscientious belief is *Thomas v. Review Board*, in which the Supreme Court ruled in 1980 that a Jehovah's

Witness refusing to work in a factory department making turrets for military tanks, instead of the steel he had previously been fabricating, should not be denied unemployment compensation by the state of Indiana. Although a fellow Witness with a laxer interpretation had advised Thomas that making weapons parts was not unacceptable, and although the Indiana Supreme Court had found that Thomas's claim was a personal philosophical choice rather than a religious one that would itself still not constitute good cause under Indiana law, Chief Justice Warren Burger for the United States Supreme Court stated that when Thomas drew a line between making sheet steel and tank turrets, "It is not for us to say that the line he drew was an unreasonable one." The free exercise guarantee is not limited to beliefs on which all members of a religious tradition agree.[53] Overall,

> Where the state conditions receipt of an important benefit upon conduct proscribed by a religious faith, or where it denies such a benefit because of conduct mandated by religious belief, . . . a burden upon religion exists. While the compulsion may be indirect, the infringement upon free exercise is nonetheless substantial.[54]

If the free exercise of religion is broadly defined to include nonconventional conscientious belief, *Thomas* favors neither one sort of religious belief over others nor religion in its narrower definition over nonreligion. Regarding same-sex marriage, if same-sex couples wish to marry civilly, whether for spiritual reasons that do or do not accord with the mainstream positions of their religious tradition(s), or for moral and ethical reasons that are not conventionally religious but occupy the place of religion in their belief systems, they should be able to do so. *Thomas* can help us understand why those experiencing same-sex attraction should be accorded not only negative freedom from interference in their private, intimate relationships, but also positive empowerment to participate civilly in an institution which is public. Moreover, while the state supports conscientious objection in specific instances, it would be a stretch to conclude that it welcomes such objections. Because, by contrast, the state obviously encourages and supports the institution of marriage, it should welcome subscribers who have previously been excluded.

Objections may be posed to treating same-sex marriage as a right of conscience under a broad definition of religion. In claiming conscientious objector status, individuals are asking the government to refrain from placing them in a particular classification, that of those of whom military service would otherwise be expected. Same-sex couples aspiring to marry, however, are asking the state positively to place them within a particular classification. As we have seen, McConnell argues that the right to free exercise of religion should not dictate the *civil* definition of marriage.[55] Or, as Justice William Rehnquist opined in his dissent in *Thomas*, when the state enacts legislation to advance its secular goals, "the Free Exercise Clause does not in my view require that the state conform that statute to the dictates of religious conscience of any group."[56]

McConnell and Rehnquist are focusing on the communal nature of religious communities, which are and should be free to solemnize or not whatever unions they choose. The *Thomas* Court, however, found for Thomas as an individual, not for Jehovah's Witnesses as a group. Although the free exercise of religious communities as such is not impeded, without civil marriage the free exercise of some individuals is blocked. The state, in the court's terms, is conditioning an important benefit upon conduct—commitment to someone of the opposite sex—"proscribed" or unavailable to individuals with a same-sex orientation on the basis of their conscientious moral and ethical beliefs. Correspondingly, the state is denying the benefits of marriage to same-sex couples "because of conduct mandated by religious belief," that is, because of the same-sex commitments impelled by these couples' deeply held convictions. Although by exclusion the state is not targeting specific conduct flowing from conscientious belief, the effect is the same as if it were, eventuating in a substantial infringement on the free exercise of these beliefs.

Moreover, those who form same-sex couples may hold moral or ethical beliefs impelling them to participate in marriage not only to attain conventionally religious legitimacy, but also to attain civil legitimacy, or the full "*Good Housekeeping* seal of approval." Insofar as civil marriage is held out as a goal to which to aspire, the inability to make this commitment not only "in the eyes of God and this congregation," but also in the eyes of the state and the hypothetical assemblage of one's fellow citizens, can thwart individuals "in the free exercise of the moral powers . . . in terms of which persons define personal and ethical meaning in living."[57] Although more states are creating legal forms for same-sex couples that bestow some or all of the material benefits of marriage on couples within those particular states, civil marriage, recognized nationwide, is still the "gold standard," and therefore understandably a status that some couples highly prize. From this perspective, then, it should not matter that the desire of same-sex couples for inclusion requires positive action rather than a refraining from action. The free exercise of conscientious beliefs may be thwarted as effectively by one as by the other.

EQUAL CITIZENSHIP AND SAME-SEX MARRIAGE

If the free exercise of conscientious belief is accorded to some while it is denied to others, the result is a failure to provide the substance of equal citizenship. The existence of the institution of marriage does not compel the participation of those who do not wish to marry, just as the existence of a particular religious organization does not require participation by those who dissent from its belief system. Although critics of the institution, disestablishmentarians of civil marriage, and nonparticipants weigh in against marriage, this does not justify delegitimizing the institution. It does, however, justify the inclusion of all adult couples who wish to participate in the institution as it currently exists. Citizens do care about what the state "thinks." Even apart from its legal and economic privileges, marriage is uniquely regarded as "an honorable estate," in the ceremonial words of religious authorities who are also invested with the public authority to preside over civil marriages.

As put by Daniel Brudney, "It is worth reflecting on the fact that people who otherwise seem hostile to state institutions, who deem them corrupt, wicked, or at best a necessary evil, nevertheless deeply want the state to endorse their point of view" as representative of "the people." He suggests that this desire underlies the arguments of both opponents and proponents of same-sex marriage. "That dispute is increasingly not about the provision of concrete legal rights and benefits . . . but about whether the term 'marriage' is to be applied to a relationship—and applied not by a minister, priest, rabbi, or imam but by an agent of the state."[58] In other words, lack of interference with private beliefs and practices is insufficient. What is wanted is positive action or approval, the provision of a context or *public* framework within which all couples may bear witness to their conscientious beliefs.

An institution of civil marriage that excludes same-sex couples is not only an establishment of a public institution in the civil sense, but also an establishment in the religious sense. In the words of Babst, the continuing ban on same-sex marriage in the United States can be attributed to a *de facto* "shadow establishment," defined as "an impermissible expression of sectarian preference in the law that is unreasonable in the light of the nation's constitutional commitments to all its citizens."[59] The prevailing understanding of the good of marriage, in his view, is a sectarian one, internal to and animated by religious convictions in general. Where Richards emphasizes the abridgment of liberty that should be guaranteed by the free exercise clause, Babst focuses on the establishment clause. "Nonpreferentialism, customized here as the *shadow establishment*, is also establishment, whereby preference is given to religion, broadly conceived yet narrowly understood as Christian and as opposed to irreligion. Expression of this preference in the law is not a legitimate, publicly justified secular purpose."[60] Another example of a shadow establishment can be found in Sunday closing laws. Although they may now provide for a uniform day of rest and family activity, they resemble the same-sex marriage ban, suggests Babst, because "both have successfully hidden the sectarian rationale for their existence behind putatively legitimate governmental purpose."[61]

Babst's point, and mine here, is not that governmental purposes are necessarily illegitimate. Rather, what *is* illegitimate is their selective and unjustified application in ways that render citizens civically unequal. Civil marriage is a public institution, and as such it is sanctioned and encouraged by the state. Yet some couples are excluded, although they wish simply to make the same kind of formal, long term commitment available to couples who are included. As described by Amy Gutmann, "discriminatory exclusion is harmful when it *publicly expresses* the civic inequality of the excluded even in the absence of any other showing that it *causes* the civic inequality in question. A court or legislature need not document harmful consequences to individual persons to establish a connection between a blocked entry and an actionable threat to civic equality of members of a group."[62] Although Gutmann makes these points in the context of a discussion of voluntary organizations, specifically party primaries, they are even more telling in the context of a public institution such as civil marriage.

The harm documented by a public expression of civic inequality is ignored in McConnell's argument about free exercise, mentioned above, that "it is one thing to say that the government may not interfere with a religious (or sexual) practice in the privacy of the home, and quite a different thing to say that the government must adjust the definition of a public institution to conform with the doctrines or desires of a minority."[63] First, the inclusion of same-sex couples does not change the definitive substance of marriage, which is the public expression of a long term commitment based on a close personal bond, and which may or may not involve the rearing of children. It simply broadens the institution's constituency by including same-sex couples along with traditional couples.

Second, marriage as currently practiced may or may not include a religious component, but it always involves a civil commitment, requiring a license to be legitimate. Moreover, religious marriages are performed by clergy who function not only as religious authorities, but also in the United States as officers vested with state authority on these occasions. Although religious authorities may deem some couples morally worthy of being united in marriage where other couples are not, the state eschews moral judgments, confining itself to objective legal criteria. If no civil institution of marriage existed and if all marriages were religious, same-sex couples would be excluded by some religious traditions, which is the latters' right. Such exclusion, however, would not instantiate a *public* expression of *civic* inequality. If, in McConnell's terms, same-sex marriage proponents are asking the government to "adjust the definition of a public institution," marriage's status as a *public* institution is exactly the reason that its constituency should be broadened to include same-sex couples. Stated simply, public institutions should be inclusive if citizens are to be regarded as equals. The exclusion of same-sex couples constitutes a public expression of their civic inequality. In Gutmann's words, "the exclusion itself *publicly expresses* the idea that they are not the civic equals of those who are included."[64]

Finally, by confining civil marriage to traditional couples, the state *is* in fact making an implicit moral judgment, one that the state is not entitled to make. Any heterosexual couple is deemed worthy of marriage if the individuals in question meet the legal requirements; in most jurisdictions, no same-sex couple is deemed worthy. The fact that many opposite-sex marriages are of remarkably short duration is well known, as in Brittany Spears's two-day marriage several years ago. Perhaps less well known but equally factual, many same-sex couples have been together for decades. Yet the exclusion of same-sex couples in effect declares the moral superiority of all traditional couples over all same-sex couples.[65] It is difficult to imagine a clearer public expression of civic inequality.

McConnell also suggests, as we have seen, that the recognition of same-sex marriage would not solve the "establishment" problem, but would only broaden it to give favored status to two "churches."[66] If we assume for present purposes, however, that the institution of civil marriage has a legitimate public purpose, is it not preferable to recognize two "churches," or two ways of accomplishing this purpose, rather than only one? Despite differences in interpretation of the religion clauses, most would agree that their existence in the First Amendment provides a positive benefit. Yet this agreement has not always prevented their interpretation in ways that have benefited some religious practices while burdening others, just as marriage has been interpreted to benefit some couples but to burden others.

A classic example may be found in *Employment Division v. Smith*, in which the Supreme Court ruled that the state of Oregon could deny unemployment benefits to members of the Native American Church for using peyote in religious ceremonies without demonstrating a compelling state interest, as the penalty was only the incidental effect of a neutral and generally applicable law. The majority held in part that consideration of a religious exemption from the effect of such laws "would enmesh judges in an impermissible enquiry into the centrality of particular beliefs and practices to a faith."[67] Despite the value of the free exercise of religion, in *Smith* generally applicable laws against the use of peyote took precedence over the religious function of peyote in Native American religious ceremonies. By comparison, however, the use of sacramental wine in Christian church services was exempted during Prohibition because this use was thought not unduly to conflict with the aims of Prohibition.

One cannot help but entertain the conjecture that the "shadow establish-ment" of Christianity, as both a majority and a mainstream religion, received a pass denied to Native Americans. In specific application, the effects of for-mal neutrality may benefit some religions while burdening others. Regarding same-sex marriage, although opposite-sex and same-sex marriage may be interpreted as two "churches," traditional marriage is both a majority and a mainstream practice. Same-sex marriage is neither. This context means that it is easier for people to view traditional marriage as congruent with public purposes than it is for them to perceive same-sex marriage similarly, just as the use of sacramental wine is more easily perceived than peyote as a legiti-mate, free exercise of religious practice. If the civil institution of marriage has a legitimate public purpose, however, absent an as-yet-undemonstrated compelling state interest in excluding same-sex couples, they should be ad-mitted. Although civil marriage is still an establishment, a broader establish-ment is preferable to a more exclusive one. We are not two communities, one of insiders and one of outsiders, but one United States with one rule of law and one type of citizen.

The problem of civic inequality may also be illustrated by recent estab-lishment clause jurisprudence. In 1984 in *Lynch v. Donnelly*, for example, the Supreme Court held that the city of Pawtucket, Rhode Island, had not violated the establishment clause by including a crèche or nativity scene in its annual holiday display in a city park owned by a nonprofit association.[68] Most relevant for present purposes is Justice Sandra Day O'Connor's concurring opinion, in which she argued that the establishment clause may be violated not only by the excessive entanglement of government with religious institu-tions, but also and more directly by "government endorsement or disapproval of religion. Endorsement sends a message to nonadherents that they are out-siders, not full members of the political community, and an accompanying message to adherents that they are insiders, favored members of the politi-cal community."[69] She believed that Pawtucket intended neither to endorse Christianity nor to denigrate other religions, but only to celebrate a public holiday by displaying traditional symbols. Interpreters may disagree with the Court's answer, but for O'Connor, the question to be asked was whether or not the display in effect conveyed a public expression of civic inequality through an implicit distinction between insiders and outsiders.

In a related case in 1989, *County of Allegheny v. ACLU*, the Supreme Court ruled that the holiday display of a crèche in the county courthouse, but not a menorah paired with a Christmas tree outside a city-county office build-ing, violated the establishment clause. Writing for the Court, Justice Harry Blackmun noted that the definition of governmental endorsement of religion has been interpreted to mean "that religion or a particular religious belief is *favored* or *preferred*," or, alternatively, promoted.[70] The prominent crèche display alone in a public building could not help but convey a religious message. The menorah display with the Christmas tree, however, rather than endorsing both Christianity and Judaism, simply suggested various ways of observing the winter holiday season.[71]

In a concurring opinion, Justice O'Connor argued that unlike the inclusion of a crèche in *Lynch* as part of a larger display, here the crèche alone on the Grand Staircase of the county courthouse "conveys a message to nonadherents of Christianity that they are not full members of the political community, and a corresponding message to Christians that they are favored members of the political community."[72] In her view, the endorsement test embodied "the essential command of the Establishment Clause, that government must not make a person's religious beliefs relevant to his or her standing in the political community" by conveying favoritism or preference for particular religious beliefs or religion in general,[73] something that may be accomplished without government proselytization or outright coercion. Correspondingly, I would suggest, the government should not make a person's sexual orientation relevant to his or her standing in the political community by conveying favoritism or preference for a particular sexual orientation. To do so is a public expression of civic inequality.

Two lessons emerge from these cases. First, when the government allows, favors, prefers, or endorses the practice of some nonharmful conscientious beliefs in the public sphere but not others, it is creating a distinction between insiders and outsiders. This in turn constitutes a public expression of civic inequality. Although making these distinctions may not cause this inequality and may not result in specific harms to individuals, the public expression of inequality by public authority, which ought to stand in the same relationship to all its citizens, compromises this relationship by suggesting that some citizens are more worthy than others. The racial policy of separate-but-equal was racist regardless of consequences. Similarly, whether related to religious belief and practice or sexual orientation and practice, the problem with civic inequality is not necessarily in what is *does*, but in what it *is*.

Second and finally, civil marriage as a public institution confers status on private relationships as nothing else can. Just as the Protestant Reformation accustomed civil authority to the idea that more than a single manifestation of religious belief and practice could be legitimate, the current desire of some same-sex couples to marry should also suggest that more than a single manifestation of long term commitment is also legitimate. The public legitimation of private practice is what Ingrid Creppell terms "public privacy." When Locke became convinced that the implementation of religious toleration would mitigate rather than exacerbate the dangers of religious identification, he suggested that God be publicly worshipped through the public presentation of private belief before the larger community, despite the fact that that the community witnessing this presentation was not unified in belief. Public privacy would legitimate an individuation of belief by protecting public presentation from interference and by creating a buffer zone between the purely private and purely public that would combine communal expression and recognition with distance and protection.[74]

In the analogy with marriage, the participation of same-sex couples in the civil institution of marriage would be, as it is for straight couples, a public presentation of identity, belief, and commitment. Marriage creates a buffer zone that shields couples from interference in their private relationships, but does so through the public affirmation of commitment in the eyes of the community. Public recognition, then, is a precondition for the protection of the private aspects of religious belief and practice as well as sexual orientation and practice. It is especially crucial for minority religions and sexual orientations, as it affords them protection that was previously unavailable. Public privacy requires not only noninterference in private relationships, but also positive action to legitimize their public manifestation. Both are required to ensure a public expression of civic equality.[75] In a polity that enshrines marriage as a public good, civic equality must apply to marriage as well as to other institutions if the public good is to be served. Failure to recognize this connection harms not only same-sex couples who wish to marry, but the rest of us as well.

NOTES

1. Janet R. Jakobsen and Ann Pellegrini, *Love the Sin: Sexual Regulation and the Limits of Religious Tolerance* (Boston, Mass.: Beacon Press, 2004), 13; see also 21–22, 47, 104, 109–10.

2. Jakobsen and Pellegrini, *Love the Sin*, 28.

3. Jakobsen and Pellegrini, *Love the Sin*, 110; see 109–10.

4. Jakobsen and Pellegrini, *Love the Sin*, 12–13; see also 111–13.

5. Michael W. McConnell, "What Would It Mean to Have a 'First Amendment,' for Sexual Orientation?" in *Sexual Orientation and Human Rights in American Religious Discourse*, ed. Saul M. Olyan and Martha C. Nussbaum (New York: Oxford University Press, 1998), 234.

6. McConnell, "What Would It Mean," 235.

7. McConnell, "What Would It Mean," 237.

6. McConnell, "What Would It Mean," 239–55.

9. *Reynolds v. United States*, 98 U.S. 145, 1870.

10. McConnell, "What Would It Mean," 249.

11. McConnell, "What Would It Mean," 250.

12. Gordon Albert Babst, *Liberal Constitutionalism, Marriage, and Sexual Orientation: A Contemporary Case for Dis-Establishment* (New York: Peter Lang, 2002), 83; see also 84.

13. McConnell, "What Would It Mean," 249.

14. McConnell, "What Would It Mean," 250.

15. McConnell, "What Would It Mean," 251.

16. McConnell, "What Would It Mean," 255.

17. Jyl Josephson, "Citizenship, Same-Sex Marriage, and Feminist Critiques of Marriage," *Perspectives on Politics* 3, no. 1 (January 2005): 271. On a related note, Gordon A. Babst suggests that gays and lesbians should be wary of being co-opted by communitarian offers of inclusivity that may amount to merely virtual, not actual, representation of their true interests ("Community, Rights Talk, and the Communitarian Dissent in *Bowers v. Hardwick*," in *"Playing with Fire: Queer Politics, Queer Theories,"* ed. Shane Phelan (New York and London: Routledge, 1997), 139–72.

18. David A. J. Richards, *Identity and the Case for Gay Rights: Race, Gender, and Religion as Analogies* (Chicago, Ill.: University of Chicago Press, 1999), 90.

19. Richards, *Identity*, 92; see also 70, 90, 126-27, and David A. J. Richards, *The Case for Gay Rights: Bowers to Lawrence and Beyond* (Lawrence: University Press of Kansas, 2005), 107-8.

20. Richards, *Identity*, 93; see also Richards, *The Case*, 108-9.

21. McConnell, "What Would It Mean," 243.

22. Jakobsen and Pellegrini, *Love the Sin*, 59; see 53–59.

23. Richards, *Identity*, 53; see also 3–4, 17–18, 22, 50, 55, 84, 86; Richards, *The Case*, 39–40, 105–6; Stephen Macedo, "Sexuality and Liberty: Making Room for Nature and Tradition?" in *Sex, Preference, and Family*, ed. David M. Estlund and Martha C. Nussbaum (New York: Oxford University Press, 1997), 90–93; Paul J. Weithman, "Natural Law, Morality, and Sexual Complementarity," in *Sex, Preference, and Family*, ed. David M. Estlund and Martha C. Nussbaum (New York: Oxford University Press, 1997), 236–40; and David O. Erdos, "Questions of Tolerance and Fairness," in *The Future of Gay Rights in America*, ed. H. N. Hirsch (New York: Routledge, 2005), 15–30.

24. Richards, *Identity*, 18.

25. Richards, *Identity*, 74.

26. Richards, *The Case*, 2005, 110; see also 103–4.

27. Richards, *Identity*, 18.

28. Richards, *Identity*, 78; see also 50, 86, 97, and Richards, *The Case*, 135–36.

29. Richards, *Identity*, 98; see also Richards, *The Case*, 69–70, 104, 135–37.

30. Richards, *Identity*, 98; see also Richards, *The Case*, 111–12, 137–38.

31. Richards, *The Case*, 141.

32. Richards, *Identity*, 88, 94; see also Richards, *The Case*, 108–9.

33. Richards, *The Case*, 116.

34. *Turner v. Safley*, 482 U.S. 78, 1987, at 96.

35. Lynne Marie Kohm, "Marriage by Design," in *Marriage and Same-Sex Unions: A Debate*, ed. Lynn D. Wardle, Mark Strasser, William C. Duncan, and David Orgon Coolidge (Westport, Conn.: Praeger, 2003), 81-90; Maggie Gallagher,

"Normal Marriage: Two Views," in *Marriage and Same-Sex Unions: A Debate*, ed. Lynn D. Wardle, Mark Strasser, William C. Duncan, and David Orgon Coolidge (Westport, Conn.: Praeger, 2003), 13–24; and Robert George, "Normality, Equality, and 'Same-Sex Marriage,'" in *Marriage and Same-Sex Unions: A Debate* ed. Lynn D. Wardle, Mark Strasser, William C. Duncan, and David Orgon Coolidge (Westport, Conn.: Praeger, 2003), 119–32.

36. Jakobsen and Pellegrini, *Love the Sin*, 98-99; see 97–101. On a related note, the authors cite Rebecca Alpert's point that "the state's refusal to recognize religiously authorized gay marriages when it recognizes other marriages performed under the same [religious] auspices is an abrogation of the free exercise of religion" (98, referencing Rebecca T. Alpert, "Religious Liberty, Same-Sex Marriage, and the Case of Reconstructionist Judaism," *God Forbid: Religion and Sex in American Public Life*, ed. Kathleen M. Sands (New York: Oxford University Press, 2000), 124–32).

37. Jakobsen and Pellegrini, *Love the Sin*, 111.

38. Jakobsen and Pellegrini, *Love the Sin*, 113; see also 105.

39. Jakobsen and Pellegrini, *Love the Sin*, 120–21.

40. Andrew R. Murphy, *Conscience and Community: Revisiting Toleration and Religious Dissent in Early Modern England and America* (University Park, Pa.: The Pennsylvania State University Press, 2001), 29; see also 240–42.

41. Murphy, *Conscience and Community*, 281; see also 282.

42. Murphy, *Conscience and Community*, 287.

43. Murphy, *Conscience and Community*, 281.

44. Murphy, *Conscience and Community*, 279.

45. Mark Strasser, *On Same-Sex Marriage, Civil Unions, and the Rule of Law* (Westport, Conn.: Praeger, 2002), 119; see also 188–21.

46. Evan Gerstmann, *Same-Sex Marriage and the Constitution* (New York: Cambridge University Press, 2004), 100–1.

47. Gerstmann, *Same-Sex Marriage*, 105.

48. Richards, *Identity*, 74. See also Martha C. Nussbaum, "Religion and Women's Equality: The Case of India," in *Obligations of Citizenship and Demands of Faith: Religious Accommodation in Pluralist Democracy*, ed. Nancy L. Rosenblum (Princeton, N.J.: Princeton University Press, 2000), 342.

49. Richards, *The Case*, 107–8; see 107-9 and David A. J. Richards, *Toleration and the Constitution* (New York: Oxford University Press, 1986), 140.

50. *United States v. Seeger*, 380 U.S. 163, 1965, at 176; see also 184.

51. *Welsh v. United States*, 398 U.S. 333, 1970, at 340–43.

52. *Welsh*, at 356; see also 357-58.

53. *Thomas v. Review Board*, 450 U.S. 707, 1981, at 715–16.

54. *Thomas*, 717–18.

55. McConnell, "What Would It Mean," 249.

56. *Thomas*, 723.

57. Richards, *Identity*, 18.

58. Daniel Brudney, "On Noncoercive Establishment," *Political Theory*, 33, no. 6 (December, 2005): 832.

59. Babst, *Liberal Constitutionalism*, 2, italics omitted.

The Religion Clauses and Same-Sex Marriage   73

60. Babst, *Liberal Constitutionalism*, 57-58.
61. Babst, *Liberal Constitutionalism*, 78; see also 72–76.
62. Amy Gutmann, *Identity in Democracy* (Princeton, N.J.: Princeton University Press, 2003), 97–98, emphasis original.
63. McConnell, "What Would It Mean," 249.
64. Gutmann, *Identity*, 97,
65. For this point I am indebted to Gordon Babst in the course of ongoing dialogue about our work.
66. McConnell, "What Would It Mean," 250.
67. *Employment Division v. Smith*, 494 U.S. 872, 1990, at 873.
68. *Lynch v. Donnelly*, 465 U.S. 668, 1984, at 683–84.
69. *Lynch*, 688; see also 690–94.
70. *County of Allegheny v. ACLU*, 492 U.S. 573, 1989, at 593.
71. *Allegheny*, 598-601, 613–22.
72. *Allegheny*, 626.
73. *Allegheny*, 627; see also 627–28, 631.
74. Ingrid Creppell, "Locke on Toleration: The Transformation of Constraint," *Political Theory* 24, no. 2 (May 1996), 227–29.
75. For a provocative discussion of the need for positive as well as negative liberty in a rich liberalism, see generally Jason Pierceson, *Courts, Liberalism, and Rights* (Philadelphia, Pa.: Temple University Press, 2005).

4

Against Neutrality in the Legal Recognition of Intimate Relationships

Carlos A. Ball*

One of the ways in which it is possible to distinguish contemporary conservatives from liberals in the United States is that the former, generally speaking, believe that there is an overlap between the spheres of politics and law on the one hand and of morality on the other.[1] In contrast, contemporary liberals (and progressives), also generally speaking, believe that it is important that the *public* sphere of politics and law be kept separate from the *private* sphere of morality.[2] In fact, many liberals view the strict separation of the two spheres as essential to protecting basic rights to liberty and equality. Liberals fear that if questions related to morality are permitted to be part of the discussion of what kinds of policies the State should pursue, it would make unpopular minorities (including sexual minorities) more vulnerable to oppression and discrimination.[3]

I have argued elsewhere that it is both necessary and appropriate for supporters of gay rights to raise explicitly moral arguments in support of their positions.[4] I realize, however, that the incorporation of morality into public policy debates makes some on the political left apprehensive. For these individuals, it may seem "strange to talk about moral values in conjunction with rights of belonging in today's political climate, with the Defense of Marriage Act and constitutional amendments prohibiting gay marriage at the top of the political agenda. Indeed, the instinctive response of most [liberals and

* An earlier version of this essay was published in volume 9 of the *Georgetown Journal of Gender and the Law* (2008). This essay is dedicated to the memory of Cristina M. Prado (1971–2008).

progressives] today is that moral values are in opposition to rights of belonging, not in conjunction with them."[5]

My goal in this essay is to seek to make liberals and progressives less apprehensive about the explicit incorporation of considerations of morality into the debate over the legal recognition of same-sex relationships. My principal argument is that when the State makes distinctions among intimate relationships in order to recognize and support some (but not all) of them, it must make assessments regarding the value and goodness of those relationships. A State, in other words, that is in the business of recognizing and protecting some intimate relationships and not others cannot remain neutral on the moral questions raised by those relationships. As a result, the essence of the ongoing dispute over the legal status of same-sex relationships is not whether the State should remain morally neutral on the goodness and value of those relationships, but is instead the underlying (and value-driven) question of whether same-sex relationships are *worthy* of legal recognition and protection.

The essay will proceed as follows. In part I, I summarize the Traditional Conservative Position (TCP) on the legal recognition of same-sex relationships and contrast it with the Traditional Liberal Position (TLP) on that same issue. I also explore a Modified Liberal Position (MLP) that, like the TLP (but unlike the TCP), calls for the legal recognition of same-sex relationships. At the same time, however, the MLP agrees with the TCP (but not the TLP) that it is proper for the State to take moral considerations into account in determining which intimate relationships to recognize.

In part II, I explain that the State could, in theory, avoid all moral questions associated with the legal recognition of intimate relationships by either recognizing *all* or *none* of those relationships. I argue, however, that the practical consequences of operating under either of these two recognition regimes are problematic. This supports my view that the State should not remain morally neutral when deciding which intimate relationships to legally recognize.

In part III, I argue that the understanding of equality which serves as the foundation of constitutional equality in the United States, namely, that the State should treat similarly those who are similarly situated, cannot be applied neutrally in the context of relationship recognition. This is the case because it is not possible for the State to determine whether a category of relationships is similarly situated to another category of relationships without making judgments about the goodness and value of the relationships in question.

Finally, in part IV, I address two objections that are likely to be raised by liberals and progressives to the idea that the State should not remain morally neutral when deciding which intimate relationships to recognize. The first objection is that the incommensurability of moral positions on controversial issues, such as those associated with human sexuality and relationships, requires that the State remain neutral as to the correctness of any one of those positions. The second objection is that if the State is permitted to take considerations of morality into account in determining which intimate relationships to recognize, it will end up legislating morality, thus threatening the liberties and rights of members of minority groups.

There are two matters that I need to address before proceeding. First, I do not, in this chapter, defend or criticize substantive positions regarding the morality of same-sex relationships. Instead, I explore the structure of arguments used in favor and against the legal recognition of same-sex relationships, with an emphasis on a particular question of political morality, namely, whether it is proper for the State to take into account considerations of morality in deciding which relationships to recognize. The question that I address here is *whether* moral arguments should be part of the debate over the recognition of intimate relationships, rather than *which* moral arguments should prevail. As a result, I do not argue here that the State should recognize same-sex relationships because they can be morally good. Rather, I defend the position that the State can appropriately inquire whether relationships have the potential for being morally good before proceeding to legally recognize them.

Second, I do not, in this essay, address which rights and benefits should accompany the legal recognition of intimate relationships. I assume that one of the reasons why the State legally recognizes certain intimate relationships is to provide them with discrete rights and benefits, including access to state-sponsored mechanisms for their dissolution if necessary. I do not, however, address the question of which rights and benefits should accompany the legal recognition of intimate relationships, or the related question of what form that recognition should take (e.g., marriage, civil unions, or domestic partnerships).

I. CONTRASTING POSITIONS ON THE LEGAL RECOGNITION OF SAME-SEX RELATIONSHIPS

In this section, I explore the structure of arguments generally relied on by advocates who argue in favor of or against the legal recognition of same-sex relationships, with an emphasis on the role of morality in those argumentations. The positions presented here are not based on the particular views of any distinct person or group, but are instead distilled summaries of the types of arguments generally relied on by those who advocate in favor of or against the legal recognition of same-sex relationships.

I begin by schematizing the Traditional Conservative Position on whether the State should recognize same-sex relationships:

Traditional Conservative Position (TCP) on
State Recognition of Same-Sex Relationships

Proposition #1: Same-sex sexual relationships, unlike different-sex sexual relationships, are (intrinsically) morally problematic.

Proposition #2: It is proper for the State to rely on moral considerations in deciding which intimate relationships to recognize.

Conclusion: The State should not recognize same-sex sexual relationships.

The moral objections raised by many conservatives to same-sex sexual conduct (and thus to the intimate relationships that can accompany that conduct) are frequently grounded in the notion that there are natural differences between men and women that are complementary and that make their unions more valuable than those of same-sex couples.[6] One of the most important of those differences relate to sexual and reproductive capabilities that, when joined, lead to the formation of a new life.[7] The fact that gay sex lacks a reproductive component means that there is no purpose to that sex other than the pursuit of physical pleasure, which makes it morally problematic.[8]

It is, of course, possible to raise objections to this moral assessment of same-sex sexual conduct, but that is not the purpose of this essay.[9] For now, the reader should simply keep in mind that the TCP's Proposition #1 is a moral claim, which, like all such claims, is subject to dispute.

While the TCP's Proposition #1 sets forth a general claim about the morality of a particular category of human relationships, Proposition #2 articulates a claim of *political* morality. It addresses, in other words, the issue of what constitutes a legitimate basis upon which to ground state action. From the TCP's perspective, it is proper for the State to make assessments regarding the morality of different categories of intimate relationships before endowing any one category with legal recognition. If the State deems the particular category of relationships in question to be immoral by concluding that they lack value or goodness, then it is proper for the State to refuse to recognize those relationships.

When we bring together the TCP's Propositions #1 and #2, there is only one possible conclusion: The State should not recognize same-sex relationships. Although both propositions can be disputed, the TCP is internally consistent because the conclusion logically follows from the two preceding propositions. If the TCP's two propositions are correct, then so is its conclusion.

Now that we have a general sense of the structure of the TCP, I can proceed to provide a schematized version of the Traditional Liberal Position:

Traditional Liberal Position (TLP) on
State Recognition of Same-Sex Relationships

Proposition #1: Same-sex sexual relationships are morally neutral.

Proposition #2: It is (in any event) improper for the State to rely on moral considerations in deciding which intimate relationships to recognize.

Proposition #3: The State should apply the principle of equality, in a morally neutral way, to the question of which relationships to recognize.

Conclusion: Once the State recognizes different-sex relationships, then it must also recognize same-sex relationships.

The TLP views having a same-sex sexual orientation, and, by extension, participating in a same-sex sexual relationship, as being morally neutral. As far as the TLP is concerned, engaging in same-sex sexual intimacy is morally akin to being left handed. Although most people are right handed, the argument goes, there is no moral value or deficit in being left handed. Similarly, although most people engage in different-sex sexual intimacy, there is no moral value or deficit in engaging in same-sex sexual intimacy.

Notice that the TLP's Proposition #1 is not the precise opposite of the TCP's Proposition #1. The former does not contend that same-sexual relationships are morally good; instead, it argues that they are morally neutral. Ultimately, however, the answer to the general moral question addressed by Proposition #1 becomes irrelevant once we transition into issues of political morality. According to the TLP's Proposition #2, the morality of relationships is irrelevant for purposes of determining whether the State should endow them with recognition. According to the TLP, *even if* the State deems same-sex relationships to be morally problematic, that assessment is irrelevant because morality is an insufficient (or illegitimate) ground upon which to base state action in the context of relationship recognition. In other words, the TLP holds that the question of morality must be bracketed from the question of state action in matters related to the legal recognition of intimate relationships. The TLP's Proposition #2, therefore, *is* the precise opposite of the TCP's Proposition #2.

The TLP's Proposition #3 is, in effect, a further elaboration of its Proposition #2. The former makes clear that the moral bracketing called for by the latter applies to considerations of equality. The TLP holds that, in the context of relationship recognition, the State can apply the principle of equality from a position of neutrality, that is, without having to take sides in disputed moral questions about particular categories of relationships. From the TLP's perspective, all that equality requires is that the State be even handed in its distribution of rights and benefits. The TLP concludes, therefore, that if the

State recognizes different-sex relationships, then it should also recognize same-sex relationships.

With a basic understanding of both the TCP and the TLP in place, I can now proceed to propose an alternative to both, which I call the Modified Liberal Position:

Modified Liberal Position (MLP) on State Recognition of Same-Sex Relationships

Proposition #1: Same-sex sexual relationships are as morally good as different-sex relationships.

Proposition #2: It is proper for the State to rely on moral considerations in deciding which intimate relationships to recognize.

Proposition #3: The State cannot apply the principle of equality to the question of which relationships to recognize in a morally neutral way.

Conclusion: Once the State recognizes one category of morally good relationships (e.g., different-sex relationships), then it must also recognize another category of such relationships (e.g., same-sex relationships).

I have argued elsewhere that same-sex relationships are morally good because they, like different-sex relationships, can serve as vehicles through which individuals meet their basic human needs and exercise their basic human capabilities related not only to sex, but also to the loving of and caring for other human beings.[10] I do not, however, elaborate on this argument here, and as a result, I do not defend the MLP's Proposition #1. Instead, my interest here is in addressing the political morality question of whether it is proper for the State to take into account considerations of morality in deciding which relationships to recognize. In answering that question in the affirmative, the MLP's Proposition #2 takes the same position as the TCP and the opposite position of the TLP. I explain in part II why I believe that the MLP and the TCP are correct on this point. I leave for part III a discussion of the connection between morality and equality in the context of relationship recognition (the issue raised by both the TLP's and the MLP's Proposition #3) and of why I believe that the MLP gets that connection right, while the TLP does not.

II. IGNORING QUESTIONS OF MORALITY IN RELATIONSHIP RECOGNITION: POSSIBLE BUT NOT APPEALING

There is no intrinsic connection between the morality of particular kinds of relationships and the question of whether they should be legally recognized.

It is theoretically possible, in other words, for the State to function under a relationship-recognition regime that calls on it to ignore moral considerations altogether. (Although those who abide by the TLP need not go this far, a morally neutral regime is consistent with the TLP.) The State could do this in one of two ways. First, it could legally recognize *all* intimate relationships. Second, it could refuse to recognize *any* intimate relationships. Although a State operating under either of these policy regimes would be able to bracket moral considerations from the question of which intimate relationships to legally recognize, both regimes are problematic for different reasons.

The problem with a regime of relationship recognition that grants legal status to all relationships is that it calls for the recognition of categories of relationships that almost everyone considers to be morally problematic because they are harmful to the individuals involved or to society (or both). An example would be sexual relationships between adults and minors. Another would be sexual relationships between parents and their children, regardless of whether the latter are adults or minors. The price of true moral bracketing, then, is a high one: it would require recognition of relationships that, because of their nature and composition, are likely to be quite harmful.

The conclusion that some sexually intimate relationships (such as those between parents and their children) lack goodness or value may seem so obvious to most of us that it may also seem as if the State, in denying them recognition, is not actually acting as a moral gatekeeper. The obviousness of a moral judgment, however, does not make that judgment any less moral. It only makes it less subject to dispute.

Once we acknowledge that it is proper for the State to refuse to recognize certain categories of intimate relationships because of their nature and composition, then the question no longer is whether the State should make moral judgments about intimate relationships, but is instead whether the State is making *appropriate* moral judgments regarding those relationships. The issue, in other words, is not whether the State should bring moral considerations to bear in determining which relationships to recognize, but is instead *which* moral considerations it should take into account.

Given that the State's recognition of all intimate relationships would lead to outcomes that are troubling, it is worth exploring a second (and possibly more appealing) way in which the State may ignore moral considerations as they relate to the legal recognition of intimate relationships. This alternative form of moral bracketing would call on the State to withhold recognition from all intimate relationships.

It is possible to question the extent to which the State, as a practical matter, could avoid altogether the recognition of relationships. For example, individuals operating under a regime in which the State withholds recognition of all intimate relationships would presumably be free to enter into contracts that would establish the rights and obligations arising from their intimate relationships. Even under this privatized model of relationship formation and organization, however, the State would still have a role to play when disagreements arose between the parties as to the enforceability and meaning of their contracts. Although the state action in such instances would be formally driven by principles of contract law rather than those of family law, the State would nonetheless have to make decisions that are analogous to the ones made by the government, under our current regulatory regime, in determining which relationships to recognize.

For example, to return to one of the morally problematic relationships already mentioned, the State would have to determine whether contracts setting forth the rights and obligations arising from sexually intimate relationships between parents and their children should be enforceable.[11] The considerations that would be taken into account in answering the question of whether those contracts are enforceable as a matter of public policy are likely to be quite similar to those that go to the question of whether the State should, also as a public policy matter, legally recognize the relationships to begin with. It is not clear, then, that moving the issue from the ambit of family law to that of contract law would remove from the analysis considerations and judgments related to the goodness and value of relationships based on their nature and composition.

Assuming, however, that an entirely privatized regime of relationship recognition would effectively bracket out moral considerations, there is still a significant limitation to that regime, at least from the perspective of sexual minorities. This limitation arises from the fact that, under an entirely privatized model of relationship recognition, there would be no legal obligation on third parties (such as employers and health care providers) to recognize the intimate relationships in question. While two individuals in an intimate relationship may be able to determine contractually many of the rights and obligations that apply vis-à-vis each other, such an agreement would not impose obligations of recognition on third parties.

As a result, the application of an entirely privatized model of relationship recognition would likely have a disparate impact on sexual minorities. If the State were tomorrow to remove itself altogether from the business of legally recognizing intimate relationships, it is likely that many entities, both public and private, would continue to recognize (and distribute benefits) to heterosexual couples in committed relationships even though they would no longer be legally required to do so. Many of these entities, however, are unlikely to do the same for intimate relationships that fall outside of the traditional heterosexual model.

In fact, one of the reasons why the gay rights movement has placed so much emphasis on gaining legal recognition for same-sex relationships has been the unwillingness of third parties to provide benefits and opportunities to same-sex couples that are, as a matter of course, offered to married heterosexual couples. Lesbians and gay men, to provide just one example, frequently find themselves unable to visit their partners in hospitals and prisons. Under an entirely privatized model of relationship recognition, there would be no obligation on the part of those institutions to provide sexual minorities with the same access given to heterosexuals. The imposition of a legal obligation not to discriminate against individuals in certain relationships might take care of this limitation, but it would also reinject the State into making distinctions between those relationships that merit legal protection (in this case, in the form of antidiscrimination laws) and those that do not.

From a gay rights perspective, then, the type of moral neutrality that would accompany a privatized model of relationship recognition comes at a significant cost because it would, by itself, do little to address existing biases and prejudices as manifested in discriminatory policies pursued by many institutions and organizations, both private and public. A privatized model, in other words, would leave the status quo largely in place, one in which different-sex relationships are advantaged and same-sex relationships are disadvantaged.

Ultimately, state neutrality on the issue of relationship recognition, while theoretically possible, ends up producing results that are problematic. Those who seek to expand the types of relationships that the government legally recognizes would be better served by articulating positive moral reasons as to why particular categories of relationships that have heretofore not been legally recognized are worthy of such recognition rather than by demanding moral neutrality from the State.

III. EQUALITY AND NEUTRALITY

A skeptic who supports the legal recognition of same-sex relationships but who does not believe that the State should make moral assessments of categories of relationships—someone, in other words, who abides by the TLP rather than the MLP—may argue that if the State were deciding, in the abstract, whether to legally recognize same-sex relationships, then considerations related to the value and goodness of those relationships might come into play. But once we pose the issue in the present social context, namely, one in which the State *already* recognizes different-sex relationships, then the principle of equality, *applied in a neutral way*, requires that the same opportunity be afforded to same-sex couples. (This is, remember, the approach defended by the TLP.)

This objection raises the fascinating and complicated philosophical question of whether the principle of equality is morally neutral. Although I cannot here give that question the attention that it deserves, it seems to me that most of the substantive understandings of equality, such as the anti-subordination perspective defended by Catherine MacKinnon and the deeply humanist and universalist conception articulated by Martin Luther King, Jr. (to name only two), are imbued with both moral claims and judgments.[12]

If there is a conception of equality that might come close to endorsing moral neutrality, it would likely be the type of formal or procedural equality which holds that those who are similarly situated should be treated similarly. It can be argued that this understanding of equality, which is traceable to Aristotle,[13] and which forms the foundation of constitutional equality in the United States,[14] is morally neutral because it does not call for the making of moral claims or judgments. Instead, it simply seeks to ascertain whether parties whom the government treats differently are similarly situated.

Note, however, that the principle of formal or procedural equality requires the asking of a question that is antecedent to its application, namely, whether the class making the equality claim is similarly situated to the class that currently enjoys the benefit that is the subject of that claim. (I will refer to this question as the "antecedent question.") It might be possible, in certain instances, to address the antecedent question from within the confines of moral bracketing, that is, by separating the issue of state action from considerations of morality. For example, it seems possible, to rely on a famous Supreme Court equal protection case, to determine whether optometrists are similarly situated to opticians, for purposes of governmental regulation, without addressing questions of morality.[15]

However, it is much more difficult, if not impossible, to answer the antecedent question pertaining to this chapter, namely, whether those in same-sex relationships are, for purposes of governmental recognition, similarly situated to those in different-sex relationships without making judgments about the goodness and value of the relationships in question. Indeed, what is ultimately at issue in the political and legal debates over the recognition of same-sex relationships is not so much what the principle of equality *demands*; instead, the disagreement is mostly about whether the principle *applies*. The dispute, in other words, is primarily about the antecedent question.

For opponents of gay rights, same-sex relationships do not deserve state recognition because they are not as good as different-sex relationships. From this perspective, heterosexual intimacy is a necessary component of valuable relationships, in part because it is through that intimacy that new life can be created. As a result, same-sex couples *are not* similarly situated to different-sex couples and, therefore, the principle of equality *does not* apply.

On the other side, there are those of us who argue that sex/gender is morally irrelevant in assessing the goodness of intimate relationships; instead what matters is the degree to which the intimacy is accompanied by other factors, such as the presence of mutuality and reciprocity. Both of these, we argue, are as likely to be part of same-sex relationships as they are of different-sex relationships. As a result, same-sex couples *are* similarly situated to different-sex couples, and therefore, the principle of equality *does* apply.

In each of the two previous paragraphs, it has been the (admittedly disputed) answer to the antecedent question that determines whether the principle of formal or procedural equality applies. The State, therefore, when deciding whether that principle applies to the recognition of same-sex relationships must take a position, for better or for worse, on the moral issues raised by the antecedent question. There is simply no avoiding it.

One of the implications of what I am suggesting here is that relying on a general nondiscrimination principle is not enough to make out a philosophically coherent case on behalf of the legal recognition of same-sex relationships. To argue, for example, that the State's failure to legally recognize same-sex relationships constitutes improper discrimination because the State already recognizes different-sex relationships assumes, without defending, the proposition that same-sex couples are similarly situated to different-sex couples.

This is not to deny that antidiscrimination arguments are politically and legally appealing, not least because they may succeed in placing the burden on the government to defend the differential treatment of same-sex couples. My point instead is that, as a theoretical and conceptual matter, something more is needed than the mere call on the government not to discriminate against same-sex couples. That "something more," I believe, must to some extent tackle the question of whether same-sex couples are as worthy of the rights and benefits that accompany legal recognition as are different-sex couples. It is, in turn, not possible to address the worthiness of same-sex relationships without taking some moral (or, at the very least, highly normative) positions about the value and goodness of those relationships.

A critic may argue that empirical information about same-sex relationships (e.g., the degree of commitment between same-sex partners; the impact on children of being raised in a same-sex household) is enough to determine whether same-sex couples are similarly situated to different-sex couples. Although empirical data can be of assistance in this regard, it can only go so far. For example, empirical information by itself cannot answer the largely normative question of whether the physical complementarity between men and women, as some conservatives argue, is a necessary element of a marital relationship.[16]

In addition, there are often values-based disagreements on the meaning (or proper interpretation) of empirical data about human relationships. To provide just one example of what I have in mind, let me briefly address the ostensibly empirical question of the impact on children of having parents who are gay or lesbian. Although most social scientists who have studied this issue have concluded that there are no differences between the children of gay and lesbian parents on the one hand and the children of heterosexual parents on the other, others have suggested—including some who support the legal recognition of same-sex relationships—that there may be differences, for example, in matters such as gender preferences and behavior.[17] Even if we could somehow empirically resolve these types of disagreements (for example, by conducting better and more accurate studies), there are still crucial values-based judgments that still need to be made regarding the meaning of the data. For instance, we need to determine whether the possible existence of differences between the children of gay parents on the one hand and those of straight parents is a cause for concern. For some, the mere existence of differences will be enough to render suspect the parenting by lesbians and gay men. In contrast, others will argue that the dispositive criterion should not be difference but rather harm.[18] And even if the latter prevail, there is still the difficult question of how to define "harm" in this instance. Does the fact, for example, that the boys of lesbian mothers may abide by fewer traditionally male characteristics and roles harm them or society? These are the types of questions that cannot be resolved simply by pouring over empirical information.

In short, it is difficult to reach ultimate conclusions about the nature and quality of the love, caring, and nurture that can be part of human relationships entirely within the parameters of empiricism. Although assessments of those relationships can clearly be informed by empirical findings, values-based judgments must ultimately be brought to bear in distinguishing between relationships that are worthy of legal recognition and those that are not.

IV. OBJECTIONS (BY LIBERALS) TO THE MODIFIED LIBERAL POSITION ON THE LEGAL RECOGNITION OF INTIMATE RELATIONSHIPS

My aim so far in this chapter has been to explain why the MLP is more relevant than the TLP to the contemporary political and legal debates over which intimate relationships the State should recognize. I have argued that the MLP's (and the TCP's) Proposition #2, namely, that it is appropriate for the State to rely on moral considerations in deciding which intimate relationships to recognize, is correct (and that the TLP's Proposition #2 is therefore incorrect). I have also taken issue with the TLP's Proposition #3, which holds that the principle of equality can be *applied in a morally neutral way* in the context of relationship recognition. Instead, I have argued, consistently with the MLP's Proposition #3, that moral considerations must first be addressed before we can determine whether the principle of equality applies.

There are likely to be several objections to my defense of the MLP by those who otherwise might agree with me that the State should recognize same-sex relationships, but who feel more comfortable operating under a relationship-recognition regime that follows the TLP rather than the MLP. In this section, I address what are likely to be two of the most important of those objections: First, that the incommensurability of moral positions on controversial issues requires that the State remain neutral as to the correctness of any one of those positions; and second, that the MLP, in effect, endorses the idea that the State should legislate morality, and as such, threatens the individual liberties and rights of members of minority groups.

A. Incommensurability of Moral Views

One argument against the incorporation of notions of morality into political and legal debates over which relationships the State should recognize is likely to be as follows: Different people have different views on what is moral and there is no objective or clear way of determining which of those positions is correct. If individuals, including philosophers and religious leaders, cannot agree among themselves as to what is moral, the argument goes, then how can we expect the State to do so?

Neutrality as a principle of political morality is appealing precisely because it offers us the hope of avoiding the disagreements and messiness that inevitably accompany efforts to define the good and the valuable in human affairs. An understanding of the State acting as a neutral arbiter making decisions from a position of impartiality is undoubtedly reassuring, especially to members of minorities (sexual or otherwise) who have traditionally been excluded from important social institutions based, in part, on moral considerations.

The reassurance offered by neutrality, however, is ultimately a false one, at least in areas of public policy where citizens ask the State to act (or not act) on matters that directly implicate contested moral views. Abortion is a good example of this phenomenon. On one side of the persistent, and seemingly intractable, debate over the morality of abortion are those who raise explicitly moral objections to the procedure based on the status of the fetus as a human life. On the other side are those who argue that considerations of autonomy and privacy require that pregnant women be permitted to make the decision of whether to carry a fetus to term.

Although pro-choice arguments are not usually understood as being grounded in explicitly moral terms, the nature of the issue requires that supporters of abortion rights take moral positions. At the very least, those who support a woman's right to choose have made an antecedent moral determination (antecedent, that is, to the public policy question of whether and how the State should regulate abortions) that a fetus, especially one that is only a few weeks or months old, does not have the status of a fully formed human life and is therefore not entitled to the protections that are usually afforded to that status. Notions of morality are also (at least) implicitly relied on by pro-choice advocates because from their perspective, the exercise of personal choice in matters of reproduction and child-bearing is a positive moral good that outweighs the interests of the fetus.

It would be nice if the State, confronted with the incommensurable views of citizens on the morality of abortion, could make the decision of whether and how to regulate the procedure from a position of moral neutrality. However, the State, whether through the decisions of elected representatives or of members of the judiciary, like its citizens, must ultimately take a position on whether abortion is a morally acceptable choice for individuals to make.[19]

Social conservatives understand perfectly well that a State which allows women to choose whether to have abortions is not being morally neutral. Liberals have a harder time coming to terms with that proposition, perhaps because one is more likely to perceive that the State is being morally neutral when it regulates in ways that are consistent with one's moral views.[20]

In any event, it may not be possible to determine ultimately and objectively whether the State, by either banning or allowing abortions, is making the correct moral choice. *But, regardless of which choice the State makes, in making a choice, it cannot remain morally neutral.*

The same is true when it comes to the question of whether the State should recognize certain intimate relationships. Like with abortion, sexual intimacy, and the relationships that can accompany it, raise seemingly intractable disagreements among citizens about what is good and valuable in matters of human sexuality and relationships. If the State chooses to maintain the status quo by continuing to withhold legal recognition from same-sex relationships, then it will side with those who believe that there is something about same-sex relationships that makes them less valuable, and therefore less deserving of such recognition, than different-sex relationships. If the State chooses to modify the status quo by recognizing gay relationships, then it will be because it has reached the opposite conclusion.

It seems, therefore, more appropriate (and intellectually honest) for liberals and progressives, rather than demanding strict neutrality on the part of the State, to acknowledge instead that the State, in deciding whether and how to regulate in matters associated with human sexuality and relationships, cannot avoid taking sides in disputed moral questions.[21]

It is important to note that once the State has staked out a moral position by, for example, allowing abortions or by refusing to recognize same-sex relationships, that position should not be viewed as a final judgment that is beyond reconsideration. In a well-functioning democracy, there will always be room for further disagreement and debate, and the State may have to re-evaluate its position as time progresses.

This is, of course, precisely what the State did when it came to the status of African-Americans in our society. For much of American history, the State, through laws and policies that segregated, and severely limited opportunities, on the basis of race, staked out a moral position regarding the inferiority of black people when compared to white people. It is clear to us today that the State, prior to the changes brought about by the civil rights era, was not morally neutral on the question of whether blacks shared with whites those basic human attributes that entitled them to equal treatment and protection under the law.

There has been, over the last fifty years, a significant reconsideration by the State of that moral question to the point where it now generally demands that all citizens be treated with equal respect and dignity regardless of race. An equal opportunity State, however, is as non-neutral as a racist state. It may seem to most of us that it is beyond moral dispute that race should be an irrelevant criterion in the distribution of legal rights and benefits,[22] but as I have already noted, the obviousness of moral judgments does not make those judgments any less moral.

B. Legislating Morality

When a committee appointed by the British Parliament in the 1950s suggested that consensual sodomy be decriminalized,[23] it led to a famous debate between two leading figures in British law on the question of whether the State should attempt to legislate morality. On one side was H. L. A. Hart, one of the most important Anglo-American legal philosophers of the twentieth century, who argued that the State should not seek to legislate morality.[24] Arguing the opposite view was Patrick Devlin, a prominent conservative judge who sat on Britain's High Court.[25]

The basic disagreement at the center of Hart's and Devlin's debate continues to this day with liberals insisting that the State should not attempt to legislate morality and conservatives arguing that it should. A liberal skeptic might thus fairly ask whether the position that I am defending in this chapter, namely, that it is proper for the State to take into account moral considerations in deciding which intimate relationships to recognize, will encourage the State, in effect, to legislate morality.

The honest answer to that question is "yes it would." I cannot deny that whenever the State makes distinctions among intimate relationships by recognizing some and not others (as when it refuses to recognize sexual relationships, for example, between parents and their children), it is to some extent legislating morality because it is taking a position as to which intimacy choices are acceptable and which are not.[26]

The concern that liberals have with the concept of legislating morality is that it can threaten individual rights to liberty and equality, in particular those of minority groups who might be viewed unfavorably by the majority. This is an understandable concern, particularly in matters related to human sexuality and relationships, given that the morality that has traditionally been reflected in public policies regarding such matters has been a conservative one that has sought to strictly limit the intimacy options available to individuals. The traditional conservative position on these questions is that only heterosexual sexual intimacy within the confines of marriage is morally acceptable.[27] From this perspective, all of the other ways in which it is possible to form and maintain intimate relationships are morally suspect.

The thrust of a liberal morality in matters of sexuality and human relationships, on the other hand, is very different. It seeks to expand rather than constrict the options and choices available to individuals. It values pluralism and diversity in the ways in which individuals go about organizing their most intimate and personal relationships. This is not to say, as already noted, that there should be *no* limits placed on which choices are recognized and supported by the State.[28] It is to say, however, that the presumption should be that individuals are ultimately in the best position to determine which types of relationships and intimacies work best for them.

This is, generally speaking, the *values-based* understanding of human sexuality and relationships that liberals (and progressives) are striving to have the State adopt. We have succeeded in some areas (e.g., the regulation of sodomy) and are still struggling in others (e.g., the legal recognition of same-sex relationships). In my estimation, individual rights to liberty and equality in these matters are better served and protected by having the State adopt into its laws and policies a distinctly liberal understanding of human sexuality and relationships, rather than by demanding that the State exercise a type of neutrality in these matters that is either unappealing or unrealistic.

Finally, I want to emphasize that what I am suggesting here is not inconsistent with the view that the Constitution appropriately places some limitations on the ability of the State to legislate morality. In the past, when the State sought to implement a conservative and traditional morality in matters related to human sexuality, it was liberals and progressives who called on constitutional provisions (such as the Due Process Clause and the Equal Protection

Clause) to protect the interests of sexual minorities.[29] If a future State were to fully implement a liberal understanding of human sexuality and relationships, those who hold traditional moral views on these matters would be entitled to rely on the same constitutional provisions (and perhaps others, including the Free Exercise Clause) to protect their interests. Indeed, it is precisely because the State cannot remain neutral on these issues that there will always be a need to protect moral minorities from moral majorities regardless of which social groups belong to the former and which to the latter.

CONCLUSION

Social conservatives have a tendency to speak about morality in the public sphere—on issues ranging from gay rights to abortion to stem cell research—as if they have a monopoly on questions related to values and the good. They seem to assume, in other words, that morality is on their side. Liberals and progressives, when participating in the public sphere, have for too long acquiesced in that assumption.

One of the reasons for this acquiescence is the view, held by many liberals and progressives, that the State should remain neutral on contested moral questions, such as those usually implicated by gay rights issues. I have attempted to show in this chapter, however, that state neutrality in the context of one particular issue that is of the utmost importance to the gay rights movement today, namely, the legal recognition of same-sex relationships, is either unappealing or unrealistic.

It is a mistake to understand contemporary debates over the issue of the legal recognition of same-sex relationships as one between a "morality-infused conservative talk" and a "morally-neutral liberal talk." Instead, the debate, at the end of the day, is about a clash between two distinct—and in many ways irreconcilable—moral outlooks. The State cannot ultimately serve as a neutral arbiter of this disagreement. Instead, the State, for better or for worse, has to take sides.

NOTES

1. The conservative position on the proper role of morality in matters of law and policy is defended in Robert George, *Making Men Moral: Civil Liberties and Public Morality* (New York: Oxford University Press, 1993).

2. In political philosophy terms, this liberal position is often referred to as the separation of the right from the good. Thus, the liberal political philosopher John Rawls argued that the right is prior to the good; that is, that fundamental principles of

justice are not connected to and are not dependent on any particular understanding of what constitutes a good life. John Rawls, *A Theory of Justice* (Cambridge: Belknap Press, 1971), pp. 30–33. Rawls believed that justice was best promoted when citizens separate their political values, which go to questions of the right, from their philosophical, moral and religious values, which go to questions of the good. John Rawls, *Political Liberalism* (New York: Columbia University Press, 1993), pp., 173–211.

3. Ronald Dworkin, for example, criticizes the incorporation of majoritarian morality into the formulation of public policy because doing so threatens the equal treatment of individuals by the State. He therefore argues that "political decisions about what citizens should be forced to do or prevented from doing must be made on grounds that are neutral among the competing convictions about good and bad lives that different members of the community might hold." Ronald Dworkin, "Foundations of Liberal Equality," in *Equal Freedom: Selected Tanner Lectures on Human Values*, ed. Stephen Darwall (Ann Arbor: University of Michigan Press, 1995), pp. 190, 200.

4. Carlos A. Ball, *The Morality of Gay Rights: An Exploration in Political Philosophy* (New York: Routledge, 2003).

5. Rebecca E. Zietlow, "To Secure These Rights: Congress, Courts and the 1964 Civil Rights Act," 57 *Rutgers Law Review* 945, 1006 (2005).

6. Patrick Lee and Robert George explain the argument as follows:

> In reproductive activity the bodily parts of the male and the bodily parts of the female participate in a single action, coitus, which is oriented to reproduction (though not every act of coitus is reproductive), so that the subject of the action is the male and the female as a unit. Coitus is a unitary action in which the male and the female become literally one organism. In marital intercourse, this bodily unity is an aspect—indeed, the biological matrix—of the couple's comprehensive marital communion.

Patrick Lee & Robert P. George, "What Sex Can Be: Self-Alienation, Illusion, or One-Flesh Union," 42 *American Journal of Jurisprudence* 135, 143–44 (1997) (footnotes omitted).

7. *See id.* at 150 ("The lack of complementarity in homosexual couples is a condition which renders it impossible for them to perform the kind of act which makes them organically one."); *see also* John M. Finnis, Law, "Morality, and "'Sexual Orientation,'" 69 *Notre Dame Law Review* 1049, 1066 (1994) (arguing that lesbians and gay men cannot, through sexual intimacy, become "a biological (and therefore) personal unit.").

8. Finnis makes this point as follows:

> Whatever the generous hopes and dreams and thoughts of giving with which some same-sex partners may surround their sexual acts, those acts cannot express or do more than is expressed or done if two strangers engage in such activity to give each other pleasure, or a prostitute pleasures a client to give him pleasure in return for money, or (say) a man masturbates to give himself pleasure and a fantasy of more human relationships after a grueling day on the assembly line.

Finnis, *supra* note 7, at 1067.

9. I address the moral objections to same-sex sexual intimacy raised by John Finnis and other new natural law theorists in Ball, *supra* note 4, at 117–25.

10. Ball, *supra* note 4, at 77-91.

11. If the children in question are minors, the contract could be voided on the ostensibly morally neutral ground that minors cannot contractually bind themselves.

12. *See* Catharine A. MacKinnon, "Sex Equality under the Constitution of India: Problems, Prospects, and 'Personal Laws,'" 4 *Int'l J. Const. L.* 181, 181–88 (2006) (contrasting the ostensible neutrality of formal equality with a view of equality that is predicated on the practice of social subordination and which assumes that no social group is inferior to any other); Martin Luther King, Jr., "The Ethical Demands for Integration," in *A Testament of Hope: The Essential Writings and Speeches of Martin Luther King, Jr.* 117–25 ed., James M. Washington (San Francisco: Harper & Row, 1986) (grounding a call for racial integration on the dignity and worth of all individuals).

13. *See* Aristotle, the Politics 307, trans. Benjamin Jowett, (The Modern Library, 1943) ("[e]quality consists in the same treatment of similar persons").

14. "Equal protection is the guarantee that similar people will be dealt with in a similar manner and that people of different circumstances will not be treated as if they were the same." 3 Ronald D. Rotunda & John E. Nowak, *Treatise on Constitutional Law: Substance and Procedure* §18.2, at 209 (St. Paul: West, 1999) (citation omitted).

15. *See* Williamson v. Lee Optical of Okla., Inc., 348 U.S. 483 (1955) (relying on health concerns to uphold law that favored optometrists over opticians).

16. *See* discussion at *supra* notes 6–8 and accompanying text.

17. *See* Judith Stacey and Timothy J. Biblarz, "(How) Does Sexual Orientation of Parents Matter?" 66 *American Sociological Review* 159 (2001).

18. *See* Carlos A. Ball, "Lesbian and Gay Families: Gender Nonconformity and the Implications of Difference," 31 *Capital University Law Review* 691 (2003).

19. Rawls argued that it was, in fact, possible to address the issue of abortion by applying three political values that he deemed to be morally neutral: "[T]he due respect for human life, the ordered reproduction of political society over time, including the family in some form, and finally the equality of women as equal citizens." *Political Liberalism, supra* note 2, at 243 n.32. Rawls concluded that "any reasonable balance of these three values will give a woman a duly qualified right to decide whether or not to end her pregnancy during the first trimester. . . . [A]t this early stage of pregnancy the political value of the equality of women is overriding, and this right is required to give it substance and force." *Id.* The problem with this line of argument, however, is that the weight accorded to Rawls's political (and so-called neutral) values flows from their moral or religious content. For example, the weight that we assign to the first factor (respect for human life) depends on when we believe a human life begins, a belief that is likely determined by our moral or religious convictions. As Michael Sandel has noted, "if the Catholic Church is right about the moral status of the fetus, if abortion is morally tantamount to murder, then it is not clear why the political values of toleration and women's equality, important though they are, should prevail." Michael J. Sandel, "Political Liberalism," 107 *Harvard Law Review* 1766, 1788 n.52 (1994).

94 *Carlos A. Ball*

20. One of the reasons why it might seem as if the State is not taking sides regarding the moral questions associated with abortion is that under our current abortion regime, it is the pregnant woman, and not the State, who decides, in any given case, whether an abortion is appropriate. Even when operating under a regulatory regime that allows for such individualized decisions, however, the State (or more specifically, the judiciary in the American context) has made a crucial prior decision, that is, it has decided that considerations of personal autonomy and privacy trump other moral considerations, including those associated with the interests of the fetus.

21. This is the case unless, as already noted, the State were to recognize all intimate relationships, or none of them. *See supra* part II.

22. The obviousness of this moral conclusion is admittedly complicated by issues related to affirmative action.

23. *The Wolfenden Report: Report on the Committee on Homosexual Offenses and Prostitution* (New York: Stein & Day, 1963).

24. Herbert L. Hart, *Law, Liberty, and Morality* (Stanford: Stanford University Press, 1963).

25. Patrick Devlin, *The Enforcement of Morals* (New York: Oxford University Press, 1965).

26. The only way of avoiding the legislating of morality in this area would be to take such authority away from the State by requiring it to recognize all intimate relationships or by prohibiting it from recognizing any of them. As already noted, however, each of these options presents its own set of problems. *See supra* part II.

27. *See, e.g.,* Finnis, *supra* note 7, at 1064–65.

28. *See supra* part II.

29. *See, e.g.,* Lawrence v. Texas, 539 U.S. 558 (2003); Romer v. Evans, 517 U.S. (1996).

II

SAME-SEX ATTRACTION AND LIBERAL DEMOCRATIC THEORY

Introduction

Emily R. Gill

The second part of this volume addresses some broader issues pertaining to same-sex attraction. Although the subject of marriage does arise here, the four contributors set their particular subjects within the broader context of liberal democratic theory. Claire Snyder-Hall argues that the 2008 California judicial decision allowing same-sex couples to marry rests squarely within the expansion of rights characteristic of the liberal democratic tradition. Jason Pierceson suggests that negative freedom from government intrusion needs to be supplemented with positive freedom, or the idea that the government has a legitimate role to play if the equal rights and freedoms of all citizens are to be secured. Samuel Marcosson focuses on those whose understandings of their religious obligations impel them to discriminate against those experiencing same-sex attraction. Valerie Lehr broadens the discussion of families headed by same-sex couples to consider the needs of young people, arguing that youths are mistakenly not attributed the status of sexual agents. Finally, Gordon Babst focuses on some implications of the concept of heteronormativity, suggesting that the true alternative to heterosexuality is not homosexuality, but sexual pluralism. All of these chapters are thoughtful contributions to the book's overall argument that individuals experiencing same-sex attraction should not simply be the subjects of grudging toleration, but should be empowered as full citizens of the liberal democratic polity.

Claire Snyder-Hall begins with the communitarian critique that liberal theory is indifferent to moral arguments, requires the setting aside of moral claims, and envisions a liberal self that is unencumbered by moral obligations to others. By contrast, she argues that liberalism does allow a moral defense of political equality for gay and lesbian citizens. Pluralism allows for the development of multiple religious and moral traditions, or comprehensive doctrines, as Rawls terms them. Her implication is that respect for the coexistence of multiple moral traditions differs substantially from an abrogation of *all* moral traditions. She also cites Locke, Kant, and Lincoln in defense of the moral equality, liberty, and dignity of all individuals.

One instantiation of this tradition is jurisprudence recognizing marriage as a fundamental right. The 2009 California decision allowing same-sex couples to marry exemplifies the application of these concepts of moral equality and freedom. The California Supreme Court noted that marriage does not exist only to serve the interests of society; if so, the state could establish or abolish this institution at will. Instead, the right to marry protects substantial interests in both personal autonomy and liberty. In sum, concludes Snyder, this decision is a moral one, preventing the *immorality* of discrimination and harm, and as such it is clearly in accord with the American political tradition.

Jason Pierceson also sets his essay within the context of the American political tradition. What he terms humanist liberalism, emphasizing negative freedom from government intrusion and ranking freedom over equality, has dominated the theoretical landscape. However, reform liberalism, embracing positive freedom and government activity to guarantee equal rights and freedoms for all, has played an equally worthy role. Pierceson traces these contrasting themes historically through several writers about same-sex attraction, then turning to ways in which the courts have developed and enhanced the richer language of reform liberalism.

He next grapples with leftist criticism of the pursuit of marriage by same-sex couples and their allies. Critics such as Nancy Polikoff argue that this strategy plays into the hands of traditionalists and reverses feminist efforts to legitimize diverse forms of family. Pierceson responds that this critique underestimates the reformist ability of liberalism. Moreover, Polikoff's implicit faith that legislators will quickly de-link marriage and public policies supporting families, once the rationality of this trajectory is presented, is misplaced. Pierceson concludes that it makes political sense for now to utilize developed policy frameworks to extend equality to same-sex couples.

Samuel Marcosson begins with the premise that because of the constitutional value assigned to religion by the First Amendment, religious arguments carry special status in our public discourse. First, he establishes the long history of religious arguments for equal rights in the historical struggles for the abolition of slavery, female suffrage, and African American civil rights. Because the government is to be neutral in religious disputes, unlike other disputes over public policy, and because the former are to remain exclusively private, however, we must be careful not to adopt public policies that risk chilling religious speakers and arguments, even those with whom or which we may vehemently disagree.

Second, although governmental neutrality towards religion might seem to require that both religious and nonreligious employers adhere to anti-discrimination laws governing sexual orientation and gender identity, the burdens they may impose on religious belief and practice permit religious exemptions to these laws. Marcosson concurs with such exemptions, given the special position of religious belief and practice in our culture. The invocation of this special status, however, does and should carry a cost. Individuals and religious groups who request and receive religious exemptions "are removing themselves from a critical part of our contemporary social contract." If the protection of religious belief and practice is a core constitutional value and a fundamental right, so also is the priority of equality that is expressed in antidiscrimination laws. Religious beliefs should be respected, but, correspondingly, religious organizations that receive public benefits should agree to relinquish exemptions from antidiscrimination laws to which they would otherwise be entitled. In sum, those who seek exemption from some of the *burdens* of respect for others' equality should not expect to enjoy all the *benefits* of equal treatment to which they might otherwise be entitled.

Valerie Lehr focuses on the often-overlooked subject of the status of young people as moral and sexual agents, arguing for a rethinking of adult and teen relationships in ways that would benefit queer and questioning youth. She begins with a discussion of the challenges faced by these young people, who are often bullied and harassed and who subsequently feel unsafe and often unsupported at home. She continues with discussion of Martha Fineman, who would have the state focus on the dependency needs of children in the mother-child relationship, and of Maxine Eichner, who suggests that dependency relationships exist between adults as well as between adults and children. Both Fineman's and Eichner's models would increase children's resources, but not their voice, and the state would intervene on behalf of young people only when children are already damaged.

Lehr argues for an extension of Eichner's own insight that the state needs to foster and protect the rights of vulnerable young people even against their own parents or caregivers. These youth deserve not only care, but also the right to express themselves under the rubric of liberty rights, an idea well developed by Laura Purdy. In Purdy's view, for example, education should not only be mandatory, but also exclusively public and focused on critical thinking. This would allow young people to resist parental indoctrination, and it might even extend to state intervention in their living arrangements if they are the gay or lesbian children of homophobic parents. These interferences may require mediation and, Lehr suggests, public agreement that young people have liberty rights and autonomy that are deserving of respect.

Finally, Gordon Babst argues that heteronormativity, or the idea that heterosexuality is the norm, misleads us into assuming that the world is divided into two kinds of people, heterosexuals and homosexuals. Heteronormativity, however, is grounded on monism, or the idea that one way of being is "normal" and that alternatives are deviations from that norm. Instead, Babst suggests that heterosexuality's alternative is human sexual pluralism, which is premised on the assumption "that humans are sexual beings, not types of sexual beings." Moreover, heteronormativity establishes a particular kind of sexuality as the norm as surely as an establishment of religion posits a particular kind of belief system as the norm, one that is superior to all others.

Babst criticizes the contemporary natural law theorists, who claim that their traditionalist understanding of human sexuality is independent of their Roman Catholic faith, as in fact sectarian in their attempt to impose their interpretation of sexuality and marriage on everyone. Physical facts about reproduction do not in themselves require exclusively opposite-sex expressions of intimacy. He also cites Kinsey's findings that human sexuality exists on a continuous spectrum, without a bright line between various types of sexuality. Babst's essay represents a provocative analysis of the meanings of human pluralism.

5

Marriage Equality and the Morality of Liberalism

The California Decision

R. Claire Snyder-Hall

As the United States Supreme Court observed in *Lawrence v. Texas* . . . "times can blind us to certain truths and later generations can see that laws once thought necessary and proper in fact serve to oppress."

—Supreme Court of California, *In re: Marriage Cases* (2008)[1]

On May 16, 2008 the Supreme Court of California eliminated unjust laws that had prevented same-sex couples from being able to marry legally, a decision in keeping with the highest moral values of American democracy. The decision was not viewed that way by all, however. Many conservatives condemn the Court for using what they see as the amoral principles of liberalism to undermine the moral principles that have undergirded American society since the founding. That is to say, because liberal political theory allows people to say, "I think you are behaving immorally, but that is your choice, and it's not the government's business to tell you how to live," it makes some people believe that it is a fundamentally amoral philosophy. In taking a liberal perspective, the Court presumably rules without regard to moral values.

In condemning Court decisions that mandate legal equality for all citizens, including lesbians and gay men, conservatives rely largely on their own religious beliefs but also on the democratic discourse of communitarianism. Communitarians often emphasize the importance of shared values as the foundation for democratic self-government and hope to reintroduce moral reasoning into political discussions. For many communitarians, same-sex marriage undermines the traditional values of communities, and so it weakens rather than strengthens democratic self-government. They condemn liberalism for allowing Court decisions to trample on the moral beliefs of the citizenry. In making the communitarian case against liberalism, however, theorists, pundits, and activists mischaracterize the liberal tradition as fundamentally amoral, when the tradition actually offers a rich vision of moral good, and one that justifies the legalization of same-sex marriage. In its essence, liberalism constitutes a political tradition that allows moral pluralism to flourish; it emphasizes important moral values, like liberty, equality, human dignity, and the rule of law; it has greatly contributed to the fundamentally moral discourse of human rights; and it stands opposed to and lessens the possibility of immoral acts such as suppression of dissent, tyranny, cruelty, and hate. America's dominant political philosophy, liberalism provides a moral justification for marriage equality, as articulated by the Supreme Court of California.

COMMUNITARIANISM AND THE DEMORALIZATION OF LIBERALISM

Liberalism, with its separation of church and state, is often viewed as antithetical to morality. For example, communitarian theorist Michael Sandel describes liberalism in a way that makes it seem, at best, amoral. Focusing his critique on John Rawls's *Theory of Justice* (1971), Sandel reduces the rich tradition of liberal political theory to three major claims. First, he argues, contemporary liberalism posits the ideal of the "neutral state" that remains indifferent to moral arguments, protecting only the rights of individuals to make their own choices about right and wrong.[2] An example of this might be the *Lawrence v. Texas* (2003) Supreme Court ruling that overturned laws criminalizing homosexual sodomy: "This Court's obligation is to define the liberty of all, not to mandate its own moral code."[3] For some the Court seems to say, "Homosexual sodomy may be immoral, but Americans should be free to do it anyway."

Second, Sandel argues that liberalism requires a "bracketing of moral claims" that takes moral controversies off the table of political discussion.[4] For example, since people disagree about the morality of abortion, the liberal state leaves it up to each pregnant woman to decide for herself whether or not to take a pregnancy to term. This approach leads to the old saw, "You can't legislate morality."

Finally, Sandel argues that liberalism presents a vision of the self that is "unencumbered" by moral obligations to others, unless those obligations are freely chosen.[5] For example, Sandel argues that liberal divorce laws allow a man to walk away from his conjugal commitments, if he no longer wants to remain married; the Court no longer considers the morality of behavior when determining divorce settlements. Thus, Sandel's portrayal of liberalism as oppositional to morality makes it seem that the political philosophy itself is amoral, if not immoral in effect.

But that is not Sandel's entire argument. He also argues that while liberalism seems amoral and claims to be neutral, it actually imposes its own set of values on public policy—values such as, toleration, freedom, and social cooperation—values that he finds inadequate to a rich moral life. Sandel argues that America's dominant public philosophy has come to allow those thin liberal values to trump other more robust moral ones. While recognizing the benefits of such a system, Sandel also suggests

it is not always reasonable to set aside competing values that may arise from substantive moral and religious doctrines. At least where grave moral questions are concerned, whether it is reasonable to bracket moral and religious controversies for the sake of political agreement partly depends on which of the contending moral or religious doctrines is true.[6]

For example, the liberal solution to the debate over abortion—"the right to choose"—makes sense only if liberals are correct in arguing that abortion is not murder; if the Catholic Church is correct and abortion is indeed murder, then it cannot be allowed under the guise of individual choice. Sandel argues that the thin values of liberalism prove inadequate in the face of serious moral questions.

Antigay conservatives often view homosexuality as a grave moral issue. For example, in March 2008 Oklahoma state representative Sally Kern proclaimed,

Studies show, no society that has totally embraced homosexuality has lasted for more than, you know, a few decades. . . . I honestly think it's the biggest threat our nation has, even more so than terrorism or Islam. . . . They are going after our young children, as young as two years of age, to try to teach them that the homosexual lifestyle is an acceptable lifestyle. . . . One of my colleagues said, "We don't have a gay problem in our community" . . . well you know what, that is so dumb. If you have cancer in your little toe, do you just say that I'm going to forget about it since the rest of you is fine? It spreads! This stuff is deadly and it is spreading. It will destroy our young people and it will destroy this nation.

When LGBT activists protested Kern's hateful speech, Peter LaBarbera, President of Americans for Truth about Homosexuality, responded by calling homosexuality "immoral sexual conduct [that] is destructive to America and harmful to children." According to LaBarbera, "Kern told Americans For Truth that 'perhaps my choice of the word "terrorism" was not the best,' but that her comments were meant to be applied to the culture (war), in this way: just as terrorists seek to destroy America, homosexual activists are destroying the moral fabric of this nation."[7] Kern and LaBarbera are not the only ones who consider homosexuality a grave moral threat and so something public policy and law should repudiate.

The communitarian critique of liberalism can and has been used to bolster arguments against marriage equality for lesbian and gay citizens. MaryAnn Glendon and Jean Bethke Elshtain, for example, both vigorously oppose the equal right to marry on communitarian grounds.[8] Both see gay rights as a problematic extension and distortion of the original concept of rights. More specifically, Glendon condemns not all rights, just the "new version of rights discourse that has achieved dominance over the past thirty years," the time during which the gay rights movement developed. For her, "a certain kind of rights talk in our political discussions is both a symptom of, and a contributing factor to, [the] disorder in the body politic."[9] Elshtain, on the other hand, explicitly concedes "that all citizens, including gays, have a right, as individuals, to be protected from intrusion or harassment and to be free from discrimination in such areas as employment and housing." She insists, however, that "no one has a *civil* right, as a gay . . . to full public sanction of his or her activities, values, beliefs, or habits"—or primary relationship. In fact, Elshtain views the struggle for legal validation as part of a destructive "politics of displacement."[10]

In opposition to this conservative version of communitarianism, Sandel actually supports equality for lesbians and gays. His problem resides with the specifically *liberal* defense of gay rights, which he thinks offers only a "thin and fragile toleration" of lesbians and gays[11]—a position that essentially says, "I don't like homosexuals but we have to tolerate them, just like we have to tolerate all degenerates." Sandel suggests that same-sex relationships should be defended on moral grounds rather than simply tolerated on the basis of equal rights.

THE MORAL VALUES OF LIBERALISM

Political equality for gay and lesbian citizens (as well as bisexual and transgendered ones) can indeed be justified on moral grounds, and contrary to the communitarian position, such a moral defense can in fact come from the rich tradition of liberal political theory, from its comprehension of moral pluralism and its practice of the rule of law.

Moral Pluralism

Liberalism originated in the seventeenth century in response to the religious conflict that developed in the wake of the Protestant Reformation. As twentieth-century liberal philosopher John Rawls puts it, "When an authoritative, salvationist, and expansionist religion like medieval Christianity divides, this inevitably means the appearance within the same society of a rival authoritative and salvationist religion . . . Luther and Calvin were as dogmatic and intolerant as the Roman Church had been."[12] The Catholic-Protestant rivalry yielded a series of bloody religious wars throughout Europe. The resulting "cruelties . . . had the effect of turning many Christians away from the public policies of the churches to a morality that saw toleration as an expression of Christian charity." Others "became skeptics who put cruelty and fanaticism at the very head of the human vices. In either case the individual, whether the bearer of a sacred conscience or the potential victim of cruelty, is to be protected against the incursions of public oppression."[13] The important values of freedom of conscience, religious pluralism, and the secular state emerged out of this milieu. Opposition to cruelty and viciousness clearly constitutes a moral position because, as twentieth-century political theorist Judith Shklar argues, these things make the exercise of human freedom impossible.

Although it provides an alternative to a religious state, political liberalism is not amoral; in fact, this political philosophy actually encourages moral pluralism within society. That is to say, by protecting freedom of thought, speech, conscience, and religion, liberalism allows space for the development of multiple religious traditions, by not allowing one or more denominations to seize political power. Under conditions of freedom, moral pluralism flourishes. That is why, for example, the American nineteenth century saw the proliferation of religious denominations. Free from governmental coercion and tyranny in matters of religion, American citizens remain free to use, what Rawls calls, their own "comprehensive" religious, philosophical, and moral belief systems to guide them as they make important decisions in their own lives, as long as they do not harm others. A "comprehensive doctrine" or belief system "includes conceptions of what is of value in human life, and ideals of personal character, as well as ideals of friendship and of familial and associational relationships, and much else that is to inform our conduct, and in the limit to our life as a whole."[14]

Political liberalism functions as an effective political philosophy for a truly pluralistic society because it protects the freedom of individual citizens to embrace a variety of religious, philosophical, and moral doctrines rather than attempting to impose one vision on everybody. As Rawls explains, "a modern democracy is characterized not simply by pluralism of comprehensive religious, philosophical, and moral doctrines but by a pluralism of *incompatible yet reasonable* comprehensive doctrines."[15] For example, Christians believe that Jesus is the Messiah, but Jews and Muslims do not. These views are incompatible, yet both are reasonable positions for believing citizens to hold. In a free society, people are going to disagree about such issues. "Political liberalism assumes that, for political purposes, a plurality of reasonable yet incompatible comprehensive doctrines is the normal result of the exercise of human reason within the framework of the free institutions of a constitutional democratic regime."[16] And it seeks to prevent the destructive conflict that sometimes results from such plurality by protecting the rights of each individual.

In other words, living in a morally pluralistic society does not mean that people give up the idea that their own moral views are the correct ones. A person may still want to save or convert other people to his way of thinking or prohibit others from expressing views or engaging in actions that he considers morally offensive. That is why liberal political theory protects the freedom of individuals to live their own lives, as long as they do not cause harm to others. As John Stuart Mill famously puts it:

> The only purpose for which power can be rightfully exercised over any member of a civilized community, against his will, is to prevent harm to others. His own good, whether physical or moral, is not a sufficient warrant. He cannot rightfully be compelled to do or forbear because it will be better for him to do so, because it will make him happier, because, in the opinions of others, to do so would be wise, or even right. These are good reasons for remonstrating with him, or reasoning with him, or persuading him, or entreating him, but not for compelling him, or visiting him with any evil in case he do otherwise. . . . The only part of the conduct of any one, for which he is amenable to society, is that which concerns others. In the part which merely concerns himself, his independence is, of right, absolute. Over himself, over his own body and mind, the individual is sovereign.[17]

Contra Kern and LaBarbera, having one's sensibilities offended does not constitute a harm—or a grave moral threat. To the contrary, it illustrates the existence of pluralism and individual liberty.

The proceduralism of the liberal state allows pluralism to develop by prohibiting any particular group from using democratic institutions to impose its own "comprehensive doctrine" as law or public policy on other people who have a different moral view. Government must remain "neutral" in the sense "that the state is not to do anything intended to favor or promote any particular comprehensive doctrine rather than another, or to give greater assistance those who pursue it."[18] This does not mean that the government must remain completely neutral towards all values. That would be impossible. As Rawls explains, it is acceptable for government to "encourage the cooperative virtues of political life," such as reasonableness, a sense of fairness, and willingness to compromise with others.[19] It cannot, however, impose a particular religious vision.

Sandel criticizes Rawls for describing the liberal state as "neutral" and argues that the ideal of neutrality and individual rights developed only in the late twentieth century. However, the political vision Rawls articulates actually finds its roots in the American founding. That is to say, in Federalist Paper #10 James Madison recognizes the inevitability of moral and ideological disagreement and oppositional interests in a free society—differences that can lead to the emergence of "factions." Discussing possible solutions to that potential problem, Madison argues that there are two ways of preventing the emergence of faction: "the one, by destroying the liberty which is essential to its existence; the other, by giving to every citizen the same opinions, the same passions, and the same interests." He condemns both strategies:

> It could never be more truly said than of the first remedy that it was worse than the disease. Liberty is to faction what air is to fire, an aliment without which it instantly expires. But it could not be a less folly to abolish liberty, which is essential to political life, because it nourishes faction than it would be to wish the annihilation of air, which is essential to animal life, because it imparts to fire its destructive agency.[20]

Madison's famous solution to factious disagreement is the proliferation of factions, so that no one can gain the power to subordinate others. The existence of a multiplicity of viewpoints is both the product of and precondition for liberty.

The Rule of Law: Liberty, Equality, and Human Dignity

The American founders articulated a moral vision based partly on the work of John Locke's *Second Treatise on Government* (1689). In Locke's theory, the formation of political society (the social contract) occurs with the establishment of the rule of law, which is implemented to better protect the life, liberty, and estate of naturally equal individuals.[21] As a philosophical concept, the *rule of law* establishes legal equality for all citizens; there must be one set of laws that apply to all people, no matter who they are. In other words, the legislature is "to govern by *promulgated establish'd Laws*, not to be varied in particular Cases, but to have one Rule for Rich and Poor, for the Favourite at Court, and the Country Man at Plough."[22] Legitimate government acts as an "Umpire" that governs "by settled standing Rules, indifferent, and the same to all Parties."[23] All must be treated equally before the law. Consequently, even though the majority rules, the concept of legal equality prohibits the majority from imposing laws that discriminate against unpopular minority groups. Indeed the American founders were quite wary of majoritarianism, and the fractured system of government they created often makes it difficult for the will of the majority to be put into law.

Moral philosopher Immanuel Kant further developed the concept of the rule of law in his writings at the end of the eighteenth century. If government should not seek to impose a particular moral vision on its citizens, but rather should leave them free to live in accordance with their own religious or moral worldviews, as liberal political theory contends, then society must be governed in accordance with human-authored laws rather than Divine law. Kant provides the philosophical explanation for how human beings can determine universal moral laws without relying on Scripture. Human beings do this, he argues, through the use of reason, the capacity that differentiates human beings from other creatures.[24] That is, the capacity for "practical reason" makes it possible for people to articulate universal moral laws in accordance with the *categorical imperative*, which states "act only on the maxim through which you can at the same time will that it should become a universal law," one that applies equally to all.[25] With this line of argument, Kant essentially secularizes the "Golden Rule" of Christianity—"Do unto others as you would have them do unto you"—a moral principle articulated in different words by most major religions. This means, for example, it is not right to act unfairly—like loudly praising the virtues and benefits of marriage, while simultaneously fighting to make sure lesbians and gay men are fully excluded.[26]

Some view the rule of law as simply neutral proceduralism; however, the rule of law as a philosophical concept entails respect for the related values of human dignity and moral equality. Equality is one of the most important values of democratic society. When Thomas Jefferson and his colleagues declared, "We hold these truths to be self-evident, that all men are created equal," they were not denying that significant differences exist among people. Instead they were insisting that despite differences of wealth, talent, and religious belief, "all men" are equal in some important moral sense, and thus they should be treated equally under the law. While the founders, despite their rhetoric, granted only white, property-owning men full citizenship, the universal language they espoused laid the groundwork for the expansion of equality and rights over the course of subsequent generations.

This emphasis on moral equality and human rights illustrates liberalism's fundamental respect for the *human dignity* of the person. In fact, contemporary political philosopher Martha Nussbaum argues that what "distinguish[es] liberalism from other political traditions is its insistence on the separateness of one life from another, and the equal importance of each life, seen on its own terms rather than as part of a larger organic or corporate whole."[27] Kant provides an excellent example of this value, when he says "the dignity of man consists precisely in his capacity to make universal law, although only on condition of being himself also subject to the law he makes."[28] That is to say, "rational beings all stand under the *law* that each of them should treat himself and all others, *never merely as a means*, but always *at the same time as an end in himself.*"[29] The dignity of the individual human being cannot be violated even in order to advance the interests of the majority.

Central to the vision of the dignified and rights-bearing person is the concept of personal liberty or autonomy—the freedom each individual has to control his or her own life. As Shklar put it, "Liberalism has only one overriding aim: to secure the political conditions that are necessary for the exercise of personal freedom. Every adult should be able to make as many effective decisions without fear or favor about as many aspects of her or his life as is compatible with like freedom of every other adult."[30] Liberalism does not seek to provide directives to people about how to live their personal lives, besides requiring behaviors such as toleration, nonviolence, and social cooperation with others, but it does respect the moral values of liberty, equality, human dignity, and the rule of law. Hence, it is an error to attribute moral vacuousness to liberalism, failing to recognize the significant moral good it seeks to advance.

IT'S NOT JUST "TALK": HUMAN AND CIVIL RIGHTS AS MORAL VISION

Human rights discourse is a moral vision that grows largely out of the liberal tradition, although it also gains support from other cultural traditions as well. In liberal social contract theory, individuals create government in order to protect the rights and liberties to which they are naturally entitled as human beings. In the *Second Treatise* Locke argues that individuals are free and equal by nature. Consequently, the government's role is to protect the rights of the people and treat all individuals equally. In fact, that is the sole purpose of legitimate government. Although it took a while for the implications of this belief to be implemented in practice—and in some areas they still have yet to be fully realized—over time the liberal belief in the equality of human rights led to the overthrow of monarchy and aristocracy, the illegalization of slavery, the formal enfranchisement of women, civil rights for African Americans, and now the beginning of marriage equality in the law for lesbians and gay men.

During the "age of democratic revolution" rights discourse was understood to be universal—the "rights of man," not only the rights of Englishman—and the moral *vision* of human freedom, equality, and dignity spread around the world, even if often not actualized in practice.[31] The French Revolution threw off the chains of the morally bankrupt *ancien regime*. The Haitian revolutionaries used "the rights of man" to terminate the vicious practice of slavery. Frederick Douglass and Elizabeth Cady Stanton used the promised "right to life, liberty, and the pursuit of happiness" in the struggle to end racial and gender oppression in the United States. Then in 1948, after the United States and its allies won the battle against Nazism, the United Nations issued the "Universal Declaration of Human Rights" that expands the moral framework of human rights to all people.

Importantly, the "Universal Declaration of Human Rights" includes marriage in its list of fundamental human rights: "Men and women of full age, without any limitation due to race, nationality or religion, have the right to marry and to found a family. They are entitled to equal rights as to marriage, during marriage, and at its dissolution" (Article 16).[32] The document as a whole articulates the basic tenets of liberalism that underlie the concept of individual rights, both civil and human. For example, Article 1 states that "all human beings are born free and equal in dignity and rights. They are endowed with reason and conscience and should act towards one another in a spirit of brotherhood." Article 7 emphasizes legal equality: "All are equal before the law and are entitled without any discrimination to equal protection of the law. All are entitled to equal protection against any discrimination in violation of this Declaration and against any incitement to such discrimination." Article 12 protects the dignity of the person: "No one shall be subjected to arbitrary interference with his privacy, family, home, or correspondence, nor to attacks upon his honour and reputation. Everyone has the right to the protection of the law against such interference or attacks." While the Universal Declaration of Human Rights does not specifically mention same-sex marriage, it clearly establishes marriage as a human right, which by definition applies to all people regardless of sexual orientation.

The United States Supreme Court also recognizes marriage as a fundamental civil right, not created by government, only protected by it. Evan Gerstmann explains that the Supreme Court has long recognized the existence of fundamental rights and that, although many such as the right to marry are unenumerated, "these rights have been elevated to a par with those rights enumerated in the Bill of Rights, including freedom of speech, assembly, and religion."[33] Fundamental rights, "deemed vital to a legally equal society," cannot legitimately be denied.[34] That is why the struggle for marriage equality is properly considered a civil rights issue.

Marriage was established as a fundamental right in the United States through a long series of Supreme Court cases. The concept of "fundamental rights" did not develop until the end of the nineteenth century. Before that time, marriage was considered a common-law right, rather than a constitutional right,[35] and marriage did not require state-sanction to be considered valid.[36] The Supreme Court first established a constitutional right to marry in *Meyer v. Nebraska* (1923). There the Court argued that liberty "without doubt" includes "not merely freedom from bodily restraint but also the right of the individual to contract, to engage in any of the common occupations of life, to acquire useful knowledge, *to marry, establish a home and bring up children*, to worship God according to the dictates of his own conscience, and generally to enjoy those privileges long recognized at common law as essential to the orderly pursuit of happiness by free men."[37] Then, in *Skinner v. Oklahoma* (1942), the Court called marriage "one of the basic civil rights of man."[38] Remarkably, neither the *Meyer* nor the *Skinner* case dealt directly with marriage. Thus, Gerstmann comments "the justices went out of their way to assert that marriage is one of the fundamental rights of humankind."[39] They may also have been simply stating a belief that was generally accepted within American culture at that time.

The idea of marriage as a fundamental right received additional support in a series of cases that actually dealt with marriage laws. Most famously, in *Loving v. Virginia* (1967), the case that overturned a Virginia ban on interracial marriage, the Court reiterated that "the freedom to marry has long been recognized as one of the vital personal rights essential to the orderly pursuit of happiness . . . one of the 'basic civil rights of man' . . . and cannot be infringed by the State."[40] This understanding was reaffirmed in *Zabloki v. Redhail* (1978): "The leading decision of this Court on the right to marry is *Loving v. Virginia* (1967). . . . Although *Loving* arose in the context of racial discrimination, prior and subsequent decisions of this Court confirm that the right to marry is of fundamental importance for all individuals."[41] Finally, an individual's fundamental right to marry was definitively established in *Turner v. Safley* (1987), which established the right of prisoners to marry. "If the Court had any doubt at all about whether the right to marry is a fundamental constitutional right, *Turner* presented it with abundant opportunity to express that doubt. Yet neither the Court nor the government expressed such doubt." Consequently, "after Turner it will be of little value to try to contest that 'the decision to marry is a fundamental right.'"[42] Consequently, Gerstmann concludes, "*the Constitution guarantees every person the right to marry the person of his or her choice*" (as long as they are adults, of course)—even gay men and lesbians.[43]

THE STRUGGLE FOR CIVIL RIGHTS

While most people may not be fluent in the history of political thought or the details of constitutional law, they would very likely recognize the discussion of liberalism and human rights offered here as the articulation of the fundamental moral principles that underlie American democracy and culture. All of the principles of liberal political theory not only justify but also require the legal recognition of same-sex marriage—legal and moral equality, individual rights and liberties, personal autonomy, human dignity, and a fair and impartial state—given the legal recognition and effects accorded the marriages of opposite-sex couples. This is not to say that all people value philosophical consistency. There are times when people allow personal religious beliefs, political expediency, material interests, or customary prejudices to interfere with the logical extension of liberal principles within the political realm. For example, Jefferson and others knew that slavery stood in direct contradiction to the revolutionary doctrine of the "rights of man" yet because of political expediency, economic interests, or racial prejudice, they allowed the institution to continue.[44]

The Civil Rights Movement of African Americans in the 1950s and 1960s exemplifies the ways in which the egalitarian ideals of liberalism can be utilized to eliminate illiberal practices, no matter how entrenched or laden with tradition they may be. Although African-Americans had been organizing for years, the Supreme Court decision in *Brown v. Board of Education* (1954) galvanized the movement for legal equality, overturning the concept of "separate but equal" and revealing as illegitimate and immoral the existence of two different sets of laws, one for whites and one for blacks.[45] Martin Luther King, Jr. made the case against racial segregation, by arguing that "an unjust law is a code that a majority inflicts on a minority that is not binding on itself." A just law, in contrast, "is a code that a majority compels a minority to follow that it is willing to follow itself."[46] While it did not come easily, legal discrimination against African-Americans was finally overturned during the 1960s through an appeal to the moral values inherent in American democracy. Fifty years later, most Americans, even the most conservative, look back upon the Civil Rights Movement as one of the great success stories of American democracy precisely because it appealed to the fundamental moral principles upon which America was founded: liberty, equality, human dignity, pluralism, and the rule of law.

Now, in 2008, at the time of this writing, American society stands in the midst of the LGBT civil rights movement. In 2003, that state of Massachusetts became the first state in the union to legalize same-sex marriage (although then-Governor Mitt Romney revived a 1913 antimiscegenation law to prevent non-Massachusetts residents from accessing marriage, a law that was finally repealed in July 2008). In the Massachusetts case, the state Supreme Court articulated the moral vision of marriage as follows:

> Marriage is a vital social institution. The exclusive commitment of two individuals to each other nurtures love and mutual support; it brings stability to our society. For those who choose to marry, and for their children, marriage provides an abundance of legal, financial, and social benefits. In return it imposes weighty legal, financial, and social obligations. . . . The Massachusetts Constitution affirms the dignity and equality of all individuals. It forbids the creation of second-class citizens. In reaching our conclusion we have given full deference to the arguments made by the Commonwealth. But it has failed to identify any constitutionally adequate reason for denying civil marriage to same-sex couples.[47]

The Court recognizes moral pluralism, when it notes that there are "strong religious, moral, and ethical convictions" on both sides of the issue. "Neither view," however, "answers the question before us. Our concern is with the Massachusetts Constitution as a charter of governance for every person properly within its reach." Quoting *Lawrence*, they conclude, "Our obligation is to define the liberty of all, not to mandate our own moral code." On May 17, 2004, more than 1,000 lesbian and gay couples were legally married in the state of Massachusetts.

While many conservatives attribute the Massachusetts court decision (and others) to amoral "activist judges," we can see from our review of liberal political theory that the court simply applied the fundamentally moral, political principles that underlie American democracy in a consistent way. Even though some Americans may not approve of same-sex marriage, that is not a legitimate reason to deny the civil right to marry to sexual minorities. In fact, the entire purpose of civil rights is that everyone gets them even if the majority does *not* approve, particularly when they do not approve. Public opinion did not support the decision of the Supreme Court that legalized interracial marriage in 1967. A 1958 Gallup poll showed that only 4 percent of the public favored interracial marriage.[48] Even in 1965, "at the crest of the civil-rights revolution, a Gallup poll found that 72 percent of Southern whites and 42 percent of Northern whites still wanted to ban interracial marriage."[49] Today, however, 90% of the people oppose "laws against marriages between blacks and whites."[50] It is the job of the Supreme Court to rule on principle, despite public opinion.

THE CALIFORNIA CASE

In the United States, marriage has long been considered a fundamental right because it is considered a morally valuable institution by many. The California

Supreme Court majority opinion begins by acknowledging that "past cases establish [the right to marry] as one of the fundamental constitutional rights embodied in the California Constitution."[51] The Court recognizes that denying lesbians and gay men the right to marry a person of their choosing violates the moral principle of legal equality, and it recognizes the right to marry as central to an individual's freedom, his or her personal autonomy, and the right to privacy that protects human dignity. The majority opinion insists that "fundamental rights, once recognized, cannot be denied to particular groups on the ground that these groups have historically been denied those rights" (72).

Moreover, in the case of marriage equality, no conflict of rights makes the decision a moral dilemma. Allowing same-sex couples to marry "does not diminish any other person's constitutional rights. Opposite-sex couples will continue to enjoy precisely the same constitutional rights they have traditionally possessed, unimpaired by our recognition that this basic civil right is applicable, as well, to gay individuals and same-sex couples" (72). In making this argument the Court rejected the creation of a supposedly separate but equal domestic partnership arrangement as immoral discrimination.

The California Supreme Court correctly recognizes the central role marriage plays in dignifying monogamous relationships and consequently the human beings who form them. As the Court notes,

> One of the core elements of this fundamental right [to marry] is the right of same-sex couples to have their official family relationship accorded the same dignity, respect, and stature as that accorded to all other officially recognized family relationships. The current statutes—by drawing a distinction between the name assigned to the family relationship available to same-sex couples, and by reserving the historic and highly respected designation of marriage exclusively to opposite-sex couples while offering same-sex couples only the new and unfamiliar designation of domestic partnership—pose a serious risk of denying the official family relationship of same-sex couples the equal dignity and respect that is a core element of the constitutional right to marry. (81)

The "opportunity to publicly and officially express one's love for and long-term commitment to another person by establishing a family together with that person also is an important element of self-expression that can give special meaning to one's life" (61).

Consequently, it is essentially immoral to deny lesbian or gay people access to an institution that can "enoble and enrich human life" (76).

As a human right, marriage cannot legitimately be denied by government. The California court explains that if the *only* role" of marriage "was to serve the interests of society, it reasonably could be asserted that the state should have full authority to decide whether to establish or abolish the institution."

However, because marriage "embodies fundamental interests of an individual that are protected from abrogation or elimination by the state" and "because our cases make clear that the right to marry is an integral component of an individual's interest in *personal autonomy* protected by the privacy provision . . . and of the *liberty* interest" in the California constitution, "the right to marry—like the right to establish a home and raise children—has independent substantive content, and cannot properly be understood as simply the right to enter into such a relationship *if (but only if)* the Legislature chooses to establish and retain it" (63). Consequently, "in light of the fundamental nature of the substantive rights embodied in the right to marry—and their central importance to an individual's opportunity to live a happy, meaningful, and satisfying life as a full member of society—the California Constitution," the justices determine, "properly must be interpreted to guarantee this basic civil right to all individuals and couples, without regard for their sexual orientation" (66).

Moreover, while the justices do not frame the issue precisely this way, their decision allows room for moral pluralism. That is, with its decision the Court refuses to impose one particular, religiously-rooted definition of marriage on the people of California, some of whom belong to denominations that allow same-sex marriage, including Unitarian Universalism, the United Church of Christ, some Episcopal congregations, and all three liberal denominations of Judaism (Reform, Reconstructionist, and Conservative). The Court decision protects religious liberty by forbidding the state from withholding recognition of marriages from an array of religious traditions. In order to allow space for moral pluralism, the justices have to put their own particular beliefs to the side. "Whatever our views as individuals with regard to this question as a matter of policy, we recognize as judges and as a court our responsibility to limit our consideration of the question to a determination of the constitutional validity of the current legislative provisions" (5). In taking this liberal position, the justices do not rule amorally. To the contrary, they act out of deep respect for moral pluralism.

Finally, the California decision is a moral one, in that it explicitly acts to prevent the immorality of discrimination and harm to persons. The Court rejects the creation of a separate institution of domestic partnership for same-sex couples, arguing that "particularly in light of the historic disparagement of and discrimination against gay persons," the existence of a separate type of institution for same-sex couples would be "demeaning to [their] dignity," and "will contribute to the perpetuation or promotion of their unfair social characterization, and will have a more severe impact upon them, since they are already vulnerable" (104). Moreover, "the exclusion of same-sex couples from the designation of marriage works a real and appreciable harm upon same-sex couples and their children" (117). While the court's decision in *In* re *Marriage Cases* (2008) may not change the social opprobrium directed against individual or partnered gay and lesbian persons entrenched in some quarters of our society, it removes the law from serving those attitudes.

CONCLUSION

With its decision to extend the fundamental human right to marry to lesbian and gay people, the California Supreme Court has not taken "rights talk" too far. To the contrary, the Court ruled in accordance with the longstanding moral values that underlie American society. Their decision protects moral pluralism by recognizing marriages endorsed by a wide array of religious denominations, and it undermines the immorality of discrimination, stigmatization, and hate. By acting in accordance with the liberal principles upon which this country was founded, the Court does not act amorally or immorally. In fact, I would argue that those who endorse state-sanctioned stigmatization and discrimination and seek to deny same-sex couples their civil rights or disrespect them as human beings are the ones who act immorally.

NOTES

1. *In re Marriage Cases* (2008) 43 Cal.4th 757 [76 Cal.Rptr.3d 683, 183 P.3d 384], www.lambdalegal.org/our-work/in-court/cases/in-re-marriage-cases.html (8 October 2008).

2. Michael J. Sandel, *Democracy's Discontent: America in Search of a Public Philosophy* (Cambridge: The Belknap Press of Harvard University Press, 1996), 7–8.

3. *Lawrence et. al. v. Texas*, 539 U.S. 558 (2003), Syllabus, 2.

4. Sandel, *Democracy's Discontent*, 18–19.

5. Sandel, *Democracy's Discontent*, 12–13.

6. Sandel, *Democracy's Discontent*, 19.

7. Peter LaBarbera, "LaBarbera Assails Homosexual Hate and Intimidation Campaign against Oklahoma Lawmaker Sally Kern," available at americansfortruth.com/news/labarbera-assails-homosexual-hate-and-intimidation-campaign-against-oklahoma-lawmaker-sally-kern.html (30 June 2008).

8. R. Claire Snyder, *Gay Marriage and Democracy: Equality for All* (Lanham, Md.: Rowman & Littlefield, 2006), chapter 6.

9. Mary Ann Glendon, *Rights Talk: The Impoverishment of Political Discourse* (New York: The Free Press, 1991), x.

10. Jean Bethke Elshtain, *Democracy on Trial* (New York: Basic Books, 1995), 54.

11. Michael Sandel, "Moral Argument and Liberal Toleration," in *New Communitarian Thinking: Persons, Virtues, Institutions, and Communities*, Amitai Etzioni, ed. (Charlottesville and London: University of Virginia Press, 1995), 86.

12. John Rawls, *Political Liberalism* (New York: Columbia University Press, 1996), xxv.

13. Judith H. Shklar, "Liberalism of Fear," in *Political Thought & Political Thinkers*, ed. Stanley Hoffmann (Chicago: The University of Chicago Press, 1998), 5.

14. Rawls, *Political Liberalism*, 13.

15. Rawls, *Political Liberalism*, xviii, emphasis mine. Rawls is careful to note that by "reasonable" he means only those doctrines that accept the validity of democratic constitutionalism. Thus he deliberately excludes doctrines that are "unreasonable," "irrational," or "even mad," such as those of the "Unabomber" or Osama bin Laden.

16. Rawls, *Political Liberalism*, xviii.

17. Mill, *On Liberty*, 13-14.

18. Rawls, *Political Liberalism*, 193.

19. Rawls, *Political Liberalism*, 163.

20. James Madison, "Federalist #10," in *The Federalist Papers*, ed. Clinton Rossiter (New York: NAL Penguin Inc., 1961), 78.

21. John Locke, *Second Treatise of Government*, in *Two Treatises of Government*, ed. Peter Laslett (Cambridge: Cambridge University Press, 1998), 324.

22. Locke, *Second Treatise*, 363.

23. Locke, *Second Treatise*, 324.

24. Immanuel Kant, *Groundwork of the Metaphysic of Morals*, trans. H. J. Paton (New York: Harper & Row, Publishers, 1956), 119.

25. Kant, *Metaphysic of Morals*, 88.

26. Linda J. Waite and Maggie Gallagher, *The Case for Marriage* (New York: Broadway Books, 2000).

27. Martha Nussbaum, *Sex and Social Justice* (New York & Oxford: Oxford University Press, 1999), 10.

28. Kant, *Metaphysic of Morals*, 107.

29. Kant, *Metaphysic of Morals*, 101.

30. Shklar, "Liberalism of Fear," 3–4.

31. See R. R. Palmer, *The Age of the Democratic Revolution, 2 vols.* (Princeton: Princeton University Press, 1959 & 1964).

32. United Nations, "Universal Declaration of Human Rights," www.udhr50.org/UDHR/default.htm (10 Sept. 2003).

33. Evan Gerstmann, *Same-Sex Marriage and the Constitution* (Cambridge: Cambridge University Press, 2004), 69.

34. Gerstmann, *Same-Sex Marriage*, 7.

35. Gerstmann, *Same-Sex Marriage*, 73–74.

36. Snyder, *Gay Marriage*, chap. 2.

37. *Meyer v. State of Nebraska*, 262 U.S. 390 (1923), 1, emphasis mine.

38. *Skinner v. Oklahoma* 316 U.S. 535 (1942), 541.

39. Gerstmann, *Same-Sex Marriage*, 67.

40. See *Loving v. Virginia*, 388 U.S. 1 (1967).

41. See *Zabloki v. Redhail*, 434 U.S. 374 (1978).

42. Gerstmann, *Same-Sex Marriage*, 83.

43. Gerstmann, *Same-Sex Marriage*, 67.

44. For a discussion of Jefferson's opposition to slavery, see Conor Cruise O'Brien, "Thomas Jefferson: Radical and Racist," *The Atlantic Monthly*, October 1999, www.theatlantic.com/issues/96oct/obrien/obrien.htm (8 October 2008).

45. Brown v. Board of Education, 347 U.S. 483 (1954).

46. Martin Luther King, Jr., "Letter from the Birmingham City Jail (16 April 1963)" in *American Political Thought*, 485.

47. *Goodridge et. al. v. Dept. of Public Health*, (Ma. 2003).

48. Carolyn Lochhead, "Pivotal day for gay marriage in U.S. nears Massachusetts move to legalize weddings may intensify backlash in other States" San Francisco Chronicle, May 2, 2004, www.sfgate.com/cgi-bin/article.cgi?file=/chronicle/archive/2004/05/02/MNGM26EHU81.DTL (3 May 2004).

49. Steve Sailer, "Is love colorblind?—public opinion about interracial marriage," *National Review*, July 14, 1997, www.findarticles.com/p/articles/mi_m1282/is_n13_v49/ai_19617224 (1 April 2005).

50. Public Agenda website, www.publicagenda.org/issues/angles_graph .cfm?issue_type=race&id=203&graph=majpropracedating.jpg (1 April 2005).

51. *In re Marriage Cases*, 5.

6

Same-Sex Marriage and the American Political Tradition

Jason Pierceson

The political, philosophical, and legal debate over same-sex marriage during the past several decades has spawned a variety of arguments and perspectives. Conservatives, libertarians, liberals, feminists, queer theorists, and others have applied these philosophical frameworks to the issue with different results. Often, these arguments are used in the public arena by advocates, elected officials, and judges. On this issue, ideas certainly have mattered. An element often missed in these discussions is that the debate over same-sex marriage has deepened, and arguments in favor continue to strengthen liberalism, the dominant, though not exclusive, political and philosophical framework in the United States. Arguments in favor of relationship equality for same-sex couples are grounded in liberal arguments that go beyond the minimal libertarianism that often dominates political and legal discourse in the United States. These arguments affirm the dignity of LGBT individuals and call for state recognition and support. They do not assert merely the right to be left alone, but a principled demand for full equality, at least in the eyes of the law.

Interestingly, legal actors have inserted these arguments into the public discourse. Although it is true enough that majoritarian politics tends to reinforce the libertarian bent of American political discourse, contrary to those who fear judicial involvement in issues of public policy and civil rights, courts are a necessary vehicle for expanding and enriching liberal discourse in the American polity. These "activist" courts have tapped into a persistent, though not always dominant, brand of American liberalism. Unfortunately, American liberalism, being dominated by libertarianism, has lacked the full potency of the transformational power of liberalism, at least in the political arena. Increasingly, courts have taken up the crucial role of challenging majoritarianism and a narrow conception of liberalism.

Of course, the liberal paradigm is disputed. Several authors in this volume address and refute conservative objections to same-sex marriage and LGBT rights more generally. An element often overlooked in this debate, however, is the objections to a liberal approach to gay rights from the left, such as the critiques by some feminist scholars and queer theorists. Later in this chapter, I will address the argument against the same-sex marriage movement offered by feminist scholar Nancy Polikoff and discuss why the liberal course taken by same-sex marriage advocates is preferable to her approach.

LIBERALISM, PROGRESSIVE CHANGE, AND THE AMERICAN POLITICAL TRADITION

The philosophical debate over same-sex marriage in the United States should be placed in the context of the debates over other fundamental questions of equality. Ironically, it seems that both the political left and the political right are reluctant to do this. The left sees the American political tradition as far too limiting and oppressive to be very useful for discussions of sexuality based equality. This is true particularly of feminists and queer theorists who argue that any attempt to work inside the system is hopelessly corrupted by deep bias and oppression. The right fears any connection to other movements will empower advocates of change by framing the issue as one of social justice. "Gay rights are not civil rights," is the common refrain. For many of these advocates, religious arguments do not point in favor of liberation from oppression; instead, they directly condemn homosexuality and prevent any state recognition of this "sin" and "perversion." This potently combines with the strong American political tendency to paint nonconformists as outsiders and threats and to use the apparatus of the state to reinforce these claims.[1] In this chapter, I hope to present an alternative that does not split the difference between the two perspectives out of some love of moderation. Rather, I will articulate an independent alternative, one that draws upon the most progressive elements of American political thought and that recognizes that any theorizing about progressive change needs to come to terms with real constraints in the American political tradition.

The basic framework for my approach is adapted from the work of J. David Greenstone.[2] Greenstone's work is a response to the theory of Louis Hartz, who argued that American political discourse is dominated by an "irrational Lockeanism." This is typified by an antistatist, libertarian liberalism, derived from the fact that the United States lacks a direct connection to the more collectivist legacy of feudalism, as opposed to Europe.[3] Many scholars have revised or argued against the Hartz thesis. Greenstone's approach emphasizes the dominance of liberalism but argues that American liberalism is more complex than Hartz's liberalism.

Essentially, according to Greenstone, there are two variants of liberalism in the American political tradition: humanist liberalism and reform liberalism.[4] Humanist liberalism is the dominant version of liberalism, and it emphasizes negative freedom, or freedom from government intrusion, and ranks freedom over equality. Reform liberalism embraces the notion of positive freedom and asserts that government has a role to play insuring equal rights and freedoms for all citizens. This difference can lead to very different politics. Stephen A. Douglas's humanist liberalism led him to assert the rights of free whites to decide, on the basis of freedom of choice, whether or not to enslave other humans. Abraham Lincoln's reform liberalism, however, caused him to see profound injustice in this position.

The richer and more egalitarian reform liberalism has been central to successful progressive reform movements, especially in the twentieth century. However, calls for a more inclusive or a more economically just polity are usually met with the libertarian response of "we must leave the private market alone" or "people have a right to their prejudices and way of life." Franklin Roosevelt's Second (and explicitly positive) Bill of Rights and Martin Luther King's call for an end to a system of segregation and white supremacy that had been based on precisely the same defense of whites and their freedoms defended by Douglas are the prime examples of the influence of reform liberalism.

Gay rights generally, and same-sex marriage in particular, fits within this framework of the constraints of libertarian liberalism. Early gay and lesbian rights movement activities of the 1950s in the U.S. were severely constrained by a moral and religious antigay majoritarianism reinforced by church and state. As a result, the language of negative rights dominated the first attempts to engage and persuade the larger polity to begin to disassemble the antigay regulatory regime of sodomy and solicitation laws, bans on government employment, and limitations on speech and assembly promulgated by the postal service and local police raids on gay bars. And yet, one can also see initial attempts to tie the gay rights cause to the cause of race-based civil rights. These themes are evident in one of the first statements of the theory of the rights of sexual minorities in the United States, Donald Webster Cory's, *The Homosexual in America*, published in 1951.

Many gay and lesbian activists in the 1950s point to reading *The Homosexual in America* as a pivotal event in their turn to political activism. Cory's goal was to normalize homosexuality and place sexual minorities squarely within the emerging minority rights and human rights paradigm, to confront what he referred to as America's "minority problem."[5] But Cory noted that sexual minorities were in a different situation from other minority groups, with a lack of full identity formation, nearly complete social marginalization, and lacking cultural and family support in the face of hostility. "The ethnic group can take refuge in the comfort and pride of their own, in the warmth of family and friends . . . But not the homosexuals . . . Constantly and unceasingly we carry a mask, and without interruption we stand on our guard lest our secret, which is our very essence, be betrayed."[6] This was a potentially more restrictive version of W. E. B. Du Bois's "dual consciousness," and Cory noted the maddening implication of the metaphor of the mask: Because of the shame and social marginalization, no one would dare challenge the status quo but leaders who are willing to do exactly that were needed to change the status quo. As he noted, "One is a 'hero' if he espouses the cause of minorities, but is only a suspect if that minority is the homosexual group."[7] In fact, it appears that Cory viewed himself as a gay version of Du Bois, taking a similar personal, cultural, historical, and sociological approach to inequality. Although Cory only cites Du Bois once, his spirit pervades the text.

Even though he expressed internal discomfort with homosexuality, he clearly saw the problem not with the gay and lesbian community, but with the majority heterosexual community. Paraphrasing Gunnar Myrdal, Cory wrote: "there are no minority problems. There are only majority problems. There is no Negro problem except that created by whites . . . To which I add: and no homosexual problem except that created by the heterosexual society."[8] The deconstruction of heterosexual privilege and hypocrisy was one of Cory's primary goals—a difficult sell in the profoundly conformist early 1950s. However, Cory viewed this as a crucial starting point in the fight for progress.

Cory's frame of analysis was clearly a liberal, rights-based framework. His demands were largely libertarian—the freedom to be left alone, the freedom to express and discuss sexuality, and sexual freedom. Indeed, his language was distinctly Millian:

> What the homosexual wants in freedom—not only freedom of expression, but also sexual freedom. By sexual freedom is meant the right of any person to gratify his urges when and how he sees fit, without fear of social consequences, so long as he does not use the force of either violence, threat or superior age; so long as he does not inflict bodily harm or disease upon another person; so long as the other person is of sound mind and agrees to the activity.[9]

Although he saw the importance of intimacy for personhood, this was not necessarily part of his political platform. He did not call for the recognition of same-sex relationships, even though he thought they might be possible; he simply felt that through a libertarian approach to sexuality, society would come to see the value of all types of sexual arrangements.

Indeed, his view of marriage was largely defined through a heterosexual prism. A bit of self-hatred and internalized homophobia was present in Cory's discussion of gay relationships. He could not quite see them the same as marriages; in fact, he argued that many gay men could continue in heterosexual marriages. Two distinct chapters of *The Homosexual in America* were devoted to the examination of the factors leading to gay men marrying women and the reasons gay men chose not to enter heterosexual relationships. Strikingly, Cory appeared to endorse the idea of heterosexual marriage for gay men as a way to have a complete life. For him, an exclusively gay life was solitary and pathetic. As he wrote,

> The married homosexuals I have known never for a moment regret the home, the family life, the mutual care and tenderness, the pursuit of common interests that have arisen from the union with a woman. They regret most of all the mask, the fact that it cannot be discarded even with the one with whom the burdens of life are being shared. But if these men could look into the inner selves of other husbands, would they not find that all people wear masks, even in the presence of their most intimate companions?[10]

Thus, sexuality was marginal to personhood for Cory. A full life could be achieved without a substantial gay relationship. Cory also dismissed "sham marriages" with lesbians, but not for the most obvious reasons, like the injustice of forcing people to live a lie. For him, the problem was that lesbians were too cold and not likely to be housewives and mothers. Gay men were seeking real nurturers, housekeepers, and mothers of their children.[11] Consequently, Cory justified the notion of compartmentalization—the idea that gay men should separate their married lives from their gay lives. He could not conceive of the notion of a fully actualized and fulfilled gay individual.

While certainly limited by the times, Cory's analysis broke through, although on a limited scale, the cultural, legal, and political hegemony of homosexuality as pure deviance. By framing the issue as a civil rights issue and connecting it to the broader political conversations concerning inequality, Cory delivered the political version of Alfred Kinsey's scientific approach of the same time. But it also shows how distant the idea of same-sex marriage was from early theorizing on gay rights.

It should be noted that liberalism was not the only framework utilized by those theorizing about the status of sexual minorities, nor would liberalism ever be the only frame. The approach of Harry Hay, who founded the Mattachine Society in 1951, illustrates an alternative framework. Hay had been a member of the Communist party, and originally intended the group to be a vehicle for radical political change. Eventually, however, due to the oppressive social and political climate the group evolved by the middle part of the decade into a social group with limited political aspirations, particularly as the radical politics of Hay and other founding members was increasingly seen as a political liability by an expanding, and more conservative, membership.[12]

Indeed, Hay's Marxist-inspired framework to the problems of sexual minorities was short-lived and suffered a Hartzian fate.[13] Hay focused on the deep structures of heterosexist domination and the resulting "false consciousness, by a hegemonic ideology that labeled their eroticism as an individual aberration," as John D'Emilio describes his philosophical approach.[14] While sharing some elements of Cory's critique, Hay and the early Mattachine members were not simply interested in libertarian freedom but more direct agitation and activism that would break the heterosexist hegemony. Ultimately, this direct confrontation was not favored as the membership of the group expanded beyond its Communist roots, and the Mattachine Society, in addition to the Daughters of Bilitis, a parallel lesbian organization founded in 1955, possessed only minimal and ineffectual political organizations in a few major cities by the early 1960s. The goal became to quietly work to convince straight, professional allies to join the cause and imbue sexual minorities with respectability.[15]

The movement took a more political and assertive turn in the early to mid-1960s, largely as the result of the actions and rhetoric of Frank Kameny. Kameny's brand of politics mirrored the increasing militancy of the civil rights movement. In fact, Kameny saw this movement as a direct model. In a speech given to the Mattachine Society of New York in 1964, Kameny outlined his vision of where the sexual minority rights movement, or the homophile[16] movement as it was called, needed to go. In the speech, Kameny focused on problems within and outside the movement. From within, he was clearly battling the internalized homophobia of the movement reflected by aspects of Cory's thought and the timid and limited tactics of the movement. Indeed, one of his explicit goals was to turn the movement away from its sole focus on self-help toward a "civil liberties-social action" approach.[17]

He was highly critical of the lack of self-confidence of the movement, instead calling for a public strategy for change: "We should have a clear, explicit, consistent viewpoint and we should not be timid in presenting it."[18] Kameny was particularly critical of the tendency of the movement to give equal status to anti-gay arguments, particularly those that came from professionals. Like Cory, he felt that central to any gay rights strategy was the challenging of elite opinion, particularly from the medical and psychiatric community. Kameny, the scientist,[19] criticized the "so-called authorities" on sexuality who demonstrated "an appalling incidence of loose reasoning, of poor research, . . . of nonrepresentative samplings, of conclusions being incorporated into initial assumptions, and vice versa, with consequent circular reasoning."[20] This empiricism was driven by the desire to eliminate the stigma of homosexuality which was central to the lack of political progress, both from within the movement and from external moralism and flawed science. As he clearly stated, "I look upon homosexuality as something in no way shameful or intrinsically undesirable."

This is clearly a big step beyond Cory's ambivalence. Indeed, Kameny was not advocating simply the right to be let alone—his framework reflected a fuller sense of individualism, one that included notions of positive freedom. Quoting from the D.C. Mattachine Society statement of purpose (which he most likely authored), Kameny asserted that the rights desired were "the right, as human beings, to develop our full potential and dignity, and the right, as citizens, to be allowed to make our maximum contribution to the society in which we live."[21]

Like Cory, Kameny viewed sexual minorities as completely equivalent to other minorities striving for equality at the time. In the speech, he emphasized the similarities to the status, treatment, and goals of African Americans and Jews. He particularly emphasized this connection while refuting the choice/change arguments made in opposition to rights for sexual minorities. "Why we are Negroes, Jews, or homosexuals is totally irrelevant, and whether we can be changed to whites, Christians, or heterosexual is equally irrelevant," Kameny stated in a clear attempt at solidarity.[22]

Kameny viewed same-sex marriage as a natural extension of his liberal reformism. In fact, he thought it was a certainty that the D.C. city council would enact a same-sex marriage law in the mid-1970s. This occurred at the same time that many same-sex couples saw this as a logical next step in the gay rights movement, with some of them bringing lawsuits challenging the state denial of their marriage license applications.

Unlike the more repressive 1950s where marriage, as represented by Cory, was viewed as much more of an essentially heterosexual institution, some liberal reformist thinkers like Kameny conceived of legal recognition of same-sex marriage as a natural outgrowth of a liberal, rights-claiming, and equality-seeking framework. They saw that intimate relationships were a part of personhood and desired not to simply be left alone by government; they wanted public affirmation and support. As Kameny described an attempt by two men to gain a marriage license in D.C. in 1972, "This is another of the efforts of homosexuals to place their relationships on par with those of heterosexuals, and to achieve full equality in society. All rights and benefits of government and law available to heterosexual citizens are, by right, available to homosexual citizens."[23] Kameny saw the opportunity created by the changing nature of heterosexual marriage, in particular the move away from procreation toward companionate marriage. In doing so, he applied liberal rationalism to the issue of same-sex marriage and anticipated the approach of judges decades later who would be equally skeptical of the "procreation justification" for heterosexual-only marriage. Abandoning tradition alone as a basis for analysis, he stated: "With the growing use of contraception and sterilization, with an absence of any ban on marriages between people physiologically or chronologically incapable of reproduction . . . , denial of marriage to homosexuals . . . is clearly untenable."[24]

This approach, of course, was political and legally naïve, with courts and legislatures (including the D.C. city council) refusing to support same-sex marriage. In addition, marriage was not favored by more the more radical gay liberationist and lesbian-feminist approaches to the movement in the early 1970s. Indeed, unlike the demise of more radical approaches in the 1950s, the gay rights movement split into distinct philosophical camps in the early 1970s with the rise of gay liberationist and feminist thought. This split continues to divide the movement on the question of same-sex marriage today, and it will be more fully addressed in a later section. By the late 1980s, however, a return to rights-based legalism would propel the issue to the center of the movement, with lawyers and courts leading the charge with a rhetoric that would build upon progressive narratives for change, as well as provide a forum to expand American liberal discourse on the topic of equality for sexual minorities.

This slight detour into mid-twentieth century gay political thought demonstrates that themes in the American political tradition recur and shape the trajectory of progressive political development. I have emphasized the thought of Cory and Kameny as representations of political theorizing within the liberal tradition. In the end, this approach may not be the most philosophically "right," but it fits within proven rhetorical avenues of political change, particularly in a polity that frames so many policy questions in terms of rights and where legalism is itself an entrenched part of the political tradition. As we will see, courts continue to frame the rights of sexual minorities in these terms.

COURTS, (RICHER) LIBERALISM, AND RIGHTS

After a period of several decades in which richer, reformist notions of liberalism were marginalized in the public and legal sphere, crowded out by libertarian, feminist, queer, and moralistic arguments, reformist arguments began to reenter the political and legal debate over LGBT rights through adjudication and court decisions. My argument in this essay is that legal language and courts have been crucial players in expanding the liberal discourse on LGBT rights and same-sex marriage claims in particular. This is a controversial notion for many scholars of the LGBT rights movement and scholars of the courts. The leading scholarly advocate against the use of courts by progressive groups, Gerald Rosenberg, argues that because of political and constitutional constraints, courts are not able to give advocates what they desire and that a backlash against their efforts is the most likely result of their litigation.[25] LGBT historian John D'Emilio has asserted that same-sex marriage litigation "has provoked a series of defeats that constitute the greatest calamity in the history of the gay and lesbian movement in the United States."[26] While the backlash against same-sex marriage litigation is real, the litigation has also allowed for an enriching of the discourse surrounding the debate over same-sex marriage and LGBT rights more generally.

In particular, courts that have ruled in favor of same-sex marriage claims have invoked language in their opinions that reflect the "reform liberalism" strain of American political thought and discourse. Before the 1990s, state and federal courts tended to address gay rights claims in the same manner as the larger political culture: through the lens of libertarianism or, more likely, through the lens of moralism. Starting with Hawaii in 1993, a richer liberalism in the context of gay rights has more fully entered the public discourse.[27] This is illustrated by the language of the Supreme Court of Vermont in 1999. That court stated that the same-sex plaintiffs "seek nothing more, nor less than legal protection and security for their avowed commitment to an intimate and lasting human relationship." Deciding in their favor was "a recognition of our common humanity."[28] Or, more recently, as the Supreme Judicial Court of Massachusetts declared: "the decision whether and whom to marry is among life's momentous acts of self-definition."[29] And this positive right to state recognition must not be denied to same-sex couples. What seemed obvious to Kameny was becoming a reality, at least in a limited context.

This richer liberalism was not limited only to a few liberal state courts. Though not directly about same-sex marriage, the U.S. Supreme Court case of *Lawrence v. Texas* (2003) invoked similar language in the majority opinion. Justice Anthony Kennedy, in striking down sodomy laws, noted that the decision to choose an intimate partner, regardless of sexuality, was protected by the Constitution. Kennedy's language was so supportive of gay individuals that Justice Antonin Scalia accused Kennedy of opening the door to the Court's eventual acceptance of same-sex marriage.

The 2008 decision of the California Supreme Court in favor of same-sex marriage was a striking example of judicial public philosophy emphasizing the need for a fuller, more robust liberalism on the question of gay rights. As the court stated,

The ability of an individual to join in a committed, long-term, officially recognized family relationship with the person of his or her choice is often of crucial significance to the individual's happiness and well-being. The legal commitment to long-term emotional and economic support that is an integral part of an officially recognized marriage relationship provides an individual with the ability to invest in and rely upon a loving relationship with another adult in a way that may be crucial to the individual's development as a person and achievement of his or her full potential.[30]

The court explicitly referenced the negative versus positive rights distinction in liberalism and framed the issue of the right to same-sex marriage as a right that necessarily transcends the dominant American emphasis on negative rights:

The substantive protection embodied in the right to marry . . . goes beyond what is sometimes characterized as simply a 'negative' right insulating the couple's relationship from overreaching governmental intrusion or interference, and includes a 'positive' right to have the state take at least some affirmative action to acknowledge and support the family unit.[31]

This type of legal language enriches the political discourse in the American polity by challenging the dominant libertarian liberalism. For much of American political history, our greatest political leaders have been broadening American liberalism, such as Lincoln's "reform" liberalism and Franklin Roosevelt's New Deal and Second Bill of Rights that called for positive economic rights to be enshrined in American policy. However, in today's climate of political timidity, even among progressive politicians, some courts have stepped in to ensure that a more robust notion of liberalism is not lost in our legal and political deliberations over gay rights. Instead of wringing our hands about counter-majoritarianism, we should welcome them into the conversation.

CRITICISM OF THE MARRIAGE STRATEGY FROM THE LEFT

In popular discourse, it is customary to reference liberal support of same-sex marriage and conservative opposition. In fact, significant opposition to same-sex marriage comes from the left, particularly from feminist and queer theorists. Michael Warner faults same-sex marriage advocates for trying to be "normal" and failing to embrace the more transgressive aspects of queer identity and practice.[32] As Steven Seidman notes, "Queer politics is scandalous politics."[33] It is hardly scandalous to want to mimic heterosexual conventions and institutions.

Nancy Polikoff, a persistent feminist critic of the same-sex marriage movement, offers an important, yet flawed, critique in *Beyond (Straight and Gay)*
Marriage: Valuing All Families under the Law. Polikoff's basic argument
is that the movement for marriage is an insufficient policy response to the
insecurity and vulnerability of a wide range of families, and it buys into the
narrative about the superiority of two-parent families. In other words, the
movement takes a normative stance toward marriage, and this stance leaves
out a wide range of family forms from policy protection, given that so much
public policy is tied to marital status.

There are two primary elements to Polikoff's argument that I wish to address. The first concerns her attempt to merge liberal, civil rights politics
with conservative family politics. Embedded in this analysis is a common
assumption of feminist/queer/critical approaches to liberalism: liberals are
the oppressor; they just don't know it. The second argument concerns her
policy analysis which I will demonstrate is underdeveloped and her solution
politically impractical.

Polikoff views the movement for same-sex marriage as too closely linked
with the conservative marriage and fatherhood movements that emerged in
the 1990s. She is concerned that both of these movements ignore feminist-
inspired critiques of the assumptions of family policy in the United States.
The same-sex marriage movement, according to Polikoff,

> positions the gay rights movement on the wrong side of the culture war over
> acceptable family structures. More alarming, the logic of the arguments made
> to win converts to marriage equality risks reversing, rather than advancing,
> progress for diverse family forms, including those in which many LGBT people
> live. The civil rights victory of marriage for those gay and lesbian couples who
> seek it may come at the expense of law reforms benefiting a wider range of
> families.[34]

Thus, liberal, civil rights politics are framed by Polikoff in opposition to the
more progressive feminist politics of total family policy deconstruction and
rebuilding.

The notion that a liberal, rights-based politics is quite limited and is, in
fact, counterproductive is implicit in this critique. Liberals, it is argued, are
blind to true power dynamics and a liberal framework is thus ill-suited to
achieving full equality. Indeed, liberalism is counterproductive by convincing its adherents to the justice of rights and rights-claiming when these rights
mask real power. This critique of liberalism has a great deal of merit, but it
caricatures liberalism and underappreciates the reformist power of liberalism, particularly a liberalism grounded in a robust defense of full personhood
and substantive, not simply formal, equality.[35] Ultimately, then, Polikiff's

rejection of the same-sex marriage movement, and her attempt to merge it with the conservative heterosexual marriage movement, is grounded in a philosophical predisposition against liberal politics.

Polikoff is absolutely correct to point out that same-sex marriage is not sufficient to protect and support a full range of family arrangements. The great contribution of her work is to demonstrate the ways in which the U.S. welfare state is tied to marriage and how those who are not married are left out of this policy framework. However, the analysis she presents neglects to take into account an understanding of ideological and policy development pathways in the United States. Her goal is to deconstruct the marriage-focused welfare state and replace it with one that is more closely linked to individual and family need.

Polikoff begins this process by examining how marriage is linked to the welfare state of other Western democracies, and she finds that in other nations, marriage is much less a prerequisite for benefits. Through this presentation, she appears to be saying, "We just need to do what they are doing." The problem with her comparative analysis is that it does not delve deeply enough: she simply points out the differences without discussing the reasons for those differences. And the reasons are everything. Policy is not made in a vacuum. To draw from the literature on comparative social policy, path dependency matters. Each nation has a unique policy trajectory that is framed by political culture, history, and institutional arrangements, to name a few important factors.

Essentially, Polikoff wishes to parachute into the U.S. policy process with a radical redefinition of social policy. I share her normative desires to create a more generous, nimble, and equitable welfare state, but I part ways with her seemingly naïve tactics. Polikoff's policy goal is to convince legislatures to de-emphasize marriage in the thousands of policies at the state and federal level linked to marriage. She desires to do by drafting and laying before legislatures model family law and other policy codes. The implication is that legislators will be so convinced by the logic of these codes and the critique of marriage-based policymaking that they will be quick to enact sweeping changes. Indeed, according to Polikoff, same-sex marriage litigation only contributes to the policy stagnation:

> Once the issue of crafting laws to protect families is before a legislature, the constraints of making legal arguments to judges disappear. In the legislature it is possible to ask for what all families need. Even if gay rights groups see their constituency as only LGBT people and their relationships, households, and families, it is possible to ask for what *they all need*, not only those that mirror married heterosexual couples.[36]

This curious formulation posits legislators as purely rational policymakers and judges as fickle and limited in their ability to make sound policy. However, legislatures are not magical places; they are filled with all of the majoritarian biases that progressives bemoan. If there is any institution that is going to uphold tradition and patriarchy, and where true marriage conservatives will have a lot of leverage, it is most state legislatures. Neither does Congress possess the greatest track record as represented by the 1996 Defense of Marriage Act and the enduring failure since 1974 to enact the Emplyoment Non-Discrimination Act (ENDA). Polikoff places too much faith in the power of deconstruction and fails to factor in real politics.

Polikoff correctly notes that if the United States offered universal health care, a large reason for same-sex marriage would be removed, because health care would be provided to individuals without regard to marital status. This example, however, illustrates the problem with Polikoff's approach. The most progressive and efficient solution to the problem of lack of coverage would be a single-payer system. But as Jacob Hacker notes, this is not likely to be enacted because of the unique policy trajectory of health care policy in the United States, particularly the existence of employer-provided health care—a system that is the U.S. equivalent of universal coverage in other nations.[37] Same-sex marriage advocates have taken a similar, pragmatic approach. They did not deconstruct a politically and culturally powerful institution; they sought to use it to expand equality and security for same-sex couples, thereby transforming the institution itself in a more progressive direction. Progressives should also be highly attentive to the issues that Polikoff outlines. However, the legal and political movement for same-sex marriage should not be abandoned for an even more politically complicated and uncertain path. Indeed, liberal, not radical, approaches often have more transformative power in the American liberal regime.

Pursing a focused, principled gradualism, then, may be more constructive than exclusively relying on feminist and queer approaches of deconstruction and ironic parody. The limitation of these approaches is that they are better at (often necessary) tearing down than building up. Even theorists from these camps concede this point. As Susan Burgess argues, "Parody and drag are central political strategies of queer theory. . . . Earnest political struggle, abstracted from a larger ironic framework, is seen as hopelessly naïve at best, and dangerously misguided at worst."[38] Destabilizing cultural norms is part of any strategy for LGBT liberation and equality, but when this trumps efforts at more pragmatic, polity-aware approaches, destabilization may be the only result. Perhaps finding a balance between the two approaches is the key, but it makes no sense to marginalize or demean political struggle in the courts and in legislatures that builds upon reform traditions in American political development.

The reason that same-sex marriage advocates have, at times, appeared to appropriate the language of conservatives results from the fact that, in the United States, marriage is such a large gateway to government economic benefits and support. It makes sense politically, especially when advocating for 4 percent of the population, to gain access to already developed policy frameworks rather than calling for a radical, though noble, change in social policy. This is particularly understandable when one tactic includes tapping into the liberal, rights-claiming and equality-reinforcing framework of constitutional litigation.

In Polikoff's analysis, the idea that same-sex relationships, or any relationship for that matter, ought to be recognized by the state as more deserving than others is profoundly suspect, and what she proposes is a rather sterile policy proceduralism. She places the relationship with one's intimate life partner on par with the relationship to a second cousin who lacks health insurance. Hers is the libertarian position on the questions of same-sex marriage: get rid of civil marriage altogether. Unfortunately for the most ardent libertarians, feminists, and queer theorists, this is a pipe dream in the American polity. It is tantamount to saying to those who are currently married (gay and straight): "We are going to civilly divorce you, but don't worry, we are in the process of revising thousands of statutes and administrative rules to ensure that you will get the same benefits from the government. And, by the way, there is nothing special about your intimate relationship. Two strangers will be able to have access to these benefits as well." Contrary to this view, politics is about construction within historical, cultural, and institutional parameters. Deconstructing policy is a good first step, but it is only an academic exercise when divorced from the larger policy context.

CONCLUSION

The movement for same-sex marriage, while not perfect, represents yet another avenue of progressive change framed by liberalism in the American political tradition. The movement has been aided by a robust legal liberalism that has expanded the discourse over gay rights. As the case of the Communist-inspired approach to the movement in the 1950s, often the best avenue for progressive change comes from a liberal, rights-based framework that challenges American social conservatism by arguing that the highest American ideals support progressive change, as Kameny did. While it is always useful to be aware of the limitations of a liberal approach, this is clearly the language of progressive political change in our polity, especially if the liberalism invoked is a robust one.

NOTES

1. James A Morone, *Hellfire Nation: The Politics of Sin in American History* (New Haven, Conn.: Yale University Press, 2003).
2. J. David Greenstone, *The Lincoln Persuasion: Remaking American Liberalism* (Princeton: Princeton University Press, 1993).
3. Louis Hartz, *The Liberal Tradition in America* (New York: Harcourt Brace & Co., 1991).
4. See Greenstone, pp. 53–63.
5. Donald Webster Cory, *The Homosexual in America: A Subjective Approach* (New York: Greenberg, 1951), 4.
6. Cory, 10.
7. Cory, 14.
8. Cory, 228.
9. Cory, 231–32.
10. Cory, 221. The gendered language used here points to the gay male emphasis of Cory's writing.
11. Cory, 212.
12. John D'Emilio, *Sexual Politics, Sexual Communities: The Making of a Homosexual Minority in the United States, 1940-1970* (Chicago: University of Chicago Press, 1983), 58–87.
13. Hartz argued that ideologies outside the parameters of America's narrow liberalism would not take hold in the polity.
14. D'Emilio, 66.
15. D'Emilio, 87.
16. This term was used by Kameny and others to de-emphasize the sexual aspects of the movement. Therefore, homophile was preferred over homosexual.
17. Franklin E. Kameny, "Civil Liberties: A Progress Report," *New York Mattachine Newsletter*, vol. 10:1 (July 1965), 7–22, 8.
18. Kameny, 11.
19. Kameny was a physicist by training.
20. Kameny, 13.
21. Kameny, 15.
22. Kameny, 15.
23. Frank Kameny, Draft press release, Mattachine Society of Washington, D.C., June 30, 1972. Papers of Frank Kameny, Library of Congress. Copy on file with the author.
24. Frank Kameny, "Action on the Gay Legal Front," unpublished manuscript, ca. 1975, 26. Papers of Frank Kameny, Library of Congress, copy on file with the author. Evan Gerstmann has noted this "rational" approach to the issue of same-sex marriage utilized by courts. "Courts, unlike the public, legislators, or executive officials, are obliged to actually consider and respond to facts and arguments presented by gay and lesbian advocates. Further, courts must publicly set out the reasons for their decisions in writing. As a result, the courts have been bastions of rationality in dealing with same-sex marriage . . ." "Litigating Same-Sex Marriage: Might the Courts Actually Be Bastions of Rationality?" *PS: Political Science and Politics*, 38:2 (April 2005), 217.

25. Gerald Rosenberg, *The Hollow Hope: Can Courts Bring About Social Change?* 2nd ed. (Chicago: University of Chicago Press, 2008).

26. John D'Emilio, "Will the Courts Set Us Free? Reflections on the Campaign for Same-Sex Marriage," in Craig A. Rimmerman and Clyde Wilcox, eds. *The Politics of Same-Sex Marriage* (Chicago: University of Chicago Press, 2007), 45.

27. *Baehr v. Lewin*, 852 P.2d 44 (Haw. 1993).

28. *Baker v. State of Vermont*, 744 A.2d 864 (Vt. 1999).

29. *Goodridge v. Dept. of Public Health*, 798 N.E.2d 941 (Mass. 2003).

30. *In re Marriage Cases*, Supreme Court of California, slip opinion, May 15, 2008, 59.

31. *In re Marriage Cases*, 64.

32. See Michael Warner, *The Trouble with Normal: Sex, Politics, and the Ethics of Queer Life* (New York: The Free Press, 1999).

33. Steven Seidman, *Difference Troubles: Queering Social Theory and Sexual Politics* (New York: Cambridge University Press, 1997, 193.

34. Nancy D. Polikoff, *Beyond (Straight and Gay) Marriage: Valuing All Families under the Law* (Boston: Beacon Press, 2008), 98.

35. For more on this argument, see Jason Pierceson, *Courts, Liberalism, and Rights: Gay Law and Politics in the United States and Canada* (Philadelphia: Temple University Press, 2005), chapters 2 and 3.

36. Polikoff, 211.

37. Jacob Hacker, *The Divided Welfare State: The Battle over Public and Private Social Benefits in the United States* (New York: Cambridge University Press), 2002.

38. Susan Burgess, "Queer (Theory) Eye for the Straight (Legal) Guy: *Lawrence v. Texas'* Makeover of *Bowers v. Hardwick*," *Political Research Quarterly*, 59:3 (September 2006), 404.

7

The Special Status of Religion Under the First Amendment . . . and What it Means for Gay Rights and Antidiscrimination Laws

Sam Marcosson

Throughout American history, important voices speaking in favor of equality have used the language of morality and religious doctrine to persuade their fellow citizens to abolish slavery,[1] expand the franchise to include women,[2] and later to end the sweeping manifestations of racial segregation and discrimination that characterized the "separate but equal"[3] era and usher in the civil rights revolution.[4] Religion had a powerful place as a force for equality in each of these movements.[5]

But what happens when religion and equality splinter apart? What are the implications of the fact that in recent years religious arguments *against* equality have been raised in the fight over lesbian, gay, bisexual, and transgendered (LGBT) rights? If the religious claims of earlier times were persuasive and powerful—and, more critically, gained legitimacy—precisely because they were religious, then the religious arguments being deployed on the anti-equality side of the LGBT civil rights struggle have the same claim to legitimacy. If, on the other hand, the strength of those historical arguments did not owe to their religious nature, but to the fact that they were on the right side of the equality fights of their time, then there is nothing worrisome about the religious nature of the modern anti-LGBT arguments.

My thesis is simple: religious arguments are special in our discourse. Their special status results from the constitutional value that is assigned to religion by the Religion Clauses of the First Amendment to the U.S. Constitution,[6] especially the Free Exercise Clause.[7] While at the narrowest level the First Amendment serves only to create limits on the exercise of government power, it (like the rest of the Constitution) also serves a constitutive function—defining the core values and shared assumptions that govern the ways in which we relate to each other, particularly in the public sphere where we debate and exchange ideas and proposals. And in my view, the Religion Clauses tell us that religion enjoys an elevated status in that public sphere, a status that does not vary depending on whether we happen to agree with the message.

Even more important, the fact that antigay Americans have brought religious arguments to bear means that they not only take the anti-equality side of the debate, but also that they often assert the right to act on the basis of their religious beliefs to discriminate on the basis of sexual orientation, in violation of the equality norms embodied in antidiscrimination laws. These assertions of religious liberty thus challenge us to decide: how "special"—if at all—is the religious claim to the right to discriminate? Should it form the basis of either a constitutional exemption from antidiscrimination laws, or at least cause the democratic majority to defer to the religious claim involved by including statutory exemptions for religious beliefs in laws that bar discrimination on the basis of sexual orientation?

I will in this chapter attempt to accomplish several tasks. First, I will try to make the case for the special status of religion and religious arguments in our public discourse, and thus for a limited, nonconstitutional exemption.[8] The special status of religion is important because I shall argue that it affords the basis for recognizing exemptions on the basis of religion that—even though not strictly mandated by the Religion Clauses themselves, and thus within our democratic discretion to grant or withhold—are ones we ought to give because of the status and importance of religion among our constitutional values. In the course of making that case, and explaining it against the backdrop of the constitutional requirement of neutrality towards religion and ensuring that neutrality is given meaningful content,[9] I will endeavor to be quite careful in making clear what that special status entails—and what it does *not* mean for those who bring religion into the debate over LGBT rights, any more than it meant for those who brought it into the earlier debates over abolition, women's suffrage, or African American civil rights.

Second, however, I will also attempt to show that this exemption comes at a price, and is not unlimited. While I support a limited right of religious actors to discriminate, it must be understood that the price of this license is the actor's entitlement to equal participation in the constitutional community itself. After all, constitutionally important values are not limited only to religious liberty, and the Religion Clauses of the First Amendment are not their only source. We as a democratically governing people have decided to enact laws to protect our fellow citizens from the scourge of discrimination. These laws have been promulgated in the service of values that are just as important (and just as constitutionally derived) as those underlying the Religion Clauses. Only the source is different—in the case of antidiscrimination laws, it is the Equal Protection Clause of the Fourteenth Amendment rather than the First Amendment. Indeed, the nation's antidiscrimination statutes have (as the Supreme Court noted in the landmark decision, *Romer v. Evans*[10]) become part of the fabric of our economic and social life, and the right to equality they provide is a critical component of making the promise of the Equal Protection Clause a reality.

Given this collision of constitutional values, it should be clear that the democratic majority—acting in the service of the constitutional values underlying antidiscrimination laws, but having chosen to defer those values because of the competing First Amendment interests at stake when religious principles are being asserted in support of exemptions—may (and, I will argue, should) place limits on the exemptions it will recognize. Specifically, those who seek to remove themselves from the *obligation* to respect the right to their fellow citizens' equality may not demand the right to continue to enjoy the *benefits* of equal treatment and participation in government programs in which they might otherwise be entitled to participate. While religious groups and individuals should ordinarily be entitled to participate in government programs on equal terms (and not be excluded because of their religious views), the government can and should condition such equal participation on compliance with nondiscrimination rules from those religious groups would otherwise (if they did not wish to participate in the program) be exempted. This is, I will argue, the proper balance between the constitutional norms of First Amendment religious liberty and Fourteenth Amendment equal protection.

I. THE SPECIAL PLACE OF RELIGION IN AMERICAN DISCOURSE: THE CONVERGENCE OF CONSTITUTIONAL TEXT AND HISTORICAL PRACTICE

To justify the claim that we should allow religious exemptions from antidiscrimination laws (even when the Religion Clauses of the First Amendment do not provide an absolute constitutional mandate for them), I begin with the premise that religion has a special status in our polity. Religion's special place is a matter of constitutional values, and it is a matter of historical practice—both of which we should honor even when the Constitution gives us the choice to regulate religion without running afoul of the First Amendment itself.

While at one level it is easy to argue that all speech is created equal in the eyes of the First Amendment,[11] there are ways in which we have recognized a meaningful special status for religion. Of course, all speech—religiously inspired or not—enjoys the protection of the Free Speech Clause. In that sense, the instinctive notion of the equal status of speech is valid. But in another sense, both the text of the First Amendment and our traditions suggest a special, elevated place for religion in the discourse.

A. The Religion Clauses of the First Amendment and the Elevation of Religious Argument

The text of the First Amendment provides an excellent starting point for considering the place of religious discourse:

> Congress shall make no law respecting an establishment of religion, or prohibiting the free exercise thereof; or abridging the freedom of speech; or of the press; or the right of the people peaceably to assemble, and to petition the Government for a redress of grievances.[12]

The framers dealt with issues of an establishment of religion in a way qualitatively distinct from the rest of the First Amendment. Instead of barring the government from "prohibiting" or "abridging," in its regulations or laws, the Establishment Clause bars any law even *"respecting"* an establishment of religion. Government, in other words, must stay entirely out of the way of religion—neither favoring nor inhibiting its practice or place in our culture.[13]

The Establishment Clause, in other words, makes clear that religion (and religious speech) is meant to be exclusively a private domain. This is true of no other area of speech in our society: government may (and often does) take sides in secular debates, putting tax dollars on the side of particular substantive messages on issues such as drugs,[14] abortion,[15] arts,[16] the environment,[17] and smoking.[18]

The government's general freedom to take policy positions on major issues—to spend our tax dollars to persuade us rather than merely stay neutral as private citizens attempt to persuade each other (and then influence elections and government policies)—is therefore an important dimension of the framework within which speech takes place. But pursuant to the Establishment Clause, that does not include religion. Religious discourse is thus uniquely private in nature.

B. The Historical Place of Religious Discourse in Campaigns Over Equality

There is a long tradition in American political discourse pursuant to which religious arguments have played a critical role. This has been particularly true when the issue on the agenda has been one focused on equal treatment: the institution of slavery, women's suffrage, and civil rights. Religious arguments have been central in each of these debates.

The fight over slavery that encompassed the entirety of the years between the ratification of the Constitution and the Civil War included an important religious dimension. Mark Noll (among others) has described how abolitionists and defenders of slavery alike wielded Biblical arguments in making their case.[19]

Similarly, religion found its voice in the campaign for women's suffrage. The decision by the Woman's Christian Temperance Union (WCTU) in the 1880s to reverse its position and fight to gain the franchise for women was a critical event in the suffrage movement, and it both had religious origins and brought religious discourse into the fight. Frances Willard, who became the WCTU's President in 1879 and led it to endorse the suffragist cause, "claimed to have experienced God's call to advocate woman suffrage."[20] Prior to this time, the religious model for women's participation in governance was for them to have indirect influence; the WCTU had previously accepted the notion of the home as the woman's sphere of influence.[21] Gradually, however, it became clear to the leaders of the organization that accomplishing their moralistic goals—including especially Prohibition[22]—could not be accomplished merely by influencing men to act in the political sphere as they believed men should. It would require actual political power in the hands of the morally superior sex—women.[23]

The problem that the WCTU faced was in how to articulate a pro-suffrage message in religious terms, consistent with the Biblical special role of women it had previously endorsed, a role which seemed to preclude the political influence that suffrage entailed. Indeed, this change of position was itself expressed in religious terminology as a "conversion," and a wrenching one at that, one that was possible only "on the strength of her personal experience of God's call to vote."[24]

Having experienced this conversion, the pro-suffrage WCTU women began to use religious themes "to reverse the arguments used against them by those who warned that woman's voting would be an act of rebellion against God."[25] As Gifford points out:

> Writings and speeches began to include many references to women of the Old and New Testaments who served God through entering the public sphere and engaging in the religious and political processes of their times. . . . Biblical women served as models of courage and power for WCTU women who were attempting to initiate new modes of behavior. They did not intend to question the authority of scripture but to enlist the weight of scripture in support of what they had experienced as the will of God for them.[26]

Of more recent vintage, the twentieth-century racial civil rights movement was suffused with religious themes, led by religious leaders, and supported by significant and effective religious rhetoric. How could it be otherwise, when perhaps the most important leadership group of the 1960s was the Southern Christian Leadership Conference (SCLC)?[27] To take but one famous example, Dr. Martin Luther King's famous April 1963 *Letter From A Birmingham Jail* was written to "My Dear Fellow Clergymen," who had criticized his protests in Birmingham as "unwise and untimely." The letter was filled with religious arguments justifying the civil disobedience in which King and his followers engaged:

> I am in Birmingham because injustice is here. Just as the prophets of the eighth century B.C. left their villages and carried their "thus saith the Lord" far beyond the boundaries of their home towns, and just as the Apostle Paul left his village of Tarsus and carried the gospel of Jesus Christ to the far corners of the Greco Roman world, so am I compelled to carry the gospel of freedom beyond my own home town. Like Paul, I must constantly respond to the Macedonian call for aid.[28]

King attempted to place his movement squarely within the Christian tradition, explaining that his followers had legitimate grievances that justified their "extremism," if the protests in which they were engaged (and for which he sat in an Alabama jail) could fairly be characterized as "extremism":

> So I have not said to my people: "Get rid of your discontent." But I have tried to say that this normal and healthy discontent can be channeled into the creative outlet of nonviolent direct action. Now this approach is being dismissed as extremist. I must admit that I was initially disappointed in being so categorized.
>
> But as I continued to think about the matter I gradually gained a bit of satisfaction from being considered an extremist. Was not Jesus an extremist in love—"Love your enemies, bless them that curse you, pray for them that despitefully use you." Was not Amos an extremist for justice—"Let justice roll down like waters and righteousness like a mighty stream." Was not Paul an extremist for the gospel of Jesus Christ—"I bear in my body the marks of the Lord Jesus." Was not Martin Luther an extremist—"Here I stand; I can do none other, so help me God." . . . . So the question is not whether we will be extremist, but what kind of extremist will we be. Will we be extremists for hate or will we be extremists for love? Will we be extremists for the preservation of injustice—or for the cause of justice? In that dramatic scene on Calvary's hill, three men were crucified. We must never forget that all three were crucified for the same crime—the crime of extremism. Two were extremists for immorality, and thusly fell below their environment. The other, Jesus Christ, was an extremist for love, truth and goodness, and thereby rose above his environment. So, after all, maybe the South, the nation and the world are in dire need of creative extremists.[29]

Those who argue to delegitimize religious discourse in the LGBT civil rights movement have an insurmountable task in seeking to explain away or distinguish away the legitimacy of Martin Luther King's place in the political history of the twentieth century. Unless, that is, they would claim that religious arguments in favor of equality (a major part of King's discourse, although by no means the whole of it) are acceptable, but religious arguments against equality (the sort made by opponents of the LGBT rights movement) are impermissible. But that claim is untenable, for it represents a viewpoint-based distinction between otherwise similar speech, and viewpoint-based distinctions are themselves anathema under the First Amendment.[30]

There is, in short, a long, historical tradition by which we have recognized the important place that religion plays in our discourse, *particularly* when it comes to matters of equality and the assertion of rights. In the face of this history, it should be difficult to take issue with the core notion that religion and religious values have a special status. That status has a claim on our attention, even in a more secular age.

C. The Limits of the Special Status: Religion's Claim to Our Regard

Text and history point us in the same direction: there is a special place for religion in the debates that the framers intended would take place, and for which the First Amendment creates the constitutional space. Moreover, when those debates have been over the great issues of constitutional equality, religion has played precisely the special role the framers envisioned.

But this special role should not be misunderstood. The fact that an argument is religious in origin or substance does not exempt it from rebuttal, nor is the religious speaker insulated from criticism for his or her stance simply because the speech comes from a religious source.[31] It is in this sense that all participants in the First Amendment forum are created equal.

Nevertheless, I believe our constitutional history and the facts that are included in it have resonance. As I have already pointed out, the Constitution allows government to take sides in all the disputes between us . . . except our religious disputes. Only these are constitutionally predetermined to be exclusively private, with the government placed on the sidelines by the Establishment Clause. While not every battle in which religious arguments are deployed is "religious" in the sense that the Establishment Clause is triggered and government is compelled to remain neutral, there is certainly an overlap, and the fact that religious arguments are on the table is at the least one indication that government must keep out—making private discourse that much more critical in the debate.

If private discourse in this area is, in short, all there is, then it becomes all the more critical to value highly that speech. We should take care to consider the impact of adopting policies that run the risk of chilling religious speakers from articulating their views in the marketplace of ideas. The question whether a government policy has a "chilling effect" on speech is an enduring and important one in First Amendment doctrine. For example, the Court employs the overbreadth doctrine to overturn government policies that have a chilling effect on protected speech.[32] While I am not arguing that subjecting religious Americans to antidiscrimination (or other) laws has a chilling effect of First Amendment proportions, it is thus worth considering the consequences our decisions in this area have on the full and free exchange of ideas.

I am not arguing (nor shall I in the next section) that the special constitutional status of religious speech, nor the special place of religious messages have held in fights over equality in our history, mean that religious employers are constitutionally entitled to exemptions from antidiscrimination laws, either in general or specifically when it comes to sexual orientation. But I am saying that what history, and the constitutional values in favor of religious liberty that emanate from the text, should matter to us in how we value and treat religion and religious freedom. My claim is an important, and I think a meaningful one, but it is not unlimited.

II. NEUTRALITY FOR RELIGION: THE PRICE OF A LICENSE TO DISCRIMINATE

Taken together, the Religion Clauses have been understood to require government to remain neutral between religions, and as between religion and non-religion.[33] But to point to neutrality as the touchstone only begins to scratch the surface. The concept plays out differently in different types of cases.

Just to take one example of the form this constitutionally required neutrality takes, the Supreme Court has made clear that, pursuant to the Free Exercise Clause, religious individuals and organizations may not be excluded from participation in forums created for expression simply because of the religious content of their message.[34] The Establishment Clause has a similar effect in producing neutrality towards religion, since as I have already discussed, it ensures that government may not take sides in either entangling itself with or endorsing religion.

What neutrality means in practice is not, however, always simple to determine. Neutrality seems to require, for example, that religious employers[35] be subject—just like any other employers—to the requirements of antidiscrimination laws covering sexual orientation and/or gender identity. But, as I will argue, the concept of meaningful equality requires us to take into account the burdens that such laws place on religious beliefs and practices. Thus, a more nuanced understanding of neutrality demands that we consider, and sometimes recognize, religious exceptions to such laws, despite their impact on their effectiveness.

Indeed, many such statutes include religious exemptions, presumably because legislatures have recognized that religious views presents a special case, more deserving of deference than the typical claim (which, by definition, the statute itself rejects) that the employer ought to be able to discriminate. Typical of these is the one included as Section 6 of the proposed federal Employment Non-Discrimination Act, which provides in relevant part:

SEC. 6. EXEMPTION FOR RELIGIOUS ORGANIZATIONS.
    (a) In General—This Act shall not apply to any of the employment practices of a religious corporation, association, educational institution, or society which has as its primary purpose religious ritual or worship or the teaching or spreading of religious doctrine or belief.
    (b) Certain Employees—For any religious corporation, association, educational institution, or society that is not wholly exempt under subsection (a), this Act shall not apply with respect to the employment of individuals whose primary duties consist of teaching or spreading religious doctrine or belief, religious governance, supervision of a religious order, supervision of persons teaching or spreading religious doctrine or belief, or supervision or participation in religious ritual or worship.[36]

It is at least arguable that such exemptions from otherwise applicable government regulations represent "special rights" for religious employers, favoring them in a way that runs afoul of the Establishment Clause's requirement that government remain neutral. However, in *Corporation of the Presiding Bishop of the Church of Jesus Christ of Latter Day Saints v. Amos*,[37] the Supreme Court upheld the religious exemption in Title VII of the Civil Rights Act of 1964 against just such an Establishment Clause challenge, saying that the neutrality required by the First Amendment can be "benevolent" towards religion and "accommodate" its practice.[38] There seems little doubt that if Congress constitutionally may free religious corporations from the generally applicable obligation not to discriminate on the basis of religion (which is what was alleged in *Amos* and the type of discriminatory conduct permitted under the exemption at issue), a legislature may similarly free them of the obligation not to discriminate on the basis of sexual orientation and/or gender identity.

While statutory exemptions for religion are clearly constitutionally permissible, the more difficult question is whether they are ever constitutionally required. That is, if a legislature chooses *not* to provide one, what is the status of a claim by a religious employer that the First Amendment affords it an exemption from the antidiscrimination obligation? Sadly, the courts have been utterly incoherent in dealing with such claims. It is, of course, critical to examine whether there is a sound basis for religious individuals to claim that, when they act as employers, they have a constitutionally-protected right to discriminate. Recall that the premise with which I began this chapter was that the general values of religious freedom that emanate from the Religion Clauses should guide our decisions in how we treat claims for religious exemptions from antidiscrimination laws; such an argument presupposes that the Constitution itself does not *entitle* religious claimants to an exemption. If their constitutional claim is valid, then we have left the realm of general values emanating from constitutional principles that ought to inform our discretionary, self-governing decisions, and entered the realm in which the Constitution actually constrains our decision-making.

It is here that we encounter the Supreme Court's controversial 1990 decision in *Employment Division v. Smith,*[39] in which the Court held that the Free Exercise Clause does not exempt individuals whose religious beliefs or practices conflict with the requirements of neutral, generally applicable laws from having to obey those laws. The Court made clear in *Smith,* and in subsequent cases, that the Free Exercise Clause protects religious practices only when government singles out religion: when, for example, the same conduct is regulated because it is engaged in for religious reasons, but not when it is practiced for nonreligious purposes.[40]

Before examining how the courts have applied *Smith* in the employment discrimination context, it is worth noting how poorly reasoned a decision *Smith* itself was. To begin with, Justice Scalia's opinion in *Smith* departed from at least two lines of precedent which had held that the Free Exercise Clause does provide an exemption from government regulations when those regulations impose a substantial burden on religious practice. (I will argue shortly that paying careful attention to the burden that laws place on religious practices is a critical dimension of the proper constitutional inquiry — and hence that the Court erred badly in *Smith.*) In *Sherbert v. Verner,*[41] the Court held that if the state cannot show that its regulations are narrowly tailored to satisfy a compelling government interest, laws must give way to religious practice.[42] In *Smith,* however, the Court limited the *Sherbert* rule to the context in which it arose (claims for unemployment compensation, in which the claimant's eligibility for benefits was conditioned on a willingness to work even if the available job conflicted with his or her religious beliefs), stating, "Even if we were inclined to breathe into *Sherbert* some life beyond the unemployment compensation field, we would not apply it to require exemptions from a generally applicable criminal law."[43]

Similarly, the Court paid little heed to its earlier decision in *Wisconsin v. Yoder,*[44] a case in which the Court did precisely what Justice Scalia's majority opinion in *Smith* claimed it had never done before: hold that the Free Exercise Clause may, under appropriate circumstances,[45] excuse an individual from compliance with an otherwise valid law.[46] In *Yoder,* the Court permitted Amish parents to withdraw their children from schools after the eighth grade, saying that the First Amendment gave them an exemption from the generally applicable state-law requirement that they remain in school. In light of *Yoder,* commentators have rejected (in sometimes stirring terms) the claim Justice Scalia advanced in *Smith* that the Court had never recognized such an exemption.[47] Nevertheless, regardless of *Smith's* consistency with prior precedent, it states a clear and definitive rule: the Free Exercise Clause does not afford an exemption for religious practices from rules of general applicability, regardless of the burden those rules may place on religion.

Despite this clear stance, the lower federal courts have quite remarkably managed to establish antidiscrimination laws as an area of the law in which one would think that *Smith* had never been decided. They have continued to recognize religious exemptions from these neutral laws of general applicability, without offering an adequate explanation for distinguishing *Smith.* As I have already noted, most employment discrimination laws include numerous exemptions written with religion in mind. For example, Congress permitted religious educational institutions to discriminate in certain hiring decisions on the basis of religion under Title VII of the Civil Rights Act of 1964.[48] But those statutory exemptions are limited, and do not permit religious entities generally to discriminate on the basis of race, sex, and national origin.

Into that breach the courts stepped—in limited fashion—to craft an exemption for churches and church-related employers that does not apply across the board, but only for ministers. The "ministerial exemption" permits employers to discriminate not only on the basis of religion, but on any and every basis that is ordinarily covered by Title VII, including race. They are, in other words, fully exempt as to the position itself.

The history of the adoption of the ministerial exemption demonstrates its roots in the "substantial burden" Free Exercise Clause test that the Court emphatically rejected in *Smith.* The exemption was first recognized in *McClure v. The Salvation Army,*[49] a sex discrimination and retaliation case in which the Fifth Circuit held that applying Title VII to the employment relationship between a minister and a church would violate the First Amendment. The *McClure* court cited[50]—among other cases—*Sherbert,* the seminal case setting forth the "substantial burden/compelling interest" test the Court rejected in *Smith.*

Thus, the ministerial exemption would have seemed vulnerable to challenge once the Court decided *Smith* and abandoned the *Sherbert* approach. And yet, it has persisted, despite being deprived of its doctrinal foundation. In fact, it has *even been extended to non-ministerial employees* who perform tasks that courts have decided are akin to those performed by pastors.[51] It is as if—alone among neutral laws of general applicability—employment discrimination laws are the only ones that governments may not enforce without running afoul of the Free Exercise Clause.

In response to the argument that *Smith* fatally undermined the doctrinal basis for the ministerial exemption, the D.C. Circuit in *Catholic University* held that the exemption really wasn't about "exempting" the religious employers from employment discrimination laws, and didn't come under the *Sherbert* line of authority after all. Instead, it was actually more in the nature of recognizing the "ability of a church to manage its internal affairs."[52] This artful (non) distinction allowed the court of appeals to move the discussion to an entirely different line of authority, exemplified by cases such as *Kedroff v. St. Nicholas Cathedral of the Russian Orthodox Church in North America*,[53] holding that churches have the authority to manage their internal affairs, including the hiring of clergy.

The D.C. Circuit cited two other cases for the proposition that, "The Supreme Court has shown a particular reluctance to interfere with a church's selection of its own clergy."[54] Neither case bears the weight the majority opinion placed on it. The first was *Gonzalez v. Roman Catholic Bishop of Manila*,[55] a 1929 case that did not involve the validity of a statutory attempt to regulate an employment relationship at all, but rather a case in which a plaintiff sought to assert his entitlement to a position as a chaplain based on an interpretation of canon law, and to have a civil court so declare, contrary to the decision made by an Archbishop. The Supreme Court made the unremarkable declaration—as quoted by the D.C. Circuit—that in such a case "it is the function of the church authorities to determine what the essential qualifications of a chaplain are and whether the candidate possesses them."[56] The fact that courts will not second-guess such theological determinations has little to do with whether religious employers in the post-*Smith* world retain the ministerial exemption from neutral, generally applicable employment discrimination laws—particularly in cases where no such theological questions are raised.

The second case cited by Judge Buckley was even less helpful to his cause. In *Serbian Eastern Orthodox Diocese v. Milivojevich*,[57] the Supreme Court rejected as constitutionally impermissible a state court's extensive review of the actions of a church, defrocking a bishop and reorganizing a diocese. As with *Gonzalez*, the Court found these to be ecclesiastical matters involving church governance, as to which civil courts must accept the religious determinations of the religious authorities.[58] At most, these cases stand for the proposition not that the ministerial exemption survives *Smith* intact, but that a piece of it might remain, in specific cases in which application of a statute would call upon a civil court to overrule or second-guess a religious determination made by a church.

That was certainly not the case in *Catholic University* itself, in which the employer specifically disclaimed any theological basis for the decision to deny Sister Elizabeth McDonough tenure. Moreover, the U.S. Equal Employment Opportunity Commission (EEOC) made clear that the relief it was seeking was only to have her reinstated into the tenure process to the point she had reached when she had been (it and she alleged) discriminatorily denied tenure. After that point, she would still have had to survive a subsequent review, which would have included an assessment by the Vatican of her theological fitness to hold a position in the Canon Law Department at the Catholic University of America.

It is perfectly possible to have Title VII apply in a case to address sex (or race, or national origin) discrimination, and still not interfere with theological decision-making. In other words, the wholesale application of the ministerial exemption in such circumstances could not be justified on the basis of the cases cited by the D.C. Circuit.[59] Its continued existence after *Smith* is a doctrinal anomaly that makes the federal employment discrimination laws a constitutional poor stepchild, uniquely unable to be applied in the way every other regulatory regime can be, so long as it is neutral and generally applicable. Nevertheless, the ministerial exemption has persisted in the post-*Smith* era, and the view of the matter in *Catholic University* has become the prevailing approach.[60]

The irony, of course, is that the problem with the ministerial exemption is its fundamental inconsistency with *Smith*. But in my view, the less currency given to *Smith,* the better, for as I have already argued, it was misguided for its own inconsistency with prior precedents like *Sherbert* and *Yoder,* and for its failure to reckon with the constitutional value the Free Exercise Clause places on avoiding government burdens on religious practice. The fact that there is a gross inconsistency in the law is, in and of itself, a bad thing. But the fact that the continued application of the ministerial exemption happens to result in consideration of the alleged conflict between religion and antidiscrimination laws is a good thing (even though the D.C. Circuit erred in applying that test and finding a conflict in *Catholic University*), and would be better still if the courts limited the exemption to cases of actual conflict between theological principles and the application of the antidiscrimination laws.

More fundamentally, the anomalous treatment of antidiscrimination laws in the post-*Smith* era indicates that what is deemed "neutrality" towards religion in this area is far more complex than the simple formula articulated in *Smith*. While the lower courts' adherence to the ministerial exemption (at least in the way they have adhered to it) is problematic for the reasons I have already explained, there are deeper reasons to carefully consider—more carefully than the Supreme Court did in *Smith*—what is required for religion to be treated "equally" when it comes to applying government regulations to religious and secular components of society. The beginning of that thorough consideration begins with examination of whether religious and nonreligious individuals are truly similarly situated when it comes to being subjected to such regulations.

Consider the parallel to race-conscious government decision-making. The Supreme Court's ill-considered decisions[61] to hold affirmative action policies designed to assist racial minorities, remedy prior discrimination, and promote diversity to the same strict scrutiny standard that has long been applied to cases challenging invidious discrimination, ignored the very reasons why that standard had been applied in the first place. Strict scrutiny is justified when majoritarian political institutions discriminate against discrete and insular minorities, because in those cases courts have special reason to be skeptical of the policies at issue, and thus to require especially strong explanations for those policies. When there is a long history of discrimination against a group, judges have special reason to suspect that the latest policy may be simply the latest example of the pattern repeating itself, and to require the government to explain the very good reason it has for enacting the policy. These justifications for strict scrutiny simply do not apply, and they certainly do not apply with equal force, to affirmative action policies.[62]

In its recent affirmative action jurisprudence, the Court has opted for a kind of surface-level equality rather than for meaningful equality. It is enough for the Court that both affirmative action and traditional, invidious racial discrimination involve racial classifications. But meaningful equality takes into account differences in the groups or individuals being assessed, and not only permits but may require differential treatment if those differences justify (or demand) it. The mere fact that a racial classification was being used when the Topeka School Board maintained a dual school system, and that race is also utilized when the City of Richmond adopts an affirmative action plan, is not alone sufficient to subject those two government actions to the same standard of equal protection scrutiny.

So it is with the principle of neutrality under the Free Exercise Clause. The fact is that when it comes to government regulations, religious and nonreligious individuals are not (or at least they may not be) equally situated, any more than government affirmative action policies are the same as segregated schools and antimiscegenation laws. Laws may impose unique burdens on religious beliefs and practices that are not felt by nonreligious individuals, or are experienced only by people with particular religious beliefs but not others. Treating them as if they are the same does not represent meaningful neutrality, and it does not serve the values underlying the Free Exercise Clause.

This point is demonstrated by the application of the law at issue in *Employment Division v. Smith*. On its face, the law applied to the religious and nonreligious alike. But in practice, only those with a religious need to use peyote would be put to the choice of giving up the sacrament involved in their worship services, or face dismissal from their jobs for misconduct (and thus ineligibility for unemployment benefits). In other words, the sacrifice involved in giving up peyote is simply not the same; both groups give up the drug, but only one gives up the drug *and religious practice.*

Under the right conditions, where it is shown that compliance with an antidiscrimination law would cause a sufficient burden on genuine religious beliefs, religious objections (including those protecting sexual minorities from discrimination, which under current norms would almost certainly be the most frequently asserted exemption) should be honored, either through exemptions written into the statutes or recognized as constitutionally required by the Free Exercise Clause (the latter limited to ministerial positions). Obviously, the objection will be raised that this privileges religious objections to legal obligations over other, secular objections—objections that may be accompanied by burdens on nonreligious practices that are just as substantial as those that are asserted in support of religious exemptions.

But it is critical to keep in mind that these exemptions are based on the premise that religion occupies a special place in our culture, a place assured to it by operation of the First Amendment itself. Mere secular objections to democratic, majoritarian decisions to protect gay men and lesbians from discrimination are not entitled to the same consideration, because the Constitution simply does not give them the same status.

Invocation of that special status is not a cost-free decision, however. Antidiscrimination laws have become part of the fabric of economic life, and the protections they provide are fundamental to every American. As the Supreme Court observed in *Romer v. Evans*,[63] discussing and invalidating a state constitutional amendment that barred such protections when provided to gay men and lesbians:

> We find nothing special in the protections Amendment 2 withholds. These are protections taken for granted by most people either because they already have them or do not need them; these are protections against exclusion from an almost limitless number of transactions and endeavors that constitute ordinary civic life in a free society.[64]

Religious exemptions from antidiscrimination laws tear at the social and economic fabric that binds us together. These laws have become a core and accepted part of the way in which we relate to one another; most Americans simply take for granted that we will not be judged in the workplace on the basis of the characteristics that these laws place off-limits. Even as I assert that exemptions are justified in the name of religious tolerance and freedom, I do not in any way detract from the extent to which those who "take" the exemption are removing themselves from a critical part of our contemporary social contract, or minimize the extent to which they strike a blow against the premise of equality that is also a core constitutional value, this one expressed by the Fourteenth Amendment's Equal Protection Clause.[65]

This is a critical point, worth reinforcing. Recall that I have argued that the exemptions I am urging we should respect for religious practice are not constitutionally required.[66] My view is that we should enact them because of the importance of the general values underlying the Religion Clauses, the Free Exercise Clause in particular. But if the question is one of constitutional *values*, not hard-and-fast constitutional requirements, then competing constitutional values can and should also be weighed in the balance—and the equality-based priorities expressed in antidiscrimination laws are a classic illustration of this, emerging as they do from the values that animate the Fourteenth Amendment.

Hence, the decision by people of faith, or entire churches, to remove themselves from the social and economic fabric that binds us together must and should have consequences. If they are asking the rest of us to honor their request to be freed of the obligation to render their fellow citizens the equal treatment to which they would otherwise be entitled under the law, then they cannot expect to receive all of the benefits that come with the entitlement to full and equal treatment. It is here that the government can, and should, take full advantage of the Supreme Court's 2004 decision in *Locke v. Davey*,[67] which I believe was wrongly decided on its facts but could be fairly applied to other situations.

Locke itself involved a Washington state scholarship program, for which students were ineligible if they intended to pursue a degree in devotional theology. In other words, certain students were—uniquely—excluded from the benefits of an otherwise generally available program simply because of the religious nature of their intended course of study.[68] The Court, quite oddly in light of the prevailing precedents, permitted Washington to exclude students from the "generally available benefit" (the scholarship program) solely on the basis of religion.[69]

The majority's explanation for its ruling was that the state had "play in the joints"[70]—that even though the state was not required by the Establishment Clause to exclude theology students from the scholarship program,[71] the state could choose to exclude them without running afoul of the students' Free Exercise Clause rights. This reasoning seemed to Justice Scalia—as it seems to me—backwards; it is precisely because the state was not constrained by the

Establishment Clause to exclude the students (i.e., it was constitutionally free to include them), that it had an obligation under the Free Exercise Clause to apply the neutral scholarship program in an even-handed way to all students, regardless of the sectarian content of their chosen course of study.[72]

The Court's answer was that Washington's exclusion of the theology students was not discriminatory, because it could properly conclude that "training for religious training and training for secular professions are not fungible."[73] But "fungibility" surely is not the test for neutrality; education in philosophy is not fungible for education in electrical engineering, but the state would be acting in a non-neutral way if it limited eligibility for the scholarship program to philosophy majors and excluded electrical engineers. And if the right to study electrical engineering had been held to be constitutionally entitled to neutral treatment at the hands of the state, then surely that exclusion could not be defended on grounds of the non-fungibility of the field.

While the Court's decision in *Locke* is difficult to defend in circumstances like those involved in that case, there are instances in which governments are justified in excluding religious participants from government programs even though they seem nominally qualified. The core premise of the argument that people and organizations of faith should not be excluded from competing for a government contract or program on equal terms with secular people and organizations is that they are not different when it comes to program eligibility, simply for being religious, than those secular competitors. If, for instance, the program involves providing drug rehabilitation services to prison inmates, the contract should go to the provider (religious or not) which can best meet the needs of the inmate population within the terms and requirements of the contract, without regard to the religious or secular character of the bidder.[74]

However, when defining the eligibility criteria, the government can and should define its interests more broadly than merely the narrow programmatic needs of the specific drug rehabilitation contract (or the scholarship program, etc.). Instead, it should also impose eligibility requirements that demand that participants be full members of the social contract that recognizes the full, equal citizenship of all persons protected by antidiscrimination laws. If they wish, for reasons of religious faith and commitment, to remove themselves from the community of equal citizens when it comes to the obligations imposed by our community, we can and should respect that decision; core Free Exercise Clause values demand it of us. But as we have seen, those values sound in neutrality and equality. Asking for the exemption represents a fundamental (and hence ironic) decision to foreswear the obligations imposed by those selfsame values, and those who do so cannot then turn around and demand to enjoy the benefits of our society's commitment to neutrality and equality, as we put into practice the values of the Fourteenth Amendment.

Thus, any government contract or program that is open to a religious partici-pant—including but not limited to so-called "faith-based initiatives"—should include a requirement that the contractor agrees to waive or forego any exemp-tion from an antidiscrimination law to which it, he, or she would otherwise be entitled as a function of religious beliefs.[75] This approach says to those who insist on discriminating, and on subjecting others to unequal treatment against the wishes of the democratic majority, that the commitment of that majority to its values is just as strong and sincere as the individual's commitment to her re-ligious beliefs. It strikes this balance: while our respect for the religious nature of your choice, and its sincerity (though not its substance), causes us to exempt you from the penalties for noncompliance with the baseline nondiscrimination requirement, we will not sacrifice those antidiscrimination values to the greater extent it would take to allow you to actually enjoy affirmative benefits from participation in programs that presuppose your full, equal status in the com-munity from whose obligations you have walked away.

In July 2008, news reports surfaced of regulations proposed by the Bush Administration that would do the opposite of what I have proposed here.[76] The regulation would deny federal funding to "any hospital . . . that does not accommodate employees who want to opt out of participating in care that runs counter to their personal convictions, including providing birth-control pills, IUDS, and the Plan B emergency contraceptive."[77] This is not precisely the same issue I have addressed in this chapter, since the religious views at stake do not lead the individual to discriminate on the basis of sexual ori-entation. But it is a close enough parallel to make the point clear: I would permit those with religious convictions against providing particular health care services the right to refuse to do so, in recognition of the importance of the religious liberty being asserted on that side of the issue. However, there are fundamental rights on the other side of the question as well, just as there are when exceptions to antidiscrimination laws compromise the equality-driven norms underlying those statutes. The right to quality health care, and to equal treatment (on the basis of sex) in the delivery of that care, is obvi-ously implicated by the decisions that the proposed regulation would force health care providers to leave in the hands of each individual employee.[78] The federal government should make exactly the opposite choice than the threat embodied in the proposed regulation, and condition participation in federal programs (and receipt of federal funding) on the recipient's guarantee that it can and will deliver all medical treatment and services on a timely and equal basis. If the desire of any individual employees (even on the basis of religion) not to participate in that treatment interferes with that goal, then that desire should have to yield. The fundamental principle is that in balancing the constitutional interests at stake, we should defer to the religious liberty being claimed where possible, and when it does not interfere with the accomplishment of competing constitutional values, but equality norms need not and should not yield completely merely because the "religion card" is played. If the devout individual wishes to have his or her beliefs respected absolutely, the answer is to withdraw to a field in which the government cannot use the fact of its own participation to impose conditions that are inconsistent with those values. Once the individual chooses to participate in the broader economic community, she forfeits the otherwise sacrosanct claim to religious absolutism, and beliefs must give way to the pull of the community's values expressed through majoritarian government action.[79]

CONCLUSION

Religion has a special place in our constitutional structure and values. Religious discourse is unique, both because of the text of the First Amendment and the historical tradition that honors its role (particularly when it comes to issues of equality). We should continue to honor that place. At least as important, that special status for religion means that we should create the constitutional space for religious beliefs to be protected, even when it requires exemptions from antidiscrimination laws that otherwise protect deeply important rights for sexual minorities. However, the corollary to that recognition is that those religious entities and individuals who avail themselves of the exemption have opted out of the essential fabric of equal treatment that we have democratically created, and which defines us as a society. While I believe we should be tolerant enough of religious diversity to accept their choice, we need not be more inclusive than tolerance demands. It demands no more than that we not penalize their choice; it does not require that we allow those whose religion preaches inequality and intolerance to benefit any further. They should thus be excluded from government programs in which others in society—religious and nonreligious alike—can participate equally.

NOTES

1. See *infra* p. 6 (discussing religious rhetoric of the abolitionist movement).
2. See *infra* pp. 6-7 (discussing religious rhetoric in the women's suffrage movement).
3. See *Plessy v. Ferguson,* 163 U.S. 537 (1896) (U.S. Supreme Court decision approving doctrine under which governments could satisfy the Equal Protection Clause of the Fourteen Amendment by providing facilities for blacks that were "separate but equal" to those provided for whites).

4. See *infra* pp. 7–9 (discussing religious rhetoric in the civil rights movement of the 1950s and 1960s).

5. I should make clear that I am not arguing that religious speakers have always been on the "right" side of important issues of equality, and that such a record gives religion a special claim to our attention and deference. They have certainly (as I will show) played an important role on many critical issues, but religious arguments have also been deployed on the side of brutal repression. See, e.g., Varun Soni, *Freedom From Subordination: Race, Religion, and the Struggle for Sacrament,* 15 Temp. Pol. & Civ. R. L. Rev. 33, 36–37 (2005) (discussing role of Catholic Church and Inquisition in banning Native American religious practices as part of campaign to enforce conversion of "savages" in the Americas). Certainly, the record is mixed at best. But the claim to a special constitutional status emerges not from the record of religion of having been historically and consistently been "right" on important issues of equality, but from our constitutional decision to accord religion such status, and our subsequent historical practice of having done so. It has been a happy result of that decision that, in practice, religion has often been deployed in the service of the constitutional value of equality.

6. U.S. Const., Am. 1 ("Congress shall make no law respecting an establishment of religion, or prohibiting the free exercise thereof. . . .").

7. See Ira C. Lupu and Robert W. Tuttle, *The Faith-Based Initiative and the Constitution,* 55 DePaul L. Rev. 1, 15 (2005) ("[T]he Constitution's text and history thoroughly support the assertion that religion is indeed a matter of distinctive constitutional import.").

8. I will also argue that in very limited conditions, the Free Exercise Clause also requires an exemption for certain religious employers making a specific class of decisions (those where there is a demonstrated conflict between specific theological principles and the application of an antidiscrimination law in an employment decision involving a ministerial employee). See *infra* pp. 16–19 (discussing proper, limited scope of constitutional "ministerial exception"). Besides this limited constitutional exception, the exemption for which I will argue is one that is not mandated by the Constitution, but rather is simply one I believe we should adopt in the service of the broader principle of religious liberty that is served, but not strictly mandated, by the Religion Clauses.

9. See *infra* pp. 19–22 (discussing what neutrality towards religion means when government policy disproportionately burden religion, and analogizing to Supreme Court's decision in *Romer v. Evans,* 517 U.S. 620 (1996), recognizing equal treatment must be understood in a deeply contextualized sense).

10. 517 U.S. 620 (1996).

11. See U.S. Const., Am. 1 ("Congress shall make no law . . . abridging the freedom of speech. . . .").

12. U.S. Const., Am. 1.

13. See Robert A. Sedler, *The Protection of Religious Freedom Under the American Constitution,* 53 Wayne L. Rev. 817, 818 (2007) ("as a matter of constitutional structure, we protect religious freedom . . . by prohibiting the government from 'advancing or inhibiting religion'—the establishment clause requires that the government pursue a policy of complete official neutrality toward religion") (footnote omitted).

14. See, *e.g.*, U.S. Drug Enforcement Agency, *What Americans Need to Know About Marijuana*, available at www.usdoj.gov/dea/pubs/publications.html (publication taking strong anti-marijuana stance).

15. See *Rust v. Sullivan*, 500 U.S. 173 (1991) (government may fund family planning programs while selectively refusing to fund those that support or even mention abortion, as part of general antiabortion government policy).

16. See *National Endowment for the Arts v. Finley*, 524 U.S. 569 (1998) (National Endowment for the Arts funding decisions may be based on statutory criteria including general standards of "decency and respect" for the values of the American people, without violating the First Amendment by excluding funding requests that run afoul of those values).

17. For example, government agencies were part of the consortium that founded Keep America Beautiful, the organization that produced and aired the classic "Crying Indian" antipollution commercial in 1971 with the famous slogan, "People start pollution. People can stop it." *See* www.youtube.com/watch?v=X3QKvEy0AIk.

18. Government agencies have been funding anti-smoking campaigns for years, without anyone ever suggesting that they are compelled to maintain by some vision of "viewpoint neutrality" under the First Amendment to also fund commercials supporting tobacco companies. See, *e.g.*, www.youtube.com/watch?v=PJAlB5Iez8I (ad produced and sponsored by the Maryland Department of Health and Mental Hygiene).

19. See Mark A. Noll, *The Civil War as a Theological Crisis* 38-72 (2006).

20. Carolyn De Swarte Gifford, *Frances Willard and the Woman's Christian Temperance Union's Conversion to Woman Suffrage*, in *Wheeler*, Marjorie Spruill, *One Woman, One Vote: Rediscovering the Woman Suffrage Movement* 117, 127 (1995).

21. *Id.* at 123.

22. See Carrie Chapman Catt and Nettie Rogers Shuler, *Woman Suffrage and Politics: The Inner Story of the Suffrage Movement* 279 (2005) (discussing the relationship between the Prohibition and suffrage campaigns, and noting that because of the perception that if women received the franchise they would vote disproportionately to support Prohibition, "[m]en indifferent to suffrage but hostile to prohibition were rendered impervious to the suffrage appeal, and men hostile to prohibition but in favor of suffrage were frightened by the continual insistence of liquor workers that woman suffrage meant the speedier coming of prohibition").

23. See Gifford, *supra note 20*, at 123–26.

24. *Id.* at 128–29 (discussing anonymous essay entitled "One Woman's Experience" breaking away from the religious arguments that women should not vote because "man was to govern, woman was to be government, and thus that woman could not vote since voting was governing"). This essay discussed the views of Rev. Horace Bushnell, a theologian who took the view that the act of voting for woman was an unnatural one of unsexing herself.

25. *Id.* at 130.

26. *Id.* at 130–31.

27. See Taylor Branch, *Parting the Waters: America in the King Years 1954-1963* (1988) (discussing the founding and role of the SCLC).

28. Martin Luther King, *Letter From a Birmingham Jail*, in *A Testament of Hope: The Essential Writings of Martin Luther King, Jr.*, James M. Washington, ed., 289, at 290 (HarperCollins 1991).

29. *Id.* at 297-98.

30. See *Good News Club v. Milford Central High School*, 533 U.S. 98, 107 (2001) (where state creates a limited public forum for groups to use—in this instance, a school used by groups for after-school activities—it must make that forum available on a viewpoint-neutral basis and any restrictions must be "reasonable in light of the purpose served by the forum," which does not include discrimination on the basis of the religious nature of the group) (quoting *Cornelius v. NAACP Legal Defense & Ed. Fund, Inc.*, 473 U.S. 788, 806 (1985)).

31. See Samuel A. Marcosson, *The "Special Rights" Canard in the Debate Over Lesbian and Gay Civil Rights*, 9 Notre Dame J. L. Ethics & Pub. Pol'y 137, 166–67 (1995) ("[A]ny claims that criticism of antigay arguments amounts to "religion bashing" should be dismissed; a bigot is not immune from the charge of bigotry merely because she asserts a religious basis for her position.").

32. See *Virginia v. Hicks*, 539 U.S. 113, 119 (2003) ("We have provided this expansive remedy out of concern that the threat of enforcement of an overbroad law may deter or 'chill' constitutionally protected speech—especially when the overbroad statute imposes criminal sanctions. . . . Many persons, rather than undertake the considerable burden (and sometimes risk) of vindicating their rights through case-by-case litigation, will choose simply to abstain from protected speech, . . . harming not only themselves but society as a whole, which is deprived of an uninhibited marketplace of ideas.") (citations omitted).

33. See *McCreary County, Ky. v. ACLU*, 545 U.S. 844, 875-76 (2005) (advancing neutrality as the critical mediating principle for both Religion Clauses of the First Amendment).

34. See *Rosenberger v. Rector and Visitors of the University of Virginia*, 515 U.S. 819 (1995).

35. I refer to religious employers for the sake of simplicity, but the basic argument would be the same in the case of a religious landlord who wishes to discriminate against a gay, lesbian, or transgender renter, or the owner of a business who seeks to close his or her place of public accommodation to LGBT customers. The question of whether antidiscrimination statutes should apply in those contexts is not meaningfully different from the question as it applies to a religious employer.

36. Sec. 6, H.R. 2015 (the Employment Non-Discrimination Act of 2007), available at thomas.loc.gov/cgi-bin/query/F?c110:1:./temp/~c110cBw7c7:e11850.

37. 483 U.S. 327 (1987).

38. *Id.* at 335.

39. 494 U.S. 872 (1990).

40. See *Chuch of the Lumumi Babalu Aye v. City of Hialeah*, 508 U.S. 520 (1993) (city ordinances that targeted ritualistic animal sacrifices when engaged in by a particular religious group, and did not apply to the same conduct of slaughtering animals engaged in by others, were not neutral and generally applicable, and thus violated the religion's Free Exercise Clause rights).

41. 374 U.S. 398 (1963).

42. *Id.* at 403.

43. *Smith,* 494 U.S. at 884.

44. 406 U.S. 205 (1972).

45. Those circumstances are defined by the application of the strict scrutiny test set forth in *Sherbert*: the regulation at issue may be applied notwithstanding the burden it places on religious practice and belief if it is narrowly tailored to serve a compelling interest.

46. See Jay S. Bybee, *Common Ground: Robert Jackson, Antonin Scalia, and a Power Theory of the First Amendment,* 75 Tul. L. Rev. 251, 304 (2000) ("By the time Scalia reached the Supreme Court, the Court had made clear that both the Free Exercise Clause and the Free Speech Clause sometimes required exemption from otherwise valid laws of general applicability . . . ."). Professor Bybee went on to cite *Yoder* specifically as such a case, implicitly rejecting Justice Scalia's reimagining of that case. *Id.* at 304-05.

47. See, *e.g., id.* at 310 ("The proposition that the Court had never thought that free exercise claims excused compliance was so outlandish that it diminished the credibility with which the Court announced its new position."); John T. Noonan, *The End of Free Exercise?*, 42 DePaul L. Rev. 567, 577 (1992) ("On a fair reading of *Smith,* nothing remained of the major decisions of the past to the extent that they upheld the free exercise of religion against state action."); Michael W. McConnell, *Free Exercise Revisionism and the Smith Decision,* 57 U. Chi. L. Rev. 1109, 1120–22 (1990) (explaining the failure of the Court's attempts to distinguish *Yoder*).

48. 42 U.S.C. § 2000e-1(a) ("This subchapter shall not apply . . . to a religious corporation, association, educational institution, or society with respect to the employment of individuals of a particular religion to perform work connected with the carrying on by such corporation, association, educational institution, or society of its activities.").

49. 460 F.2d 553, 558-60 (5th Cir.), *cert. denied,* 409 U.S. 896 (1972).

50. *McClure,* 460 F.2d. at 558.

51. See *EEOC v. Catholic University,* 83 F.3d 455 (D.C. Cir. 1996) (applying ministerial exemption to affirm dismissal of complaint filed by faculty member who alleged sex discrimination after she was denied tenure by sectarian university's Canon Law Department).

52. *Id.* at 460.

53. 344 U.S. 94 (1952).

54. *Catholic University,* 83 F.3d at 460.

55. 280 U.S. 1 (1929).

56. *Id.* at 16.

57. 426 U.S. 696 (1976).

58. *Id.* at 721 (criticizing the Illinois Supreme Court for "substitute[ing] its interpretation of the Diocesan and Mother Church constitutions for that of the highest ecclesiastical tribunals in which church law vests authority to make that interpretation. This the First and Fourteenth Amendments forbid.").

59. The ministerial exemption has been defended on alternative grounds, as an expression of the limits that the Establishment Clause places on the jurisdictional

authority of the government vis-à-vis religion. See Ira C. Lupu and Robert W. Tuttle, *Sexual Misconduct and Ecclesiastical Immunity*, 2004 B.Y.U. L. Rev. 1789, 1815–16. Professors Lupu and Tuttle argue (emphasis added):

> Because the state is forbidden from being the author or coauthor of religious faith, it may not adjudicate or regulate the ways in which communities of faith are organized. Nor may the state select the voices which lead these communities, nor the lessons they communicate. Religious entities cannot waive this jurisdictional limitation, which we believe resides most comfortably in the Establishment Clause (even as it furthers Free Exercise values). Hence the district court judge correctly decided to stop the trial on the merits of Sister McDonough's claim. Moreover, *no state assertion of countervailing state interests, compelling or otherwise, may operate to set aside this limitation.* The Catholic University decision remains correct, regardless of the governmental interest in combating sex discrimination in employment.

This argument posits the Establishment Clause as a unique constitutional provision in that the limits it imposes on governmental power are absolute, subject to no balancing of interests, regardless of how compelling those secular interests may be. The Supreme Court has, properly, never interpreted either the Establishment Clause or the Free Exercise Clause in this fashion, for it would elevate sectarian interests far above all others. Moreover, it assumes that every application of employment discrimination laws to positions like that held by Sister McDonough would constitute the government becoming "the author or coauthor of religious faith," a claim that is not borne out by the facts of that specific case and which paints with too broad a brush in exempting *all* religious employer from *all* applications of Title VII to positions that courts have labeled "ministerial" in nature.

    60. *See, e.g., Petruska v. Gannon University*, 462 F.3d 294 (3d Cir. 2006) (former chaplain's Title VII sex discrimination and retaliation claims barred by ministerial exemption).

    61. *See Richmond v. J. A. Croson Co.*, 488 U.S. 469 (1989) (holding that affirmative action program enacted by city was subject to strict scrutiny because it used race); *Adarand Constructors, Inc. v. Pena*, 515 U.S. 200 (1995) (extending holding in *Croson* to federal affirmative action programs).

    62. *See Adarand*, 515 U.S. at 243–45 (Stevens, J., dissenting) ("The Court's concept of 'consistency' assumes that there is no significant difference between a decision by the majority to impose a special burden on the members of a minority race and a decision by the majority to provide a benefit to certain members of that minority notwithstanding its incidental burden on some members of the majority. . . . The consistency that the Court espouses would disregard the difference between a 'No Trespassing' sign and a welcome mat.").

    63. 517 U.S. 620 (1996).

    64. *Id.* at 631.

    65. U.S. Const., Am. XIV ("No State shall . . . deny to any person within its jurisdiction the equal protection of the laws.").

    66. It is true that I have argued for a limited, constitutionally-required exemption, in that I would support a modified version of the ministerial exemption, limited to

cases in which application of the antidiscrimination law would actually conflict with the theological beliefs of the employer, assuming that the Court restored the pre-*Smith* "substantial burden" test for Free Exercise Clause cases. In such cases, the balancing test I will advance in the text would not apply, because the exemption is actually mandated by a proper reading of the Free Exercise Clause, rather than a justifiable policy choice subject to being balanced against other values and policy considerations.

67. 540 U.S. 712 (2004).

68. *Id.* at 726 (Scalia, J., dissenting) (criticizing the majority opinion for "sustain[ing] a public benefits program that facially discriminates against religion").

69. *Id.* at 726-27 (Scalia, J., dissenting) (discussing cases such as *Hialeah*, 508 U.S. 520 (1993), and *Everson v. Board of Ed. of Ewing*, 330 U.S. 1, 16 (1947)), which established the principle that government "cannot exclude individual Catholics, Lutherans, Mohammadens, Baptists, Jews, Methodists, Non-believers, Presbyterians, or the members of any other faith, because of their faith, or lack of it, from receiving the benefits of public welfare legislation").

70. *Id.* at 719 (majority opinion) ("These two Clauses, the Establishment Clause and the Free Exercise Clause, are frequently in tension. . . . Yet we have long said that 'there is room for play in the joints' between them. . . . In other words, there are some state actions permitted by the Establishment Clause but not required by the Free Exercise Clause. This case involves that 'play in the joints' describe above.") (references omitted).

71. In some earlier cases, governments had argued that they were required by the Establishment Clause to exclude religious individuals or organizations from government programs, because including them would constitute an endorsement or perceived endorsement of religion. In those cases, the Court rejected the notion that the inclusion of religion on a neutral basis would raise significant Establishment Clause concerns. See, *e.g., Witters v. Washington Dep't of Services for the Blind*, 474 U.S. 481 (1986) (state may provide vocational rehabilitation assistance to blind student who would apply it to studies at Christian college, and who intended to become a "pastor, missionary, or youth director" without violating the Establishment Clause); *Rosenberger v. Rector and Visitors of the University of Virginia*, 515 U.S. 819 (1995) (state university violated first amendment rights of student group when it denied funding to them based on the religious perspective of their speech, and a fear of violating the Establishment Clause had the religious speech been included did not justify the viewpoint-based exclusion of the students).

72. See Thomas C. Berg and Douglas Laycock, *The Mistakes in Locke v. Davey and the Future of State Payments for Services Provided By Religious Institutions,* 40 Tulsa L. Rev. 227, 235-36 (2004) (arguing that the Court erred in *Locke* because it failed to see that on matters of religion, unlike other issues as to which the government may take sides, the state must remain neutral).

73. *Locke v. Davey,* 540 U.S. at 721.

74. See, *e.g.,* 42 U.S.C. § 604a(c) (the Charitable Choice Act, requiring that, if a state administers part of its public assistance program utilizing private service providers, they must make "religious organizations . . . eligible, on the same basis as any other private organization, as contractors to provide assistance, . . . so long as the

programs are implemented consistent with the Establishment Clause of the United States Constitution").

75. Of course, this waiver requirement would be neutral in the sense that all contractors (religious or not) would be subject to it. In practical terms, of course, its effect would be felt only on the religious participants, since they are the only ones who would benefit from the religious exemptions they are being asked to waive as a condition of participation in the program.

76. See Rob Stein, *Workers' Religious Freedom v. Patients' Rights: Proposal Would Deny Federal Money if Employees Must Provide Care to Which They Object*, The Washington Post, July 31, 2008, at A1, *available at* www.washingtonpost.com/wp-dyn/content/article/2008/07/30/AR2008073003238.html.

77. *Id.*

78. See generally Heather A. Weisser, Note, *Abolishing the Pharmacist's Veto: An Argument in Support of a Wrongful Conception Cause of Action Against Pharmacists Who Refuse to Provide Emergency Contraception*, 80 S. Cal. L. Rev. 865 (2007) (discussing the massive impact on women of refusal by pharmacists to provide needed reproductive services).

79. See Robert N. Cover, *The Supreme Court 1982 Term: Foreword: Nomos and Narrative*, 97 Harv. L. Rev. 4, 26-33 (1982) (giving credence to the Free Exercise Clause arguments of the Amish in *Wisconsin v. Yoder* precisely because they were based on the separate community the Amish had established and their lack of integration into the broader legal and economic life governed by generally applicable legal rules).

8

Supporting Queer Youth

A New Vision of Child, Family, and State

Valerie Lehr

Feminist and gay and lesbian theorists of family have gone far in rethinking the role that family plays in society and new ways that the state should form and support families if it is to enhance, rather than restrict, equality. Despite this, in most discussions of family within both literatures, children receive little attention, unless it can be argued that they will benefit as a result of better recognizing and supporting parental relationships. For example, in discussions put forth by advocates of gay marriage, this argument is made for multiple reasons: (1) marriage would enable more young people to live in two-parent families; (2) more visible gay and lesbian families would change the image of homosexuality; (3) normalizing gay relationships might allow more gay and lesbian couples to adopt children who otherwise remain in state care; (4) the visibility of children of gay and lesbian parents and the demands of gay and lesbian parents would force schools to acknowledge gay families in new ways.

Each of these points strikes me as at least somewhat true, though they also can potentially reinforce dominant values that might be better questioned, such as the idea that children should live in two parent families or that schools should structure their curricula around the demands of parents. Equally importantly, the focus on gay adult relationships within gay and lesbian work on family fails to explore the panoply of sexuality issues that young people, including questioning and queer youth, face. Feminist discussions of family often focus on how care needs within families can be met in ways that do not overburden women and that do not reinforce the view that women should be primary caretakers. Here, too, the focus on adults means that children's needs and rights go unexplored. These literatures, however, sometimes point in

directions helpful for theorizing a vision of family and the state that can include youth as moral agents whose needs for care should not lead to denying
them essential human rights, particularly liberty rights. Such a vision could
result in policies that would enhance the lives of many queer youth.

The development of theory and politics that can help to support queer
youth must begin with the recognition that unlike in most other oppressed
communities, queer young people are largely not raised in communities
that present a counterimage to the dominant culture. In many cases, this
means that a young person has to confront invisibility; in the worst cases, it
means that a young person has to confront both public and private hostility
with ambivalent cultural approval. To the extent that parental rights remain
dominant, this can be a highly negative situation for queer youth, as well as
for heterosexual young people whose knowledge and choices are limited by
parental right discourses.[1] The question that I want to consider is how family
might be reconceptualized to increase the freedom of teenagers, including
their sexual freedom.[2]

My intent is to explore how works that seek to rethink intimate adult relationships in order to both critique traditional marriage and argue for lesbian
and gay equality might provide a foundation for also rethinking adults and
teen relationships in ways that would benefit queer youth. In the first section,
I will briefly discuss some of the issues that face queer teens. Following that,
I will begin to explore how progressive theories of family, even when they do
not fully critique current models of parent-child relationships, can point us in
important directions. Next, I will explore a number of theorists' articulations
of children and rights in order to both highlight the strengths of these arguments and the weaknesses that arise when youth are not understood as having
rights in the present, rather than in the future. I will then discuss how a vision
of youth/teenagers that understands them as full human beings better fits with
the feminist vision of family/state relations developed earlier and how such
an understanding would benefit teens whose sexuality rights are limited by
current understandings of family and parental rights.

QUEER YOUTH: STRENGTHS AND CHALLENGES

In developing this section, my focus will largely be on the forces that deny
sexual agency to young people. However, it is also important, from the out-
set, to be clear that most queer teens grow into well-adjusted and successful adults. Thus, we need to be aware of the factors that contribute to this
growth and development, even as we come to describe the forces that also
limit the lives of youth. Further, it is important to be aware that research in

this area is incomplete, and that the picture one sees can easily be an artifact of those who show up in any given study. With that caveat, it strikes me that researchers in this field would agree with the following: (1) young people are both questioning their sexuality and defining alternative sexualities and gender orientations at younger ages than in the past; (2) overall, teens who question their sexuality have more positive resources from which to draw than in the past, since they have a culture that presents a wider array of sex/gender images and most seem to have some peers to whom they can be honest about their sexuality and receive support; and (3) the parents of these young people are more likely to see leading a positive life as a gay person as more possible than in the past, not the least because possibilities for positive relationships with partners and children are more clearly visible now. This constellation, along with interviews with many youth who are doing quite well, leads Savin-Williams to suggest that the almost exclusive focus on negative characteristics in the lives of queer youth is misplaced and dangerous. Alternatively, "[d]escribing these young people as resilient acknowledges the developmental assets they've accumulated over their life course—abilities, traits, and ways of circumventing adversity and health-damaging behaviors and promoting outcomes that are better than one would expect given the amount of risk factors they have. The risk factors have been well-documented; the protective factors, which can be innate or environmental (including good schools and families) have not."[3]

I do not, therefore, want to suggest that all queer teens face developmental problems somehow inherent to defining nonnormative sex or gender identities. Nevertheless, too many of these young people continue to face challenges that would be less problematic if we lived in a society that took the rights of young people more seriously and that understood young people as sexual. Among these challenges is harassment in schools.[4] Nearly two-thirds of students who participated in the 2005 GLSEN National School Climate Study report that they did not feel safe in their schools; 75.4 percent report "hearing remarks such as faggot or dyke frequently or often at school,"[5] as well as other forms of harassment, such as having property stolen or "being the target of rumors or lies," 'cyberbullying.'" These issues affect transgender youth even more. Most of these incidents are not reported, at least in part because less than a quarter attend schools that have a policy that explicitly bans harassment on the basis of sexual orientation, while only a tenth of schools ban harassment on the basis of gender expression.[6] When harassment is reported, it is dealt with in a satisfactory way less than half of the time.[7] The environment has an impact on grade point average and future aspirations. Those who feel the most unsafe and least supported have a grade point average about 0.5 points lower than that of those who feel supported and "about

20 percent of those with no supportive faculty/staff reported that they did not plan on going to college compared to 12.2 percent of students with a few and 7.1 percent of those with many supportive faculty/staff."[8] It is important to also note that among those planning to pursue higher education, "those planning to pursue a graduate degree was higher than among the general population."[9] Overall, these students are vulnerable when they lack support, with this vulnerability affecting both present and future planning. Those who feel supported, Savin-Williams notes, are still harassed, but they are able to fight back, and to be empowered by the experience of fighting back.

Harassment in schools is sometimes hard to deal with because the person being harassed does not want his/her family to know about either the harassment or the sex/gender issues. In the GLSEN Survey, 55 percent did not report harassment to family members. When students did report harassment to parents, 43.6 percent did not intervene.[10] The worries that young people have about revealing their sexuality/gender identities are not groundless, as estimates suggest that as many as 25 percent of adolescents who come out to their parents are thrown out of their homes. Although this figure seems high, there are a number of studies that indicate that 25 to 40 percent of homeless youth identify as lesbian/gay/bisexual/transgendered (LGBT). The fact that these young people end up homeless is not surprising, since those who have been in the foster care system find it to be generally hostile and homophobic.[11] These problems might be eased somewhat if social service systems tried to match teens who become homeless as a result of sexuality issues with gay, lesbian, bisexual, transgendered, and queer (GLBTQ) adults, but few states do this. Young people also need to be concerned about their parent(s) right to involuntarily commit them for mental health treatment.[12] In each of these cases, the rights of the child are denied. Although each of these issues can be confronted on its own—for example, it is possible to argue that since homosexuality is not a mental illness, a parent has no legitimate right to institutionalize a child for "Conversion Therapy"—I want to suggest that an alternative way of confronting this panoply of problems is to foster a different vision of children. Such a vision could and should be part of rethinking family.

RETHINKING THE FAMILY

There have been two primary approaches to addressing feminist and queer family issues. One is to transform the current institutional arrangements in order to open up greater possibilities for women and for LGBT people within the institutional structure of marriage. A second approach has been to argue that marriage, as an institution, has traditionally served state interests by locating the responsibility for both financial support and nurturance squarely in the private realm so that state resources contribute minimally to the reproduction of life. This has had a particularly negative impact on women, who are assumed responsible for providing care labor within the private sphere, and people involved in same gender relationships, who are excluded by the gender division on which the family rests. By arguing for a radical rethinking of family, this latter group of theorists has provided a critique of the institutions of family and marriage with the potential for providing a foundation for rethinking not only the roles of adults within the institution, but also the roles of children.

Through a discussion of the work of Martha Fineman, a proponent of removing the state from marriage and increasing public support for those who meet dependency needs, and the work of one of her critics, Maxine Eichner, who argues that Fineman makes a significant contribution, but that she underestimates the extent to which adult relationships are often about meeting dependency needs. I will explore how children have been excluded from such critiques in ways that maintain adult power. Since both Fineman and Eichner draw from the same children's rights theorist, Barbara Bennett Woodhouse, as they develop their analyses of family relationships, I will look at the ways by which Woodhouse's arguments are limited for developing a fuller vision of children's potential, and the rights that they require to meet this potential.

One of the most extensive challenges to the dominant norm of family in feminist and queer writing comes from Martha Fineman.[13] Fineman suggests the family needs to be radically reconceptualized by starting from the premise that the central relationship that needs state recognition and support in families is not the sexual relationship between adults, but rather the mother-child relationship. Since the marital relationship (or the domestic partnership or the civil union) is between two adults, there is no reason, she argues, for the state to set the terms of the relationship. The very intervention of the state in this relationship upholds the construction of marriage as an institution that enforces civil status, rather than the individuality of the two individuals and the relationship that they wish to create. Yet, where dependency relationships are central, as in the parent-child relationship, Fineman argues, state support and intervention is compelling and necessary. As Fineman recognizes rethinking the family in this way requires rethinking the public/private line. Marriage, as she points out, has been defined as a realm of privacy within which the state has no right to interfere, regardless of negative behaviors within the family unit. The traditional assumption was that men would control what happened in the privacy of their homes. With dependency safely located in the private sphere, the state could assume that the family would satisfy the needs of all individuals contained within it, with dependency needs being largely met by women.

One of Fineman's central arguments is that these dependency needs are ones that should be recognized not as private matters that women should take care of, but as public matters. This is necessary because it is clear that the fact that women—particularly mothers—have entered the workforce in increasing numbers has not adequately challenged the notion that dependency needs should fall to women. And, "as a result the social, economic, and cultural implications motherhood remains very different from those of fatherhood. Of course, within individual families we may see signs of successful struggle over sharing responsibilities. Some men are actually attempting to redefine their own behavior and society's expectations for fathers. Studies show that when they do, they suffer some of the same disadvantages and negative consequences as mothers."[14] Thus, the only solution is to create social policy that supports caretakers, with the primary model for caretakers being mothers. Caretakers would be supported in ways that allow them to be both in the labor market and caring for children; Mothering could be done by both men and women without either paying a price for this labor.

Maxine Eichner is sympathetic to Fineman's argument in *The Autonomy Myth*. She agrees with Fineman that dependency needs must be reframed as public and, therefore, state supported. "In my view, however," Eichner writes, "Fineman weakens her case by conceiving this public responsibility as stemming directly from the fact of dependency and, alternately, as a debt that results from the future expected contribution of the child. I argue instead that public support is better justified based on the state's responsibility to protect the vulnerable."[15] As she points out, most people would be horrified at the idea that the state must only be responsible for those children who will live long enough to repay a debt. This "is because we intuitively conceive public responsibility for caretaking to spring from something other than the likelihood of society receiving a future economic return."[16] Rather, we tend to believe that vulnerable people need support, though this begs the question of who is responsible for that support. In making the argument that the State has responsibility for providing a share of the necessary support, Eichner discusses the extent to which family success and failure rests on state policies:

> The modern administrative state built on this foundation has no neutral, isolated position into which it can retreat to wait while families exhaust their responsibility to care for dependents 'before' the state acts. Therefore, insofar as the state has a responsibility to protect the vulnerable, it is conceptually and chronologically incoherent to conceive that responsibility as being triggered only after the state waits for the family to act. Instead, the responsibility must be deemed to exist simultaneously with families' responsibility to do the same. This does not mean that the state's responsibilities in this regard are identical to families.[17]

This point leads Eicher to revise Fineman's overall argument in two ways that are important for my argument. First, Eichner clearly recognizes that dependency relationships exist not simply between children and adults, but also between adults: "Such caretaking occurs in "horizontal" relationships between adults as well. . . . This sort of caretaking produces a society in which adults are knit into webs of care that help to support one another."[18] Eichner moves from here to suggest that the state has some interest in not only parent-child relationships, but also adult relationships:

> The state has an interest in supporting long-term horizontal relationships in which care-taking occurs, including relationships between couples who are not necessarily monogamous, or, on the opposite end of the spectrum, those whose relationships are not sexual. By the same token, the state has an interest in supporting caretaking in family groupings that involve more than two adults.[19]

In other words, the state has an interest in fostering and supporting relationships between those who are interdependent. In this sense, the parent-child relationship is not unique, but rather connected to a wider set of relationships. In fact, many children play extensive caretaking roles in families.[20] As a result, it may make sense to see the parent(adult)/child relationship as one that becomes less and less vertical as the child becomes a teenager and an older youth. The state, then, would need to recognize that parent-child relationships change over time, and that childhood dependence (other than financial) remains a necessary part of childhood for a much shorter period of time than U.S. law and (most) policy now recognizes. Yet this leaves open the question of what rights children and young people should have as they develop.

Interestingly, when both Fineman and Eichner talk about parent-child relationships, they draw from children's rights theorist Barbara Bennett Woodhouse. Fineman draws from Woodhouse when she considers how privacy might be recast in her revision of family and state. It is important that Fineman's discussion of how children fit into her theory as something more than dependents only comes in the Postscript to *The Autonomy Myth*. Here, she attempts to define what privacy could mean in the family as she reenvisions it. The obvious difficulty is to navigate between reinforcing an understanding of privacy that excludes the state based on the currently dominant assumption "that parents possess what the child lacks in judgment,"[21] with "concern with abuses associated with state intervention and regulation of intimacy."[22] It is here that she turns to Woodhouse's arguments for "need-based rights." "These rights," she argues, "are not associated with children's rights to autonomy or independence, but are the basis for a positive claim for basic nurture and protection."[23] In distinguishing between the two arguments, Fineman notes:

My claim is a communal one—entity focused and based on a sense of entitlement or right originating as a result of the societal work of caretakers. Woodhouse's model is not a compensatory one, but is based on the status of the child
as a future citizen. She positions the child as the claim holder and, in doing
so, conceptually breaks up the family into individual and therefore potentially
competing interests. This paves the way for claims of collective supervision and
monitoring of parental stewardship.[24]

Such claims, Fineman argues, are potentially destructive of the parent-child
relationship, a relationship that in the remainder of the postscript is conceived
as Woodhouse suggests it should be at its best: as one in which the parent recognizes the increasing independence of the child and provides the child with
the voice necessary to develop in a positive way.[25] Fineman suggests that the
family unit needs privacy in order for this relationship to flourish, and state
subsidies should generally be seen as properly going to the unit:

> Units may make mistakes, but if it is not abuse or neglect (we can argue about
> where to draw to the line later) then the unit as recipient of the subsidy should
> decide how it is to be used. This way of looking at what is an appropriate focus
> for policy also gives value to the caretaking labor. The dependent may be the
> beneficiary, but the labor of the caretaker is what has societal value.[26]

Although this model would provide children with more resources than in the
present, they may well have no more voice. Many queer youth would, therefore, be no better off than they are currently since they remain embedded in a
"unit" that may not recognize their sexual/gender interests and needs.

Eichner's discussion in "Children, Parents, and the State: Rethinking the
Relationships in the Child Welfare System," presents a compelling argument that the current policy of defining families as entities that only require
intervention when they are failing is deeply flawed, largely because it fails
to recognize that the state is influencing families all along. She suggests that
we reframe the role of the state as "supportive state," a redefinition that is
both logical and would offer significantly greater protection to all members
of families.[27] The failure to envision the state role in this way leads, as Eichner details, to significant failures and destructive failures, since the state is
more focused on solving problems after they have developed (and at a time
when there is little evidence that the state can intervene in a positive way)
than in providing resources that might keep problems from developing.
State intervention comes when children are already harmed, and then acts
in ways that are more likely to exacerbate the harm than to address it. In
articulating an alternative, she too turns to Woodhouse and ends in a position that is very close to Fineman's in that she argues that the state should

provide resources to parents in a way that does not interfere with the parent-child relationship:

> The current approach to the child welfare system pits parents and the state in a zero-sum game: as the state becomes more involved, it increasingly wrests children away from the control of their parents. In contrast, a major goal of the supportive state model is to align the interests of the state and parents; in it, the state assures parents the resources that they need to parent without taking control from them.[28]

It is here that I think Eichner might better apply her own insights from her critique of Fineman.

What is most striking to me about the "supportive state" argument is that the state is understood to foster positive parental control, rather than viewed as needing to act in ways that foster, protect, and recognize the rights of the vulnerable, yet still fully human, child. This is an argument that is unimaginable in relation to most other caretaking relationships today, at least in feminist theory, where the recipient of care is generally seen to be an active agent whose voice (if it is at all possible) needs to be recognized and valued.[29] I want to ask whether parent/child relationships can be reconceptualized as relationships between people, one of whom is often more vulnerable than the other, partially because of natural differences and partially, as legal scholar and children's theorist William Geimer observes, because of constructed differences.[30] That is, can we take Eichner's critique and use it to develop a theory that complicates the relationship between the family or caretaking and the state because it does not begin from the assumption that the quintessential dependence relationship is one of control for those who will be future citizens, but rather one of vulnerability and interdependence between human beings with rights? Further, what would this conceptualization require of the state in relation to children? How would this need to change as children's evolving capacities develop and as they become more fully agents in their own right? In addressing these questions. I want to suggest that Woodhouse (and, as a result, Fineman and Eichner) does not go far enough in recognizing the expressive rights of young people and that these rights need to be acknowledged, an acknowledgment that would be important for many queer youth who need to be able to make demands of the state on their own behalf.

BALANCING CARE AND EXPRESSION

Woodhouse argues that a central problem in U.S. family policy is that children continue to be understood as the property of their parents.[31] She suggests that we draw from and expand a counter-discourse, that of parent as fiduciary guardian of the child. One argument that she makes is that the Convention on the Rights of the Child could be a mechanism for encouraging the United States to accentuate the fiduciary argument, which would enable children to be seen as persons, while minimizing the property argument.[32] Thus, she argues that those who see the CRC as a threat to American values are incorrect; the Convention would simply (though importantly) draw from a strand of already existing values: "Despite the arguments advanced by those opposing it, the Convention is not antifamily, and does not threaten either the U.S. Constitution or existing laws in this country."[33] She goes on to suggest four points in support of this position, of which the middle two are particularly relevant to my discussion: "Second, the Convention actively protects the family and the parent-child relationship as an integral elements of the rights of children. Third, by characterizing parents as the guardians of children's rights, the Convention reflects a child-centered perspective on the rights of parents, viewing the relationship as one of trust, rather than of ownership."[34] Woodhouse focuses on Articles of the Convention (Articles 5, 9, 14(2), 16, and 19)[35] that do in fact define parents as particularly important guardians of their children's rights, with the important observation that states have an important role to play in helping parents to meet their obligations in relation to their children.

Interestingly, though, Woodhouse fails to discuss those Articles that explicitly grant rights to children that are not at all clear within American law, for example, Article 12 (freedom to express views, and the right to participate in judicial hearings); Article 13 (expands freedom of expression to the right to seek information); Article 14 (freedom of conscience and religion);[36] Article 15 (freedom of association); Article 24 (right to health care, including the mandate that states should act "to abolish practices prejudicial to the health of children"[37]); and Article 31 (right to participate in "recreation, cultural life, and the arts."[38] As children's rights scholar Bob Franklin notes, not discussing such provisions is not uncommon in relation to the CRC or children's rights more broadly: "These two kinds of rights [welfare rights and liberty rights] can conflict and are at the center of much of the controversy which surrounds discussion of children's rights. . . . Children's claims to protection rights have rarely been contested. Their claims for liberty rights invariably are."[39] To take the latter seriously is to recognize that children have rights not simply in the future, but also in the present. In this sense, the perspective that Woodhouse develops, and that both Fineman and Eichner adapt, focuses too much on how the state can foster the future citizenship of children by focusing the ways by which the state can support parents as they raise children, rather than on how the state may recognize the interdependence of adults and children in ways that acknowledge the participation rights of young people in the present. Young people's expression and participation rights can be taken seriously without this meaning that we abandon children completely to their own devices, and that if we read the CRC fully, although it has flaws, it actually does lead in this direction. Thus, unlike Woodhouse, I believe that it does pose a threat to U.S. understandings, but it is a threat that we must face if our attempts to rearticulate family and private life are not to leave teens behind, particularly queer teens.

In order to explore the implications of seeing young people as deserving not simply guarantees of care, but also expression, or more broadly liberty, rights, I want to briefly discuss two areas where debates about children's writes often come up against questions of parental rights: in making decisions about education and in the possibility that children could "divorce" their parents. In relation to each, I will discuss the arguments of Laura Purdy.[40] Purdy provides a detailed exploration of some of the conflicts that arise in parent-child relationships and potential ways by which the state could intervene. Her explicit goal is to counter arguments by "child libertarians" in order to suggest that children should not have equal rights with adults, an argument that is really about whether children should be given exactly the same rights as adults. Although she concludes that they should not and that parental rights largely should be respected, she also provides significant grounds for asserting that there are in fact situations in which children's expressive or liberty rights need to be recognized to a far greater degree than is currently the case. I want to explore her arguments in some detail because although she argues that expanding the rights of young people is important because, her desire to not grant too much freedom and to preserve parental rights makes it hard for her to fully address the needs of queer youth. This, I will suggest, would require a more explicit statement of liberty rights for young people.

Within United States' law the right to determine where a child goes to school is a parental right. There are various positions on how this might be modified to recognize the voice of young people. Purdy argues that schools can provide an important counterbalance to parents, preventing them from indoctrinating their children into their belief system. Therefore, schooling should be both mandatory and public. A public education in a system that focuses on critical thinking would allow young people to resist parental indoctrination,[41] while also helping to counter the segregation and prejudice that continue in the United States.[42] If we conclude that public schools should be mandatory *and* that students should have participation rights within them, it would significantly change the balance between the state and the school to a balance between the state, the student, and parents. And, rather than treating the child as a future citizen, it would treat them as "meaning-makers" in the present.[43] In relation to queer teens who are challenging schools to combat heteronormative assumptions, such a vision is critical. GLSEN reports that "Students who reported an LGBT inclusive curriculum were also much more likely to feel comfortable talking to their teachers about LGBT issues—about half (55.8 percent) of the students without a curriculum felt comfortable compared to three-quarters (75.8 percent) of students with an inclusive curriculum."[44] The presence of such curricular changes is itself often the result of students working with sympathetic teachers. Purdy does not develop what it would mean for youth to have participation rights in schools, and the extent to which this would require encouraging democratic participation by students in schools. These are, though, critical components of making schools safe places for all students.

The possibility of giving young people significant rights in the public sphere of school must also raise the question of what happens when such freedom allows youth to develop identities and beliefs that contradict their parents beliefs and values. Purdy recognizes that the child-parent relationship itself sometimes needs intervention from outside, and that it is not always possible, even with intervention, to preserve the relationship. In identifying some of the situations where these problems may arise, she asks:

> What sort of complaints bring children to the point of seriously considering other living arrangements? Most people would probably agree that who are beaten to the point of physical injury or who are being sexually abused at home have a good case for leaving. In such cases children should be permitted or even encouraged to terminate relationships with their parents. Other situations would be much more controversial, however. What, for instance, are we to do about gay children of actively homophobic parents? Many such children now run away from home or are thrown out, but what about those who feel trapped in a situation where they are made to feel like the scum of the earth? Or, what about children who feel the weight of their parents' sexist stereotypes especially strongly? What if a parent undermines a girl's attempt to be strong and independent? Or repeatedly punishes a boy for crying or allegedly sissy interests? More generally, what about the many fundamental conflicts that may arise in matters of religion or politics?[45]

These are compelling questions and ones that I think deserve serious consideration, particularly by those concerned by the abuse homelessness of queer youth. In trying to find a way to resolve situations such as these, Purdy walks a fine a line between recognizing the seriousness of the situations and the clear harm that they do to young people and reinforcing the centrality of adult-defined institutions for decision-making. She suggests that the state needs to provide a child agency to mediate between parents and children[46] and sometimes may need to be even more active in finding permanent, suitable parents, thus obviating the need for the child to have the right to act on his/her own behalf.[47] In cases where no resolution is possible, the state may need to develop "children's houses" where young people could live in well-ordered homes with clear rules and expectations, thus providing the structure necessary for the young person and making it unlikely that children will want to move into these houses if they simply resent the fact that their parents' have rules. Yet it is hard to imagine public authorities intervening in parent/child conflicts in ways that respect young people's right to define their sexuality or politics without explicit agreement in the public sphere that young people have liberty rights that must be taken seriously. That is, Purdy's resolution does not actually seem to fully address the kinds of conflicts that she identified as deeply harmful to many young people because although she hints at the ways by which young people need to be recognized as having rights, she does not develop this framework.

In sorting through similar issues, ethicist Hugh LaFollette[48] suggests that it would be helpful to begin to think through the different forms of autonomy that might be appropriate at different ages. In part, I think that the way that LaFollette discusses autonomy is quite similar to what Woodhouse, Fineman, and Eichner assume is dominant within many families. And, although for many this may be the case (which would explain why most children grow into at least relatively pro-social adults), it does not mean either that we do not need a legal system that explicitly recognizes such rights or that dominant social institutions, such as schools, would not be forced to change if we formally recognize such developing autonomy in law and family policy. LaFollette sets forth a vision of the development of autonomy from administered to monitored to minimally constrained. In the latter, "the parent may still intervene from time to time, but only infrequently, and even then not with a heavy hand. The parents will knowingly let their child make more significant errors than they would have at earlier stages, although they might still intervene in ways they might not intervene in the life of another adult. Moreover if the parents have taken the child through the first two stages, then typically they can intervene best by simply talking with the child."[49] He makes another critical point as he argues that the state has a role to play in fostering the autonomy of children: "Even if the legal system does not get into the business of deciding how every parent should treat every child, legal pronouncements can set appropriate expectations that would make it more likely that children are given increasing normative autonomy."[50] This may, in fact, be a way of articulating the Convention on the Rights of the Child's requirement that the child's evolving capacities be recognized in a way that begins to move the agent of recognition from simply and solely being the parent. In fact, we might see leaving decisions such as whether to attend a sex education program to the child as one way by which the state can signal that the child is developing autonomy. For teens, this could evolve into giving students a significant voice in determining what they wish to discuss in such programs. Certainly the state could guarantee that a teen could not be institutionalized without a voice in the matter and without a review process that seriously asks whether parents have raised the child in such a way as to recognize and encourage her/his autonomy.

LaFollette recognizes that many (including, I would suggest, Purdy) might object that recognizing the autonomy of some children requires that the autonomy of all be recognized, and this may result in some children who would otherwise be well-off with their parents making impulsive and damaging decisions. Further, because children would know that they have rights, it might interfere in their relationship with their parents. To the first point, he observes that most children are not going to try to leave their parents, and that even those who did would need to persuade a court that this was really necessary. His response to the latter is worth quoting at some length because it takes us far toward articulating a new way of recognizing the rights of the child. LaFollette writes:

> These are legitimate worries. Injecting rights talk into an intimate relationship can certainly damage it. That is true not only of relationships between children and parents, but also of relationships between partners. The proper response, though, is not to deny that each party to such relationships is autonomous. Rather we should find new ways to describe and understand such relationships. We should understand that both parties have the ability and authority to make choices about matters that profoundly affect them, even though they need not (regularly) resort to the language of rights. Intimates should care for and respect one another. Parents should likewise love and respect their children. To fully respect one another means we must sometimes let them choose for themselves, even when we may think their decisions are misguided.[51]

In considering what this means for relationships, I think LaFollette is pointing to the fact that we might understand autonomy not in terms of independence, but in terms of interdependence. In this sense, I think it is possible to connect his argument to Eichner's revision of Fineman. To the extent that autonomy is a myth, it is a myth when it serves to deny interdependence and the humanity of all. And, in this sense, Eichner is correct in asserting that Fineman's focus on the parent-child relationship as the quintessential caretaking relationship denies too much continuity between this particular relationship and other human relationships. Once we begin to see these continuities, it becomes harder to deny that young people, like adults, may be both autonomous and interdependent. Youth need privacy not simply as the member of a unit, but as people with the agency to form meaningful relationships and contribute to their own well-being and society.

The model that I am developing suggests that young people should have significant decision-making rights, both in the private sphere of the family and the public sphere. Most people—whether child or adult—make decisions within social contexts and relationships. These contexts both signal to the individual what level of participation and expression is acceptable and provide resources to supplement individual decision-making capacities. As Tom Cockburn recognizes as he draws on the social constructionist psychology of Rom Harre, this is a radically different developmental psychology than that which is embedded in liberalism and liberal institutions: "Developmental psychology seemingly buys into the quasi-political doctrine of individualism. The social constructionist viewpoint advocated by Harre sees becoming a competent person not as a matter of 'injection of a dose of subjectivity from one mind to another, but rather the appropriation from a common public realm of whatever is needed to round out and inform the mind of the developing individual.'"[52] Harre's research, as Cockburn discusses throughout his essay, suggests that children are aware from a very young age of the situations in which they can assert themselves and those situations where they should wait for the "guidance" of others. Much additional research supports the idea that young people have the cognitive development necessary to make significant decisions, and that they are likely to draw from supportive relationships to make such decisions. Writing in relation to teens decisions in relation to abortion, Rhonda Hartmann summarizes the research of Bruce Ambuel and Julian Rappaport:

> The researchers report that adolescents aged '14-17 appear to be similar to legal adults in both cognitive competence and volition' and that they 'remain competent decision makers when facing an emotionally challenging real world decision.' They further report that adolescents often consult with adults when making monumental personal decisions, and that state mandates, such as parental notification and consent, pose serious risks for adolescents.[53]

They suggest that instead of privileging parents, courts need to recognize the decisional autonomy of youth and allow them the agency to consult with those whom they most trust. This is also the foundation of the AAUW's position on the Child Custody Protection Act.[54] The challenge, then, in law and public policy, is to allow teens to decide for themselves whom they can trust when making important decisions. Encouraging and helping young people to see decision-making as both one's responsibility and connected to relationships is important for fostering skills that serve adults, as well as children and teens, well.

CONCLUSION

Sexual identities exist within historical moments. Given that we live in a time period when disputes over sexual rights and relationship are central to politics, the need for youth to define their sexual/gender identities and preferences is both demanded and hotly contested. Those who oppose young people having such rights have focused on abstinence-only sex education (which largely defines homosexuality out of the curriculum), on having parents assert their rights to determine what their children learn and when they learn it, and continued portrayals of youth as too immature to make such important decisions. At the same time, it positions adults who would like to enable young people to be sexual agents as predators and recruiters. Since schools are unable to ban Gay-Straight Alliances from forming, groups opposed to them are trying a new strategy: requiring parental permission for attendance. So, for example, the Provo Utah school board accepted such a requirement, and it has had a chilling effect, "Provo High Principal Sam Ray said about thirty students attended an informational meeting about the club in October, but only about half showed up at a second meeting after parental permission slips were required to attend."[55] Using such a policy to target gay and lesbian groups means, however, that parental permission would be required for all non-curricular clubs is an attempt to meet legal standards.

Trying to limit the rights of teens in one area, then, has broader ramifications, particularly for young people who may not have very good relationships with their parents.

Restricting the decision-making rights of queer youth, I have argued is harmful, but in concluding, I want to suggest that increasingly all young people need greater authority to develop and exercise decisional autonomy. German social theorist Ulrich Beck describes current society as a "post-employment society," indicating that we must find identities outside of employment and that all people must be able to negotiate relationships individually, outside of the institutional and status constraints of the past.[56] Anita Harris discusses how the changes that Beck identifies affect young people: "It is young people who must try to forge their futures by mastering the anxieties, uncertainties, and insecurities conjured up by unpredictable times . . . young people are newly obliged to make good choices for themselves and set themselves on the path to success with little support or security outside the private sphere."[57] For some youth, those with family resources and family support, the chances of succeeding are relatively good, but for many others who lack this privilege, failure will be seen as the fault of the individual. In such an atmosphere, fighting for the material support of children and teens, as Fineman, Eichner, Woodhouse, and Purdy each agree is necessary, is surely critical. But if these young people are going to contribute to building a humane society despite the changes that Beck and Harris discuss, they will also need to develop their agency. The state can play a role in this not only by supporting caretakers, but also by supporting young people as rights-bearers who need to have a say in how they are treated not only for their future, but also in the present. Only if it does both is it truly a "supportive state." Gay and lesbian advocates of new and changing visions of family could support youth rights as part of their rethinking of family, but often the focus on securing autonomy for adults either ignores the similar needs of youth or reinforces constructions of children that prevent us from believing that children can and should exercise agency. This leaves us less able to support the development of policies and programs that can expand the "protective factors" that help youth, but particularly queer youth, to combat homophobia and sexism.

NOTES

1. The Senate's July 2006 passage of the Child Custody Protection Act is an example of the ways by which parental rights can be used to justify social policy that harms young women. This act would have made it illegal for family members other than parents to help a teen to obtain abortion services in another state unless she has met parental notification requirements of her own state. This is, therefore, an act that discourages young people from turning to family members other than parents to seek support and assistance.

2. I will use the terms teenagers or youth to refer to people between the ages of thirteen and eighteen. I discuss this age group for two reasons. First, these are critical ages for constructing sexual identities, with the lower end of the age range a time when teens begin to think about sexual attractions and make sense of them and the latter the time period in which many begin to define themselves as having a sexual identity. Between these ages, as developmental psychologist Ritch Savin-Williams discusses, many young people resist labeling themselves (2005). Secondly, this is an important age range because parents continue to have significant rights in relation to their children. Savin-Williams, Ritch. 2005. *The New Gay Teenager*. Cambridge, Mass.: Harvard University Press.

3. Savin-Williams (2005, 183).

4. Although I will draw from the 2005 Gay, Lesbian, and Straight Teacher's Network report on American schools, it is also important to point out the excellent work done by Human Right's Watch in drawing attention to the issues confronted by LGBT young people in schools in the United States and their framing of these issues as human rights abuses in their *Hatred in the Hallways* to these issues as human rights abuses. See Human Rights Watch. 2001. *Hatred in the Hallways: Violence and Discrimination Against Lesbian, Gay, Bisexual, Transgender Students in U.S. Schools.* New York, N.Y.: Human Rights Watch.

5. Kosciw, Joseph and Elizabeth Diaz. 2005. *The 2005 National School Climate Survey: The Experiences of Lesbian, Gay, Bisexual, and Transgender Youth in our*

Nation's Schools. A Report from the Gay, Lesbian, Straight Educators Network. www.glsen.org/binary-data/GLSEN_ATTACHMENTS/file/585-1.pdf (December 12, 2006), xii.

6. Kosciw and Diaz (2005, 65).
7. Kosciw and Diaz (2005, 37).
8. Kosciw and Diaz (2005, 78).
9. Kosciw and Diaz (2005, 45).
10. Kosciw and Diaz, xiv.
11. Many of these young people have family problems outside of sexuality issues, but sexuality issues exacerbate these other issues. See Cull, Mark, Platzer, Hazel, and Ballock, Sue. (2006). "Out on My Own: Understanding the Experiences of Needs of Homeless Gay, Lesbian, and Transgender Youth." Health and Social Policy Research Centre, School of Applied Social Science, University of Brighton. www.ucalgary.ca/~ptrembla/gay-lesbian-bisexual/01c-full-text-gay-school-prostitution-aids.htm (May 24, 2008). see Mallon, Gerald P. 1998. *We Don't Exactly Get the Welcome Wagon: The Experiences of Gay and Lesbian Adolescents in Child Welfare Systems*. New York: Columbia University Press; Casciano, J., Sullivan, C., Pumo, D., and Kern, J. 2000/2001. "Symposium Proceedings: Client-Centered Advocacy on Behalf of At-Risk LGBT Youth." *New York University Review of Law and Social Change*. 26: 221–43.
12. See Caincaitto and Cahill. 2004 Cianciotto, Jason, and Sean Cahill. 2006. *Youth in the Crosshairs: The Third Wave of Ex-Gay Activism*. National Gay and Lesbian Task Force Policy Institute. www.thetaskforce.org/downloads/crosshairs.pdf (August 4, 2006).
13. Fineman, Martha. 1995. *The Neutered Mother, the Sexual Family, and other Twentieth Century Tragedies*. New York: Routledge, and Fineman, Martha. 2004. *The Autonomy Myth: A Theory of Dependency*. New York: New Press: Distributed by W. W. Norton.
14. Fineman (2004, 172).
15. Eichner, Maxine. 2005b. "Dependency and the Liberal Polity: On Martha Fineman's The Autonomy Myth." *California Law Review* (July) library.law.unc.edu/faculty_services/working_papers.html#eichner. (July 28, 2006), 38.
16. Eichner (2005b, 43).
17. Eichner (2005b, 46).
18. Eichner (2005b, 58–59).
19. Eichner (2005b, 66).
20. For example, Alridge and Becker note that "there are currently as many as 50,000 children in Britain who are providing substantial and regular care for an ill or disabled parent or other relative in the home" (2002, 208). Discussions of these caregivers tend to frame the young people as either angels or victims, rather than as individuals with rights in need of social support (Alridge and Becker 2002, 218). Alridge, Jo, and Saul Becker. 2002. "Children Who Care: Rights and Wrongs in Debate and Policy on Young Careers." In *The New Handbook of Children's Rights*, ed. Bob Franklin. London and New York: Routledge, 182–95.
21. Fineman (2004, 298).

22. Fineman (2004, 299).

23. Fineman (2004, 302).

24. Fineman (2004, 302).

25. See Woodhouse, Barbara Bennett. 1998. "From Property to Personhood: A Child-Centered Perspective on Parents' Rights." *Georgetown Journal on Fighting Poverty* 5 (Summer): 313–19. Woodhouse, Barbara Bennett. 2001. "Child Abuse, the Constitution, and the Legacy of Pierce v. Society of Sisters." *University of Detroit Mercy Law Review* 78 (Spring): 479–89.

26. Fineman (2004, 306-307).

27. Eichner, Maxine. 2005. "Children, Parents, and the State: Rethinking the Relationships in the Child Welfare System." *Virginia Journal of Social Policy and Law* 12: 448–74.

28. Eichner (2005b, 20).

29. See, for example, Tronto, Joan. 1993. *Moral Boundaries: A Political Argument for an Ethic of Care.* New York: Routledge.

30. Geimer, William. 1998. "Juvenileness: A Single-Edged Sword." *Georgia Law Review* 22: 949–73.

31. Woodhouse 1998.

32. The United States is one of only two countries that has not ratified the Convention on the Rights of the Child. The CRC is, of course, not in itself able to transform how children are seen and treated in law, yet there is evidence that it has had an impact on debates about state policy in relation to children and children's rights in a number of countries. For example, Peter Newell points out that as a result of the CRC, ten states have banned all corporal punishment (2002, 383). Newell, Peter. 2002. "Global Progress Towards Giving up the Global Habit of Hitting Children." In *The New Handbook of Children's Rights,* ed. Bob Franklin. London and New York: Routledge, Additionally, Lansdown traces the prevalence of ombudsmen or Children's Rights Commissions in many European countries to the Convention, in combination with the advocacy of human rights organizations (2002, 285–86).

33. Woodhouse (1998, 315).

34. Her first and fourth points are: "First, the Convention is a human rights charter, not a domestic relations statute. Its intent is to strengthen the status of children as persons with basic rights, not to displace domestic laws regarding the family. If the ratification of the Convention by the United States were to have any impact on contemporary American family law, this impact would be gradual. . . . Finally, the primary effect of the Convention would be to ratify the human rights foundation undergirding family rights. The provision of human rights is not a zero sum game; acknowledging that children have human rights serves to strengthen, rather than to diminish, the human rights of their parents" (1998, 315).

35. UN Convention on the Rights of the Child. (1989). UN General Assembly Document A/RES/44/25.

36. Although Woodhouse paraphrases Article Fourteen, she stops before she gets to what I believe to be a key phrase. She writes: "Article Fourteen which protects children's rights of thought, conscience and religion and protects the roles of parents as their guides and teachers." In fact, Article 14, clause 2 reads: "2. States Parties shall

respect the rights and duties of the parents and, when applicable, legal guardians, to provide direction to the child in the exercise of his or her right in a manner consistent with the evolving capacities of the child. As I will suggest below, the necessity that parents limit their role based on "the evolving capacities of the child" is a critical limitation on parent's rights.

37. This was largely intended to combat practices such as genital mutilation. Yet homophobia has a clearly negative impact on health.

38. UN Convention on the Rights of the Child. 1989.

39. Franklin, Bob. 2002. "Children's Rights and Media Wrongs: Changing Representations of Children and the Developing Rights Agenda." In *The New Handbook of Children's Rights: Comparative Policy and Practice*, ed. Bob Franklin. London and New York: Routledge, 21.

40. Purdy, Laura (1992, 1999). Purdy, Laura M. 1999. "Boundaries of Authority: Should Children be Able to Divorce their Parents?" In *Having and Raising Children*, eds. Uma Narayan and Julia J. Bartkowiak. University Park, Pa: Penn State Press, 153–62. Purdy, Laura Martha. 1992. *In Their Best Interest?: The Case Against Equal Rights For Children*. Ithaca, N.Y.: Cornell University Press.

41. Purdy (1996 157). Interestingly, Fineman makes a similar argument, all the while recognizing that this argument goes against her more general suggestion that parents should control decisions affecting their children: "In considering education, however, my inclinations are the opposite. I want a more active state and more well-defined public presence" (2003, 241n1). Fineman, Martha. 2003. "Taking Children's Interests Seriously." In *Child, Family, and State, NOMOS XLIV*, eds. Stephen Macedo and Iris Marion Young. New York: New York University Press, 234-42.

42. Purdy (1996, 156–57).

43. (Verhellen, 187) Verhellen, Eugene. 2001. "Facilitating Children's Rights in Education: Expectations and Demands on Teachers and Parents." In *Children's Rights in Education*, eds. Stuart Hart, Cynthia Price, Cooper, Martha Farrell, and Malfrid Flekkoy. London: Jessica Kingsley Publishers, 187. See Jeffs (2002) for a discussion of the ways by which British schools violate students' rights. Jeffs suggests that unless schools are made more democratic institutions, children should be able to opt out of them. Jeffs, Tony. 2002. "Schooling, Education, and Children's Rights." In *The New Handbook of Children's Rights: Comparative Policy and Practice*, ed. Bob Franklin. London and New York: Routledge, 45-59.

44. Kosciuw and Diaz, 82.

45. Purdy (1999, 156–57).

46. Purdy (1999, 159).

47. Purdy (1999, 158).

48. Lafollette, Hugh. 1998. "Circumscribed Autonomy: Children, Care, and Custody." In J. Bartkowiak and Uma Narayan, *Having and Raising Children*. University Park, Pa.: Penn State Press, 137-152.

49. Lafollette (1998, 149).

50. Lafollette (1998, 151).

51. Lafollette (1998, 147).

52. Cockburn, Tom. 1999. ""Children, Fooles, And Mad-Men": Children's Relationship To Citizenship In Britain From Thomas Hobbes To Bernard Crick." *The School Field: International Journal of Theory and Research in Education,* X (Autumn/Winter), 73-74.

53. Throughout her essay "Adolescent Autonomy: Confronting an Ageless Conundrum," Rhonda Gay Hartman cites studies that indicate the developed decision-making skills of youth. See footnotes 88, 248, 361 in Hartman. Hartman, Rhonda Gay. 2000. "Adolescent Autonomy: Clarifying an Ageless Conundrum." *Hastings Law Journal* (August): 1265-362.

54. American Association of University Women. 2006. "Child Custody Protection Act." www.aauw.org/issue_advocacy/actionpages/positionpapers/childcustody_protection.cfm (August 8, 2006).

55. Chang-Yen, Anna. 2005. "District Oks Policy that Permits Gay Club to Stay," *Provo Daily Herald,* November 8. (August 4, 2006).

56. See Beck, Ulrich, and Elisabeth Beck-Gernsheim. 2001. *Individualization.* London: Thousand Oaks New Delhi: Sage, and Beck, Ulrich, and Johannes Willms. 2004. *Conversations with Ulrich Beck.* Cambridge, UK; Malden, Mass.: Polity Press.

57. Harris, Anita. 2004. *FutureGirl: Young Women in the Twenty-first Century.* New York; London: Routledge, 5.

9

Consuming Its Own?

Heteronormativity *contra* Human Plurality

Gordon A. Babst

[T]he human condition of plurality . . . [is] the fact that men, not Man, live on the earth and inhabit the world . . . the human condition is not the same as human nature, and the sum total of human activities and capabilities which correspond to the human condition does not constitute anything like human nature . . . . The problem of human nature . . . seems unanswerable . . . nothing entitles us to assume that man has a nature or essence in the same sense as other things. In other words, if we have a nature or essence, then surely only a god could know and define it . . . attempts to define human nature almost invariably end with some construction of a deity . . . the fact that attempts to define the nature of man lead so easily into an idea which definitely strikes us as "superhuman" and therefore is identified with the divine may cast suspicion upon the very concept of "human nature."[1]

While Hannah Arendt would identify human beings firstly by their sharing the human condition, a condition characterized by plurality and a peculiar sameness—"we are all the same, that is, human, in such a way that nobody is ever the same as anyone else who has ever lived, lives, or will live"[2]—she insists that ascribing to human beings some sort of "nature" widely misses the mark, dangerously reducing human beings to a oneness that is not their condition, and is in fact injurious to it. Totalitarianism dovetails from such oneness in practice, which makes human beings in their plurality superfluous, as she herself experienced and famously tried to illuminate.[3] In this chapter I will attempt to reveal normative heterosexuality as monistic and opposed to human plurality, and, in addition, destructive of the latter.

"Heterosexuality" is both a term used to describe male-female sexual relations, and a normative notion assigning ethical value to male-female sexual relations, and then usually within a specific range of sexual activities. Despite the concept's schizophrenia, it has endured partly because many of its users apprehend it without a thought, or find its meaning obvious, transparent.[4] Feminist theorist Diane Richardson contests the coherence of the concept, and the stability and uniformity of the heterosexual subject and community; she writes that "[w]ithin social and political theory little attention has tradition-ally been given to theorizing heterosexuality . . . [it] is rarely acknowledged or, even less likely, problematised."[5] "Heterosexuality" has been said to have four aspects: "its institutionalization within society and culture, the social and political identities associated with it, the practices it entails and the experi-ence of it . . . as institution, practice, experience, and identity, heterosexuality is not merely sexual."[6] Carol Smart writes of being "struck by how, at this time of recognition of diversities and differences, heterosexuality is always presented as a unitary concept."[7] I regard "heterosexuality" as bifurcated into the descriptive/empirical and the normative, the latter being regarded as its heart by folks hostile to sexual pluralism.

As a normative notion, heterosexuality is not limited to ascribing value to the physicality of male-female sexual relations, or to reproduction in the hu-man species; indeed, the latter may have an ethical significance that the term "heterosexuality," oddly enough, may obfuscate, given the considerable other baggage it carries. Foucault comments on this peculiar aspect of the concept of sexuality generally in his 1977 essay "Power and Sex:"

> [H]ow is it that in a society like ours, sexuality is not simply a means of repro-ducing the species, the family, and the individual? . . . How has sexuality come to be considered the privileged place where our deepest "truth" is read and expressed? . . . In Christian societies, sex has been the central object of exami-nation, surveillance, avowal and transformation into discourse.[8]

In this chapter I focus attention on "heterosexuality" in the second sense, as a normative notion, as in "heteronormativity."[9] I will argue that "hetero-normativity" is, or includes a powerful ethical preference for the same, or for sameness, and as such is antithetical to humanity's pluralism, which by contrast is implied when the term "heterosexuality" signifies reproduction in the human species, a species in which no two members are in fact the same, a fact key to the survival of the species. In the course of making my argument I will discuss heteronormativity as destructive, not creative, despite its alleged rootedness in procreativity; the anti-pluralist, God-infused monism hetero-normativity rests on; and, finally, the fluidity of human sexuality.[10]

While my understanding of human plurality in this chapter is framed by Arendt, some Nietzschean observations will help to frame my discussion of the power of normativity, because he understood that morality is a form of power wielded over others both directly, punishing violators of the moral law, and indirectly, through widespread coercion or subtly insisted upon subscription to the same moral code. The idea of morality indirectly coercing includes the observation that subscription to customary morality may not be consciously given, such that adherence to it is not likely to liberate, but tends to enslave, and that even when not consciously chosen the moral code no less powerfully than when consciously chosen determines to a great extent the judgments of value a people make, or believe they are supposed to make about human goods. For Nietzsche, the dominant morality in the West consumes people's freedom to perceive different ways of valuing themselves, others, and humanity itself, which he believes has been rendered unworthy of belonging to.

Heterosexuality as a morality or normative code must consume its others in order to sustain itself; it is predatory on members of the so-called opposite sexuality, and on its own members, when conceived as more than baby-makers, as sexual beings with legitimate sexual dimensions beyond procreation.[11] Purporting a monopoly in morally correct value judgments, the heterosexual ideal can be used to justify the consumption of nonheterosexuals both literally (e.g., through violent hate crimes), and figuratively, through its obliviousness to the hurt and suffering it inflicts while asserting itself. The alternative to heterosexuality is not homosexuality, its purported eternal and unnatural nemesis, but human sexual pluralism, which is to say, no sexuality or sexual orientation in particular as we have come to understand the term, freighted with value judgments. And, the alternative to heterosexual persons is not homosexual persons, or any other nonheterosexual, but simply understanding that humans are sexual beings, not types of sexual beings.

It is not homosexuality that refutes heteronormativity, but human plurality, in which context heterosexuality in its first, descriptive sense remains just as meaningful, or just as stale in terms of generating universal normative meaning as is homosexuality as such. That some persons live their lives as gay or lesbian, and so live their sexual lives with a difference, is the manifestation of the refutation, the most in-your-heteronormative-face challenge to the often predatory, unhappy-making uniformity or renewable unoriginality that heterosexuality can lay claim to. It is high time to assail the taken-for-granted authenticity of heterosexuality itself.

HETEROSEXUALITY AS CORROSIVE OF HUMAN PLURALITY

What is tradition? A higher authority which one obeys, not because it commands what is *useful* to us, but because it *commands.*—What distinguishes this feeling in the presence of tradition from the feeling of fear in general? . . . Originally all education and care of health, marriage, cure of sickness, agriculture, war, speech, and silence, traffic with one another and with the gods belonged within the domain of morality: they demanded one observe prescriptions *without think-ing of oneself* as an individual. Originally, therefore, everything was custom. . . . The most moral man is he who *sacrifices* the most to custom. . . . Self-overcom-ing is demanded, *not* on account of the useful consequences it may have for the individual, but so that the hegemony of custom, tradition, shall be made evident in despite of the private desires and advantages of the individual: the individual is to sacrifice himself—that is the commandment of morality of custom.[12]

While "cannibalism" refers to the literal act or habit of eating one's own kind, heterosexism does this in a figurative sense when, in the course of propagating the heterosexual ideal for itself, nonheterosexuality is consumed either through the violent destruction of others whose sexual orientation does not turn on their procreative capacity, or through elimination of a moral space for their being in the world, itself continuously remade in heterosexuality's own image through millions of apparent opposite-sex performances that, in reality, reduce to the one—a narrowly circumscribed sexual act upon which is built a many-layered normative edifice that stretches from penile-vaginal union to God himself. While human cannibalism might be excused in cases of extreme emergency, when for some who are still strong to continue to live others who are less strong must be consumed, no such emergency exists across humanity to warrant foreclosing human sexuality and moral space for being in the world only to affirmed heterosexuals, or to those who are pre-sumed to perform exclusive heterosexuality.

Hence, even in the naturalized sense of referring to human reproduction, as a concept "heterosexuality" cannot help but go beyond the given and so is subject to human interpretation, manipulation, and improvisation; it is produced, or so Judith Butler successfully has argued.[13] While there may be no original heterosexuality there to copy, except as an ideal that occurs in the minds of those who believe it and who may contend that its originality owes to the act of divine creation, a religious assertion that is beyond confirmation, certainly physical, male-female sexual relations have been endlessly copied in the sense of hostile ejaculate invading and penetrating egg, beginning a biological chain of events that frequently has produced one or more human beings, each one of whom is unique.

It is this reproductivity at the heart of heterosexuality that its supporters claim anchors its normative dimension, its capacity to produce a good, a ca-pacity that went unnamed until the late nineteenth century, when the second sense of heterosexuality, its normative sense, was layered onto the biology of human reproduction, inscribing a medical discourse where beforehand an understanding overdetermined by religion provided the nameless norm for human sexuality. But while this new discourse eventually brought human sexuality across a range of sexual behaviors within the arc of its ambit of explanation, de-prioritizing the intentional reproductive act as the essence of human sexuality, the normative dimension of heterosexuality gradually was thrust into prominence. Increasingly vocal advocacy of heteronormativity has been a way to recapture the hegemony of the heterosexual ideal, a heretofore unnamed hegemony, and its primary task is to avoid reproduction of the cache of values presumed exclusively to characterize heterosexuality from being extended anywhere outside the site of male-female sexual activity. While heterosexuality in its first sense might reproduce, as heteronormativity it is predatory on human pluralism, on any other sexuality being accorded value and status; it would consume its nonheterosexual offspring by contrast to which it is itself identified and implicated in producing in the first place, most clearly in its descriptive sense.

It is my argument that heteronormativity is either a dressed-up biologism and nothing more, or it is a normative outlook that ultimately is predatory on human pluralism. It is monistic in its ascription of ethical value, as is its theological grounding ultimately in monotheistic Christianity. While a later section specifically addresses the new natural law argument as an ultimately unsuccessful attempt to bridge the gap between these two understandings of heterosexuality as an ethical outlook, the monism of will be considered first.

THE MONISM OF HETEROSEXUALITY

It is a common accusation that being gay or lesbian is simply a chosen identity, a willful affront to God. It is far less common to note monotheism's role as collective identity-former, and rarer still to note that religious affiliation is just as willfully chosen an identity as sexual orientation—by which is meant homosexual orientation—is alleged to be.[14] Both religion and sexual orientation are layered onto behavior, offering oneself and society at large a means to describe and interpret self, society, or the cosmos. But, some interpretations have iconic status, or are "compulsory," to use Adrienne Rich's famous phrase. It can be argued that identity-formation is an inherently exclusionary process that may work violence on "the Other," whoever that happens to be or include.[15] There is an economy to an identity-formation, when a people adopt exclusive allegiance to a principle of oneness. Any violence associated with the process is authorized by the favorite monotheistic deity, excising "the Other's" difference or heathen foreignness, itself, of course, a prior construct.

There is scarcity in this economy of ethical understanding, and the actual or, more likely, symbolic characteristics of the favored group warrant the denigration of "the Other," a violent denigration portrayed in the Hebrew Bible as the wish of God, sanctified in the requisite way of all norms at this level. This sanctification is necessary, because otherwise treating persons in the way partners to same-sex activity historically have been treated in the West would have been deemed immoral. Heterosexuality as a norm has been grounded in this Hebrew Bible, the *Ursprung* of three of the world's major religions. Or, perhaps better put, it is grounded in the heterosexual canon within the canon of this tripartite religious tradition.[16] The violence to "the Other" associated with monotheism and the community identified by it, Schwartz contends, is time-specific:

> Violence is not only what we do to the Other. It is prior to that. Violence is the very construction of the Other. . . . Ironically, the Other is believed to threaten the boundaries that are drawn to exclude him, the boundaries his very existence maintains. Outside by definition but always threatening to get in, the Other is poised in a delicate balance that is always off balance because fear and aggression continually weight the scales. Identity forged against the Other inspires perpetual policing of its fragile borders.[17]

The identity forged by heteronormativity, to the extent that it is moored in religion, is forged antithetically to any rival, with just the same consequences for pluralism in thinking about sexuality as the Hebrew Bible allowed for any rival religious identity. While monotheism and the monistic ethic I am arguing constitutes heteronormativity busily construct an identity against a possible plenitude of religious or sexual identities, "as though there were a finite amount of identity itself,"[18] humanity turns out always to have been all along more pluralist in its religious understandings, as well as in its actual sexual practices, whether sanctioned or not.

The monistic interpretation of either religion or human sexuality is the aberration, and it has always involved an extension of power to compel uniformity, a uniformity defeated in fact, a fact occluded by the presumed naturalness of heterosexuality, and corresponding disparagement of pluralism in both sexuality and ethics. But, "[i]n the myth of monotheism, pluralism is betrayal, punishable with every kind of exile . . . even alienation from the earth itself."[19] That is to say, despite pluralism in fact, for the monist it is not simply error, but a moral failing that is to be met with an unequivocal, decisive response. Homosexuality and sodomy before it were regarded as indicating the same phenomenon as heresy, that the perpetrator was dead to God's purpose and so fearfully outside the relevant human community of ethical consideration. Schwartz portrays the traditional biblical injunctions against homosexuality as, in reality, directed against the "threat of parricidal displacement," ultimately threatening "monotheism's chief tenet . . . [to] love the Lord thy God with all thine heart, and with all thy soul, and with all thy might."[20] There is no moral space here for an alternative ethic, or for sexual practices that are not in keeping with matrimonial heterosexual desire.

The opposite-sex heterosexual partners are united, or ought to be according to the traditional Christian vision, by their love of the same God, not by their love for each other, the criterion of love itself being a nineteenth-century innovation in the legitimation of marriage.[21] Yet, it is in no way necessary that these specific two individuals come together sexually. Given the accidental nature of the union of this man and this woman, the union could have been of this man and some other woman, or that woman and some other man. The point here being, the pluralism inherent even in heterosexual sexuality is displaced, deemphasized, in favor of the monistic interpretation that gives sexuality its value. The legal effect of this monism is as follows: "In the United States, heterosexuality is also a de jure established sexuality."[22] The social effect is to create an oppressive environment that subjects nonheterosexuals to social meanings that are false for them, if not for everyone, but relegates only them to living a life not by their own lights, one in which their interest in pursuing their own good is thwarted (e.g., through denigration of their self-respect), or made extremely difficult (e.g., a heteronormative culture everywhere supports their presumed lack of moral worth), burdening only them as a class along with any heterosexual dissenters, with the ethical challenge to secure a site, a moral space from which to contest it.[23]

The horror at how legitimating same-sex relations might change society, is matched by the horrible punishments meted out on those who engage in this behavior, for the God of the Hebrew Bible is a jealous God, oddly enough, given its monotheism.[24] This monistic understanding of the deity and of ethical conduct makes sense, once the religiosity is admitted. The parallel to heterosexuality, isolating its normative aspect, would be to note that no rival sexual identity can be accorded any value. However, as regards heterosexuality as a notion describing male-female sexual relations, the monism becomes problematic, because it requires interpreting the ancient biblical injunction to "be fruitful and multiply" to mean "reproduce more of the same." Yet, it is through those very same male-female sexual relations that human differences, including in sexuality, also are reproduced, regardless of the presence, absence, or relative strengths of any genetic or/and social components of sexuality, whether the procreators are married or not, and whether the child is raised by one or both biological parents, or not.

That is to say, male-female sexual relations produce both heterosexual persons and nonheterosexual persons, upon whom later is layered the normative dimension and its respective positive and negative valences. In Foucauldian terms, the heterosexual human subject is not prior to power and so its potential author; rather, he or she is formed within one or more networks of power relations that reflect discursive, normative power that is already there and poses unchallengeable. "Bionormative activity" is ascribed value beforehand; hence, it can extend its positive valence to the elderly and other opposite-sex couples whose sexual relations could not themselves actually result in any further propagation of the human species.[25] This is another sense in which the two senses of heterosexuality—as a site of procreative sexual activity and as a normative notion—are distinguishable, separate, and subject to critical scrutiny that I would argue should lead to rejection of the concept as an ethical touchstone, certainly as a criterion for judging nonheterosexuals.

REGARDING THE OBJECTION FROM THE NEW NATURAL LAW THEORIST

Custom represents the experiences of men of earlier times as to what they supposed useful and harmful—but the *sense for custom* (morality) applies, not to these experiences as such, but to the age, the sanctity, the indiscussability of the custom. And so this feeling is a hindrance to the acquisition of new experiences and the correction of customs: that is to say, morality is a hindrance to the creation of new and better customs: it makes stupid.[26]

New natural law opponents of homosexuality, such as John Finnis, lately have been emboldened by the politicized issue of same-sex marriage.[27] Indeed, same-sex marriage and homosexuality permeate recent new natural law writings, where these topics garner inordinate attention, which may suggest that the new natural law edifice is built on heteronormativity.[28] New natural law theorists do not present religious arguments per se, but are suspect nonetheless because without being grounded in a personal deity, or in an anthropomorphized notion of "nature," theirs no more an authoritative interpretation of the natural world than any other.[29] While natural law theorists would offer their ethical understanding and interpretation of human sexuality as independent of their Roman Catholic faith, their secular, almost scientific pose deploys a naturalized heterosexuality that blurs the distinction between nature and artifact.[30] Although natural law arguments, of course, do not derive from the natural sciences, it is important to point out that they do perform a trick with respect to brute data from the natural world. To this view, the biological fact of penis-vagina fit, as it were, portends an entire edifice of teleological ethics, enough to ground a heteronormative regime able to determine inherently immoral acts.[31] We should not let ourselves be confused by the natural law theorist's use of the term "function," as the theory of function in biology, based in established, empirical fact, is distinguishable from the theologian's theory of function, even where linked to established, empirical fact; nor should we conflate the two uses of function, as is often done.[32]

In an important passage in the first volume of his *History of Sexuality*, Foucault interrogated the very notion of "sex" because of its conflation of the biological and the ethical, and the perception of human biology possessing a double capacity both to reproduce life and to generate its meaning at the same time:

> [T]he notion of "sex" made it possible to group together, in an artificial unity, anatomical elements, biological functions, conducts, sensations, and pleasures, and it enabled one to make use of this fictitious unity as a causal principle, an omnipresent meaning, a secret to be discovered everywhere: sex was thus able to function as a unique signifier and as a universal signified. Further, by presenting itself in unitary fashion . . . it was able to mark the line of contact between a knowledge of human sexuality and the biological sciences of reproduction; thus, without really borrowing anything from these sciences, excepting a few doubtful analogies, the knowledge of sexuality gained through proximity a guarantee of quasi-scientificity; but by virtue of this same proximity, some of the contents of biology and physiology were able to serve as a principle of normality for human sexuality.[33]

The natural law emphasis on procreation borders on biologism, reducing human sexuality to human genitalia, and it relies not merely on the phenomenon of sex difference, but on that as a biblically-rooted fact as per the *Genesis* creation narrative. "In traditional theological terms the question is whether the [male-female] distinction constitutes an ontological truth about marriage."[34]

Here we encounter what I have elsewhere elaborated as the *shadow establishment*, because the entire edifice of the natural law approach cannot be separated from its culture-bound, religious moorings.[35] Indeed, one can argue that were it not for the authoritative voice of the Catholic Church, the fact/value distinction-blurring connections between reproductive functions and moral rightfulness, or between naturalness and normativity would be voiced by only a few.[36] The institution of marriage is the "hegemonic form" of heterosexuality, its contemporary model; its support in laws across the United States is the shadow of religious establishment.[37]

Perhaps the ablest rendition into contemporary terms of the medieval natural law position is Robert P. George and Gerard V. Bradley's "Marriage and the Liberal Imagination."[38] The reliance by George and Bradley on the Catholic natural law tradition and its recent explication in works such as Germain Gabriel Grisez' *The Way of the Lord Jesus Vol. 2: Living a Christian Life*, however, suggest that theirs is by no means a non-sectarian argument, but a comprehensive, consistent ideological framework we are under no obligation to establish in the law.[39] At any rate, we encounter this tradition's familiar language of duty to consummate the marriage, or annulment for reason of inability to meet this requirement; the intrinsic good and perfection of marriage; the derogation of pleasure, itself not viewed as an intrinsic good, so that the emotions do not commandeer a spouse away from the rational motivation in marriage; the proper approach to "reproductive functioning," identified as "inseminatory union," the aim of which is *not* procreation for the reason that having this aim instrumentalizes the procreative act and places the human good of integrity at risk; concern for fulfillment and actualization of the marriage through the "truly unitive, and thus marital" act that is at its heart deeply "interpersonal communication;" understanding children to be "gifts;" and, the "grave moral defect" nonmarital sex suffers. The natural law theorist teaches that the sex organs have one primary, if not exclusive purpose, which line of thought feminist thinkers have been foremost to challenge:

> Almost from the very beginning of our lives, we are all taught that the primary male sex organ is the penis, and the primary female sex organ is the vagina. These organs are supposed to define the sexes, to be the difference between boys and girls. We are taught that the reason for the differences, and the use to which the sex organs are put, has to do with making babies. This is a lie. In our society only occasionally are those organs used to make babies. Much more often they are used to produce sexual pleasure for men . . . . The penis and the vagina can make either babies or male orgasms; very rarely do the two together make female orgasms. Men, who have benefited greatly from both orgasms and babies, have had no reason to question the traditional definition of penis and vagina as true genital counterparts. Women, on the other hand, have. . . . Think clitoris.[40]

George and Bradley's focused exposition clarifies this classic perspective, one confounded by the clitoris, but in no way does it provide us with a warrant for establishing it in public law for reason of its excellent articulation. Its restricted understanding of marriage as the spouses' "reproductive-type act" of male-female genital union with ejaculation may or may not be worthy of respect. But the law of the land does not turn on this determination, nor should it even entertain this dubious ethical position.

Same-sex unions, as well as most heterosexual unions are certainly characterized by a great many valuable "goods," at least from perspectives which are undoubtedly more widely shared than George and Bradley's. Why should the nation or the world's peoples accept as truly marital only their shrunken interpretation to the condemnation of any other, *irrespective* of sexual orientation? More to the point, the natural law edifice does not speak to the political issue at hand; namely, why not extend government's blessing to same-sex couples, since (1) we cannot without great difficulty ascertain whether any existing marriage fulfills their conception, and (2) we can be sure that most people do not affirm their conception, but instead identify marriage with a variety of goods other than their narrowly circumscribed marital act of "two-in-one-flesh communion." Since the law rewards many marital goods other than George and Bradley's definitive one, a good which it may be no legitimate business of the law to determine, why not permit extending this status and these rewards to same-sex couples, who no less than married opposite-sex are alike in not meeting natural law's stringent marital requirements, but for whom these rewards are equally valuable? George and Bradley fail to convince that their normative order of morally correct opinions usefully describes marriage *for anyone*, much less do they demonstrate that it warrants exclusive constitutional protection. The latter they arguably cannot do in a regime where freedom of conscience and from arbitrary rule are as highly prized as in the United States. By contrast with that rendition of the natural law approach, Professor of Moral Theology Richard Peddicord, for example, relies on the American Catholic theologian John Courtney Murray, among others, to argue against any necessary connection between the Aristotelian-Thomistic view and antipathy towards gay persons, and instead to argue for gay and lesbian rights.[41] This pluralism in theological interpretation is not considered valuable in some quarters, and makes monists everywhere uncomfortable.[42]

The natural law argument, taking as its basis the (on some accounts cursed) necessity of sexual union between a male and a female to the propagation of the species, either misunderstands sexuality to be exclusively about reproduction, in which case it is a physical fact of human existence, regrettable to some traditionalists, or it misunderstands sexuality to require exclusively opposite-sex relations of affection, relations laden with normative value. Biological "oppositeness" (if male and female sex organs, or men and women themselves are "opposite" anywhere but in our understanding of them) does not entail complementarity, nor does biological "sameness" (if two men or two women are simply the "same" to each other) preclude it.[43] These are all human notions that go beyond the given, and ought to give us pause when they result in misunderstanding, denigration of human sexual pluralism, or the suffering of others under misplaced shame.

THE KINSEY STUDY AND THE FLUIDITY OF SEXUALITY

The beginnings of a science of sexuality were also the beginnings of the use of science ultimately to normalize what had been thought to be unnatural such that, rather than confirming the earlier religious understanding, the trajectory of scientific inquiry came to refute it. While what we may understand by the heterosexual ideal had seemed to map perfectly onto what we (thought we) knew and valued in human sexuality, especially its life-giving and life-affirming aspects (e.g., an idealized American family life built upon heterosexual coupling), scientific inquiry slowly revealed the constructed aspects of assumed "natural" human sexuality, aspects further revealed by researchers in the social sciences and humanities, who arrived at histories of sex and sexuality that challenged traditional, nonchalant wisdom. This was not unexpected, for, according to Foucault, "[t]he search for descent is not the erecting of foundations: on the contrary, it disturbs what was previously considered immobile; it fragments what was thought unified; it shows the heterogeneity of what was imagined consistent with itself."[44] The heterosexual ideal actually purports to possess a simple identity with all that is truly virtuous or good in humanity, rendering the nonheterosexual bad or evil. Hence, it stands in an intimate relation to its purported opposite, a relationship that is in practice predatory.[45]

Findings from the initial Kinsey studies of male sexuality (1948) and female sexuality (1953) hit Americans like a firestorm, though they may not have been aware of the studies' deeper implications.[46] Most Americans were surprised to learn that approximately 10 percent of them engage in exclusively same-sex behavior, or are exclusive homosexuals, because this number of respondents was positioned at the highest point on the Kinsey Scale. This suggested to a population with emerging Cold War mentality that there must be closeted homosexuals in their midst, alongside those more obviously gay or lesbian as perceived at the time. The news was scary, and the reaction an example of what Stanley Hoffman has called the politics of fear, with homosexuals getting rooted out of the federal government because, given their ability to pass themselves off as heterosexuals in a fiercely heterosexist society, they might successfully be recruited by the nation's communist enemies and so become its agents, traitors, once threatened with being unmasked.[47]

But the Kinsey studies had a deeper implication that should have made a lot more Americans a lot more uncomfortable, and this resides in the graduated nature of its findings. As is well-known, the Kinsey Scale did not simply represent human sexuality as an either/or proposition, either heterosexual (a Kinsey "0") or homosexual, but, rather, as a continuous spectrum. The Kinsey Scale arrayed human sexuality by degree across a seven-point scale, suggesting that a good number of individual American men and women were primarily heterosexual (say, 72 percent of the time), but somewhat homosexual (the other 28 percent of the time), such as the 'incidental homosexual' or itinerant homosexual across his or her life-course. One could not be sure whether others were genuinely heterosexual, should they hover around 50 percent heterosexual or homosexual; hence, ordinary persons who were not clearly heterosexual just might not be, especially if they didn't perform it satisfactorily.[48] This should have intensified Senator McCarthy's infamous hunt for communists and homosexuals in the State Department, but, fortunately, it did not—perhaps the deeper implications of the Study were too subtle for this original, allegedly heterosexual Cold Warrior to grasp.[49]

Even more to the point, each individual person who was less than 100 percent heterosexual, had some homosexuality to own up to. Each straight or gay person who devalued homosexuality (however understood) had either to patrol and exterminate that aspect of him or herself, or repress and shunt into some subterranean hole this aspect of his or her sexuality (however understood). Into which category of response renowned straight and gay homophobes such as McCarthy, Cohn, Hoover, and their ilk actually fall may not be as important as noting alongside their behaviors that were destructive of others, whether or not homosexual, also the self-destructive aspects of their way of being in the world. Indeed, some have speculated that the self-destructiveness of those most destructive of others was believed to get a reprieve precisely through participation in activities such as the persecution of others, or overly extolling the heterosexual ideal, a category into which so-called "ex-gays" and maybe not a few clergy over the ages might fall.

That is to say, preying on others of their own kind, so to speak, was necessary to keep on living and considering oneself a moral enough person not to warrant the discrimination if not extermination generously meted out on deserving others who were not as self-regulative and/or did not know enough how best to respond to their own self-loathing.[50] Performance of the heterosexual ideal as validated in their contemporary society was understood to require both external and internal monitoring so that any dint of homosexuality could be ferreted out and destroyed. This means, of course, ferreting out and destroying others people's lives, as well as deadening that within oneself. In the case of this original predatory homosexual, then, the desire to live is closely associated with a desire for death of the same homosexuality in others, which is a perverse sense or appropriation of heterosexuality in its first sense, that connected with human reproduction or life-giving. But, it may well be in keeping with heteronormativity.

In the first volume of his *History of Sexuality* Foucault questioned heterosexuality's commitment to life, seeing it in another light:

> Sex is worth dying for. It is in this (strictly historical) sense that sex is indeed imbued with the death instinct. When a long while ago the West discovered love, it bestowed on it a value high enough to make death acceptable; nowadays it is sex that claims this equivalence, the highest of all. And while the deployment

of sexuality permits the techniques of power to invest life, the fictitious point of sex, itself marked by that deployment, exerts enough charm on everyone for them to accept hearing the grumble of death within it.[51]

Of course, for the Christian and also in some natural law contexts, human beings through their sexuality don't actually create a new human life, because only God can do that. This religious understanding suggests that heterosexuality's *prima facie* connection with life-giving is far more problematic than commonplace understanding would suggest. It suggests that what's of value is God's granting life, derivatively through the vessel of human procreative activity and that, therefore, heterosexuality is not to be valued for its own, independent life-giving capacity, but for its participation in God's activity or plan.

In the theological terms of the heteronormative tradition, what's sacred is the quality of unreproducibility, as in the one, mysterious, unduplicable original act of creation, a singular act of God, the value of which is found in the mundane universe in a plurality of ways, or so it seems to the ethical pluralist, but not to the heteronormativist, who sees this value in only the one way and only as coterminous with heterosexuality in its descriptive sense, exclusively as reproductability. On the take of the ethical pluralist, the fact that in human society exclusive homosexuality is present but cannot propagate itself should not detract from its unreproducibility as suggested above, or capacity to reproduce human values and to be esteemed for its original quality; any goods it generates are human goods, not goods just for gay people. This alternative way of being in the world, one unconnected with reproductability, is no less capable of generating value, except for the heteronormative monist's objection, one that I argue can only be based in heterosexuality in its first sense, as an empirical notion that only dubiously generates meaning, especially where its supporters lack political power. Again, perhaps we should unmask heterosexuality as either a term referring to an empirical fact regarding human propagation, and acknowledge that, by the very same route of determination so too is homosexuality (an empirical fact regarding human propagation), or reveal it as a purely normative notion, where it is extremely problematic because the human goods it associated with it cannot be divorced from homosexuality, or because it is in reality a stand-in for, or grounded in a theological premise, and likely a monistic one at that. Gay persons are no less capable than are non-gay persons of serving values, or not serving them. Heterosexuality as reproductability, connected with the important, but bare existence of humanity, doesn't reproduce any values; rather, it reproduces value-producers and defenders, both gay and non-gay alike.[52]

Homosexuality *per se* does not entail reproductability, though gay individuals may well procreate with gay or straight opposite sex partners, but it does not exclude reproducibility, the on-going production and then protection of valuable human goods in meaningful ways other than through sexual reproduction.[53] But, heterosexual reproductability does not reproduce God's non-sexual, act of creation, and so should not itself be thought of as capable of reproducing the universe of moral and other types of meaningful goods that God's unique act did. Reproductability provides the potential for reproducing meaningfulness, which heteronormativity in its inimical stance towards nonheterosexuality shrinks or would disappear altogether. Heterosexuality, then, as a normative regime reproduces the same, a stance against moral pluralism that is not grounded in reproductability. Homosexuality, in its affront and challenge to heteronormativity, multiplies difference, difference from the sameness that heteronormativity would reproduce of heterosexuality in its first sense, as a guardian for the monistic understanding of the moral universe as grounded in reproductability.

The Kinsey Scale can be used to challenge a variety of age-old assumptions and the folk wisdom associated with the heterosexual ideal, such as the one that nonheterosexual males hate women and are a threat to their ability to reproduce the species, withholding their semen some or all of the time. Learning that a good number of men are not exclusively heterosexual, yet also not exclusively homosexual, or are not exclusively heterosexual during their entire lives, hatred of women cannot logically be inferred (assuming it ever could be) from nonheterosexual status. This allows for the possibility that hatred of women can range across the Kinsey Scale, possibly even to characterize none too few male heterosexuals. Heterosexuality may be not be woman-friendly at all, or have anything to do with being woman-friendly, as some lesbian theorists have long maintained; *mutatis mutandis*, (male) homosexuality may not be woman-hating at all, or have anything to do with being woman-hating. The point here is that the peacefulness and good care for the human species attributed to heterosexuality, may be a mis-association that is both false on its own terms, and downright dangerous as the grounding for an ethical norm.

SOME CONCLUDING REMARKS

How many are there who still conclude: 'life could not be endured if there were no God!' (or, as it is put among the idealists: 'life could not be endured if its foundation lacked an ethical significance!')—therefore there *must* be a God (or existence *must* have ethical significance)! The truth, however, is merely that he who is accustomed to these notions does not desire a life without them: that these notions may therefore be necessary to him and for his preservation—but what presumption is it to decree that whatever is necessary for my preservation must actually *exist*! As if my preservation were something necessary! How if others felt in the opposite way![54]

If the ratiocinations and musings of this chapter have been near the mark, or at least stimulating, then the status of a heteronormative ethic being nothing like the "opposite" of homosexuality, but instead corrosive of human plurality, should be clear enough.[55] Some consequences of this view may include, first, that the overarching sexual identity binary of heterosexual/ homosexual should be euthanized and buried in as undignified a way as possible, outside the gates of respectable intelligent conversation, because human sexuality is so much greater and different that what this binary purports to express. Secondly, heterosexuality, as a blend of both the empirical and normative, neither is, nor can be a valid ethical ideal because it is either a misreading (here, a reading in too much) of human biology (or, "nature"), and so a possibly willful misrepresentation of the imperative of sexual intercourse to humanity's survival as a species, or it is in practice a necessarily oppressive, authoritarian, and, in most hands, cruel regime of power because its exclusiveness does not correspond to the pluralism in humanity, and, worse, may be antithetical to it. And, thirdly, heterosexuality as a normative concept rests on an unacceptable, unarguable ethical basis, as it is a religious notion, or ultimately is grounded in one and so is unsatisfactory as a universal ethical ideal for all people, and, in the liberal-democratic setting, its validity can only illegitimately be rendered into law and compelled (directly or indirectly) on nonbelievers.

Notwithstanding that all physically fit human beings possess the ability to reproduce irrespective of their sexual orientation, reproductability could never exhaust the category reproducibility. It is heteronormativity's mistake to equate reproductability with reproducibility, just as it is any heterosexual person's mistake, which the gay person knows, to suggest that human families, or the good of human family life, are not reproducible outside of the heterosexual context, without any members participating in human sexual reproduction. While the practices of not a small number of heterosexual families are corrosive of their own families and their values, which American talk shows have made the world familiar with (e.g., through spousal abuse, child neglect, all manner of sadistic beatings, infidelities), this spiral of destruction that many of us recall from our or other people's childhoods may be the product of heteronormativity just as surely as is the violence directed and redirected towards others from this site.

Heteronormativity looms tyrannical over *all* human sexuality, and the challenge to it begins with questioning its credentials where they have been assumed to be at their most powerful—at the level of their explanation of, or contribution to the propagation of the human species and the protection of valuable human goods. I have attempted to cast a skeptical eye on heterosexuality's presumptive close connection with human difference (and homosexuality's corresponding presumptive distinctive feature of being centered on sameness) by contesting its affinity for human plurality and, as an ethical norm, suitability for serious thinking about the human condition.

NOTES

1. Hannah Arendt, *The Human Condition*, (Chicago: University of Chicago Press, 1958), pp. 7, 9–11.

2. Arendt, *The Human Condition*, p. 8.

3. See her *The Origins of Totalitarianism*, (New York: Harcourt, Brace & Co., 1951).

4. An excellent treatment of the complex, under-theorized, historically constructed, and generally unremarked concept of heterosexuality, which initially referred to a pathological desire for the opposite sex, is Jonathan Ned Katz, *The Invention of Heterosexuality*, (New York: Dutton/Penguin, 1995).

5. See her essay "Heterosexuality and social theory" in Diane Richardson, ed., *Theorising Heterosexuality: Telling it straight*, (Buckingham, Pa.: Open University Press, 1996), p. 1.

6. See Stevi Jackson, "Heterosexuality and feminist theory," in Richardson, *Theorising Heterosexuality*, p. 30.

7. See her essay "Collusion, collaboration and confession: on moving beyond the heterosexuality debate," in Richardson, *Theorising Heterosexuality*, p. 170.

8. See Michel Foucault, "Power and Sex," in Lawrence D. Kritzman, ed., *Michel Foucault. Politics, Philosophy, Culture. Interviews and Other Writings 1977–1984*, (New York: Routledge, 1988), pp. 110-111. Foucault comments further along these lines in the interview "Sexual Choice, Sexual Act: Foucault and Homosexuality," in *Ibid*.

9. So far as I know, the term "heteronormativity" is original with Michael Warner. See his Introduction to his edited volume *Fear of a Queer Planet: Queer Politics and Social Theory*, (Minneapolis: University of Minnesota Press, 1993), pp. xxi–xxv.

10. While I link heteronormativity and religious or value monism, Foucault discussed the Christian sexual ethic in terms of its having achieved a "monopoly" in the Middle Ages. See Michel Foucault, *The Care of the Self. Volume 3 of The History of Sexuality*, (New York: Vintage/Random House, 1986).

11. And neither procreation nor the desire for parenthood map onto sexual orientation such that one can assert that being homosexual means a person does not desire to procreate or rear children.

12. Friedrich Nietzsche, Aphorism 9 in *Daybreak: Thoughts on the prejudices of morality*, tr. R. J. Hollingdale, (Cambridge: Cambridge University Press, 1982 [orig.: 1881]).

13. See her classic, interdisciplinary work *Gender Trouble: Feminism and the Subversion of Identity*, (New York: Routledge, 1990).

14. See Emily R. Gill, *Becoming Free: Autonomy & Diversity in the Liberal Polity*, (Lawrence: University of Kansas Press, 2001), chap. 6, for a useful discussion of the chosen or not issue as regards both sexuality and religion.

15. This is just the line of argument pursued in far greater detail in Regina M. Schwartz, *The Curse of Cain: The Violent Legacy of Monotheism*, (Chicago: University of Chicago Press, 1997), where the humanity-friendly credentials of monotheism are interrogated and rejected.

16. This notion of a "canon with the canon" is taken from Patricia Beattie Jung and Ralph E. Smith, *Heterosexism*, (Albany: State University of New York Press, 1993), pp. 53-54. Whether this interior canon of traditional condemnation of homosexuality in any of the three Abrahamic traditions is well-grounded, accurately reflects a tradition, or is impervious to reinterpretation is another set of issues, as is its usefulness for guiding public policy and lawmaking in the modern polity.

17. See Schwartz, p. 5.

18. See Schwartz, p. 20.

19. See Schwartz, pp. 46–47.

20. See Schwartz, pp. 111, 112.

21. For example in the earlier period the love that matters is love of God, to be proclaimed loudly, not the "love that dare not speak its name."

22. See Janet R. Jakobsen and Ann Pellegrini, *Love the Sin: Sexual Regulation and the Limits of Religious Tolerance*, (Boston: Beacon, 2004), p. 105.

23. An oppressive culture characterized by heterosexism works a fraud on its victims, cheating them out of becoming aware of their equal moral worth as human beings, or so it is argued in Andrew Kernohan, *Liberalism, Equality, and Cultural Oppression*, (Cambridge: Cambridge University Press, 1998), pp. 8, 10.

24. The jealousy seems directed at human beings who turn away from this God, while in a polytheistic system gods could be jealous of each other, whether or not any of the gods are jealous of human phenomena. I'm not sure where continuing to think this through might lead, except to say that arguments to support the force of law should in no way turn on anyone's understanding of god's personal characteristics, likes or dislikes, whether petty or grave.

25. The phrase "bionormative activity" is taken from Ladelle McWhorter, *Bodies and Pleasures: Foucault and the Politics of Sexual Normalization*, (Bloomington: Indiana University Press, 1999), p. 157.

26. Nietzsche, Aphorism 19 in *Daybreak*.

27. See his essays "Law, Morality, and 'Sexual Orientation,'" *Notre Dame Law Review* 69(1994): 1049–76; and, "Reason, Faith, and Homosexual Acts," in *Catholic Social Scientist Review* VI (2001), at www.catholicsocialscientists.org/Symposium. Perhaps the most comprehensive reply to the new natural law theorists' views on sexuality, and rebuttal to their limited perspective on human flourishing is Nicholas C. Bamforth and David A. J. Richards, *Patriarchal Religion, Sexuality, and Gender: A Critique of New Natural Law*, (Cambridge: Cambridge University Press, 2008).

28. See, for example, Christopher Wolfe, *Natural Law Liberalism*, (Cambridge: Cambridge University Press, 2006), where liberal theorists such as Joseph Raz are subjected to criticism from Wolfe's natural law perspective for failing to acknowledge the harmfulness of the homosexual lifestyle, or obscuring its moral worthlessness, suggesting that this topic is a litmus test for adequate moral or ethical reasoning.

29. While sodomy has been called the "crime against nature," this phrase may more appropriately be applied to plunder of the environment, or so some might argue against the tradition's putatively unanimous understandings of the term. See Robert F. Kennedy, *Crimes Against Nature*, (New York: HarperCollins, 2004).

30. Prominent natural law advocates are discussed as "essentially dressing up a sectarian religious argument in philosophical garb" in William N. Eskridge, *The Case for Same-Sex Marriage: From Sexual Liberty to Civilized Commitment*, (New York: Free Press, 1996), pp. 96–98 (passage in quotes taken from p. 98).

31. For a well-done, point-by-point critique of this approach, see Paul J. Weithman, "Natural Law, Morality, and Sexual Complementarity," in David M. Estlund and Martha C. Nussbaum, eds., *Sex, Preference, and Family: Essays on Law and Nature*, (New York: Oxford University Press, 1997), pp. 227–46.

32. See John V. Canfield, "The Concept of Function in Biology," *Philosophical Topics* 18, no. 2 (Fall 1990): 29–53. The confusion is also likely theological, at least according to Systematic Theology Professor William Stacy Johnson, who presents a biblical evidence-based argument that the 'two-in-one union' dating back to *Genesis* referred to becoming one family. See the third chapter of his recent work *A Time to Embrace: Same-Gender Relationships in Religion, Law, and Politics*, (Grand Rapids: William B. Eerdmans, 2006).

33. Michel Foucault, *An Introduction. Volume 1 of The History of Sexuality*, (New York: Vintage/Random House, 1978), pp. 154–55.

34. See Jung and Smith, *Heterosexism*, p. 146, who argue that it does not.

35. See my *Liberal Constitutionalism, Marriage, and Sexual Orientation: A Contemporary Case for Dis-Establishment*, (New York: Peter Lang, 2002). A similar understanding of the legitimating grounds of the American sexual regulatory regime is presented in Jakobsen and Pellegrini, *Love the Sin*, p. 19: "It is not simply that religion is the context for public debates and policy making around sex; rather, in a fundamental sense, the secular state's regulation of the sexual life of its citizens is actually religion by other means."

36. This line of argument is pursued in Don E. Marietta, Jr., *Philosophy of Sexuality*, (Armonk, N.Y.: M. E. Sharpe, 1997), pp. 32–34.

37. On marriage as hegemonic, see Jo VanEvery, "Heterosexuality and domestic life," in Richardson, *Theorising Heterosexuality*.

38. *Georgetown Law Journal* 84, no. 2 (December, 1995): 301–20.

39. See esp. chap. 9 of this work (Quincy: Franciscan Press, 1993).

40. See Alix Shulman, "Organs and Orgasms," in Vivian Gornick and Barbara K. Moran, eds., *Women in Sexist Society: Studies in Power and Powerlessness*, (New York: Basic Books, 1971), pp. 198, 205. Johnson makes a similar point in his discussion of the meaninglessness of pleasure without procreation in the new natural law perspective, one that limits acceptable expressions of sexuality to sexual functionality and so cannot ascribe any meaninglessness to the female orgasm during intercourse. See *A Time to Embrace*, p. 51.

41. See Richard Peddicord, *Gay and Lesbian Rights*, (Kansas City, MO: Sheed & Ward, 1996), pp. 44–51, 178–86. A Christian religious argument in favor of gay and lesbian rights is also provided in Jung and Smith, *Heterosexism*.

42. Perhaps unnecessarily in the case of Catholic monists, because in the past the Church has shown itself quite capable of revising its approach to what are regarded as deep moral questions, though not always willingly initially or when the path ahead was beclouded by its hierarchy's entrenched, traditional patriarchialism. See Bamforth and Richards, *Patriarchal Religion, Sexuality, and Gender*, pp. 332–33.

43. This line of argument is discussed in an essay by Martha Nussbaum in her "Commentary on Parts III and IV," in Estlund and Nussbaum, eds., *Sex, Preference, and Family*, p. 327.

44. Quoted in Jennifer Tolbert Roberts, *Athens on Trial: The Antidemocratic Tradition in Western Thought*, (Princeton: Princeton University Press, 1994), p. 3.

45. An alternative take on this is to maintain the identification between humanity and heterosexuality by placing nonheterosexuals outside the group identified by "humanity," a move some have theorized and/or taken to practice. Certainly the rhetoric of some of the most ardent antigay rights advocates, with their dire warnings of the imminent collapse of western civilization or the loss of society's moral compass, or morality itself, would need little, if any twisting before it served to justify violent antigay practices such as the worst hate crimes.

46. Although my appropriation of the Kinsey Studies is favorable, it is not unmindful of problems associated with this body of work. See Vern Bullough, "The Kinsey Scale in Historical Perspective," and Vivienne C. Cass, "The Implications of Homosexual Identity Formation for the Kinsey Model and Scale of Sexual Preference," two essays in David P. McWhirter, Stephanie A. Sanders, and June Machover Reinisch, eds., *Homosexuality/Heterosexuality: Concepts of Sexual Orientation*, (New York: Oxford University Press, 1990).

47. The sodomy—treason nexus is centuries old. See the discussion in Byrne Fone, *Homophobia: A History*, (New York: Picador/Henry Holt and Company, 2000), pp. 189–91.

48. Then again, there are those people who appear to perform heterosexuality all too well, who turn out to be otherwise, sometimes even confusing themselves. Who would have thought, for example, that David Palmer, widower and former keyboard player of the classic rock group "Jethro Tull" would now be living life as platinum blonde "Dee," following a transgender operation? As reported in the Sunday magazine *Parade* (August 8, 2004): 2. If "Dee" now wishes to marry a man, she ought to avoid the State of Florida, where an appeals court ruled that postoperative transsexual people cannot legally marry. See "Transgender People Can't Wed as New Sex, Court Says," *Los Angeles Times* (July 24, 2004): A–16.

49. Apparently, McCarthy's homosexuality was an established fact within a small circle of his associates, according to the depiction given in the historical film *Point of Order* (New Yorker Films, 1964).

50. Others responses were to be openly gay or lesbian, thus meriting severe public censorship, or to be overcome by their self-hatred, perhaps committing suicide.

51. Foucault, *An Introduction. Volume 1 of The History of Sexuality*, p. 156.

52. Unless, of course, normative ethics is itself exclusively grounded in the biological fact of human reproduction, that this opposite-sex act when done by two heterosexual persons is itself a primary value for humankind. On the interpretation

presented here, heterosexuality as a normative regime, as heteronormativity, doesn't in fact hold this, but occludes this untenable locus of value or of valuing, an occlusion I would cast in the light of day and subject to critical interrogation.

53. For example, same-sex couples may nurture and cherish their children, even if they are not their biological children, as do otherwise childless adoptive parents. It is unreasonable, and probably downright mean to suggest that protecting the valuable human good of childhood is somehow not in the makeup of homosexual persons.

54. Nietzsche, Aphorism 90 in *Daybreak*.

55. The same would apply to "homo-normativity," and applies as well to most any "ism."

Conclusion

The Moral Values Project:
A Call to Moral Action in Politics

*Chai R. Feldblum**

MORAL ARGUMENTATION: SHOULD WE EVEN GO THERE?

Anyone interested in pursuing a line of moral argumentation on behalf of gay equality would do well to read (or reread) Michael Sandel's brief fifteen-page article, *Moral Argument and Liberal Toleration: Abortion and Homosexuality*, first published in the California Law Review in 1989.[1] In that article, Sandel makes the argument that solidifying the right to an abortion or the right to engage in homosexual sex might require engaging with normative moral assessments of such activities. In this concluding chapter, I refer back to that groundbreaking article and intermix political argument with my own experience in the legislative and judicial arenas to make the claim for infusing moral action in politics. By doing so, I hope to add some additional poignancy to the claims made in this book that complete and full equality for sexual minorities will be achieved only on the basis of moral argumentation.

In this volume, R. Claire Snyder-Hall forcefully presents the counter-story to Sandel, arguing that the moral values inherent in political liberalism are sufficient to justify full gay equality.[2] Carlos Ball, in his succinct and targeted contribution to this volume, sets forth the counterarguments to those claims, highlighting the problems many of us believe remain intractable if complete and full equality for LGBT people is sought solely based on the moral values of political liberalism, without the concomitant substantive claims that LGBT

---

* Parts of this chapter are derived from a monograph written for a meeting convened by the National Gay and Lesbian Task Force in 2006. That monograph benefitted from the work of Michael Boucai, Amy Simmerman, and Alyssa Rayman-Read.

people are *good* and that government has a role in supporting the advancement of certain normative goods.[3]

In his 1989 article, Michael Sandel considered the ways in which people argue for laws against abortion and homosexual sodomy, as well as how they argue against antiabortion and antisodomy laws. People make what Sandel noted might be called "naïve" and "sophisticated" arguments:

> The naive view holds that the justice of laws depends on the moral worth of the conduct they prohibit or protect. The sophisticated view holds that the justice of such laws depends not on a substantive moral judgment about the conduct at stake, but instead on a more general theory about the respective claims of majority rule and individual rights, of democracy on the one hand, and liberty on the other.[4]

Sandel's goal was, as he put it:

> to bring out the truth in the naive view, which I take to be this: The justice (or injustice) of laws against abortion and homosexual sodomy depends, at least in part, on the morality (or immorality) of those practices. This is the claim the sophisticated view rejects. In both its majoritarian and its liberal versions, the sophisticated view tries to set aside or 'bracket' controversial moral and religious conceptions for purposes of justice. It insists that the justification of laws be neutral among competing visions of the good life.[5]

Sandel proceeds to make his argument by dissecting the analysis of the Supreme Court in both its abortion and sodomy cases, with the latter focused on *Bowers v. Hardwick*. I had started my judicial clerkship with Justice Blackmun in July 1986, just after the *Hardwick* decision had been handed down in June 1986, replete with (from my perspective) an eloquent and commanding dissent from Justice Blackmun. I was particularly struck, therefore, by how Sandel unpacked and critiqued Justice Blackmun's dissent in that case.

In *Hardwick*, Justice White had easily dismissed the asserted constitutional right of privacy to engage in homosexual sodomy by cavalierly announcing: "No connection between family, marriage, and procreation on the one hand and homosexual activity on the other has been demonstrated, either by the Court of Appeals or by respondent."[6] His assumption, of course, was that whatever was common among activities such as having a family, getting married, and having children—all activities that had previously been held by the Supreme Court to be protected under a constitutional right of privacy—was definitely not present when people were engaged in the activity of homosexual sex.

But as Sandel points out, the panel of the Eleventh Circuit Court of Appeals in that case had argued precisely for recognizing a similarity between such activities. As Sandel summarized the lower court's analysis:

The marital relationship is significant, wrote the court of appeals, not only because of its procreative purpose but also "because of the unsurpassed opportunity for mutual support and self-expression that it provides." It recalled the Supreme Court's observation in *Griswold* [*v. Connecticut*] that "marriage is a coming together for better or for worse, hopefully enduring, and intimate to the degree of being sacred." And it went on to suggest that the qualities the Court so prized in *Griswold* could be present in homosexual unions as well: "For some, the sexual activity in question here serves the same purpose as the intimacy of marriage."[7]

In stark contrast to the line of reasoning adopted by the Eleventh Circuit, however, which relied on a positive normative assessment of the goodness inherent in intimate same-sex relationships, the dissent by Justice Blackmun (the eloquent and commanding dissent of my Justice!) was strikingly timid and shrinking in Sandel's view.

Justice Blackmun's dissent did conclude that there was a constitutional right of privacy that protected homosexual sodomy and prohibited its criminalization. But, as Sandel trenchantly points out, Blackmun rested his analysis on a voluntarist and individualist line of reasoning—one that had its intellectual roots in *Stanley v. Georgia*,[8] a case that protected a person's right to read pornography at home, rather than in *Griswold v. Connecticut*,[9] the case which rested on a ringing endorsement of the human good of marriage. Under this approach, while there was a constitutional right of privacy to engage in homosexual sodomy, that was not because sex between a gay couple should be understood as partaking of the same moral good as sex between a married couple. Rather, it was because our society protects our right to engage in intimate, personal activities in private that do not harm others—even if those activities are somewhat distasteful, such as the reading of pornography.

Of course, timid reasoning or not, had Justice Blackmun been able to convince just one more Justice to adopt his reasoning and join his opinion, the Supreme Court in 1986 *would* have recognized a constitutional right to privacy to engage in homosexual conduct and laws criminalizing sodomy across the nation *would* have been invalidated. That is *not* a small matter.

Moreover, had Justice Blackmun grounded his opinion on the rationale that gay sex was morally equivalent to heterosexual sex, he would probably not only have had difficulty pulling in a fifth Justice, he probably would have had difficulty pulling in *himself*. During July and August of 1986, the first few months of my clerkship, Justice Blackmun talked a fair amount about homosexuality to his clerks, given the large amount of mail he was receiving at that time as a result of his dissent in *Hardwick*. Based on his comments, it was clear to me that Justice Blackmun was not particularly comfortable with the idea of homosexuality. He seemed to view homosexuality as an unfortunate aberration that afflicted some people and for which they should not be punished. But he did not view homosexuality as a way of being that was morally equivalent to, and equally healthy as, heterosexuality.[10]

Sandel himself sets out the utility and appeal of an approach that brackets the morality of homosexuality. Of key importance, people do not have to change their views as to whether gay sexual activity is morally problematic, or even to engage in such a conversation, in order to extend rights to gay people. "By insisting only that each respect the freedom of others to live the lives they choose, this toleration promises a basis for political agreement that does not await shared conceptions of morality."[11]

And yet, I remain uncomfortable with the timid approach of the Blackmun dissent. There is something incredibly important that is absent in the pure voluntarist case for toleration. First, as a practical matter, Sandel argues, "it is by no means clear that social cooperation can be secured on the strength of autonomy rights alone, absent some measure of agreement on the moral permissibility of the practices at issue."[12] That is, perhaps people are really only ready to extend toleration once they have *already* come to believe that the underlying activity is morally permissible. And second, there is a real difficulty in "the quality of respect [the voluntarist case for toleration] secures."[13] By definition, a moral bracketing approach leaves all negative views of homosexuality unchallenged. How much respect does that ultimately gain for gay people?

Sandel concluded his 1989 article as follows:

> Defining privacy rights by defending the practices privacy protects seems either reckless or quaint; reckless because it rests so much on moral argument, quaint because it recalls the traditional view that ties the case for privacy to the merits of the conduct privacy protects. But as the abortion and sodomy cases illustrate, the attempt to bracket moral questions faces difficulties of its own. They suggest the truth in the "naive" view, that the justice or injustice of laws against abortion and homosexual sodomy may have something to do with the morality or immorality of these practices after all.[14]

I was convinced by Sandel's arguments—hook, line, and sinker. It is not that I did not perceive the many tangible political advantages in arguing for gay equality through resort to the moral values of political equality, espoused by thinkers such as John Rawls and Ronald Dworkin, and articulated so well in their application to gay equality by Claire Snyder in this volume. Indeed, in the almost twenty years since reading Sandel's article, I have operated in the legislative and judicial worlds in various roles—helping to write pro-LGBT legislation, arguing against anti-LGBT legislation, negotiating deals on both types of legislation, and writing amicus briefs. Invariably, I have used almost solely the tried and true political arguments of neutral equality. Those arguments are *very* powerful, and they often *work*.

For example, when I testified on behalf of the Employment Nondiscrimination Act (ENDA) in 1994, I turned to the power of moral bracketing in responding to a line of questioning from Senator Nancy Kassebaum (R-KA) about the possible ramifications of passing a nondiscrimination law that protected behavior. After trying to assert that the sexual behavior of a gay person should be seen as equivalent to the religious behavior of a person of faith (and getting nowhere fast with that line of argument), I then asserted:

> There are clearly people . . . who believe that it is entirely appropriate for employers to be able to fire someone just because he or she is gay. [But] you know, 70 percent of the American public when they are surveyed say they do not think so. *They do not like gay people particularly,* . . . they do not really want their sons and daughters to be gay. . . . *But they think it is [wrong] for people to be fired from their jobs. And that is really all that we are saying with this piece of legislation.* (emphasis added.)[15]

Matt Coles, Director of the ACLU Lesbian and Gay Rights Project, tells a perfect story about moral bracketing. Coles talked about a visit he made to a black fundamentalist congregation in California. The audience, deeply biased against his position, finally "got it" when he insisted that "you can't make my housing, my job depend on whether you *like* me."[16] And James Esseks, a lawyer with the ACLU Project, noted that many people who accept the principle of nondiscrimination in employment do not accept that straight and non-straight people are or should be equal. In Esseks' view, "ENDA could pass without 'gay is good.'"[17]

Coles and Esseks are correct that moral bracketing is very much in play when a gay civil rights law is being considered. For example, the reality is that many Americans still believe homosexuality is immoral. In a Gallup poll taken in May 2007, 49 percent of respondents said they found "homosexual relations" to be "morally wrong," while 47 percent called such relations "morally acceptable." While the percentage of people who are saying that homosexual relations are morally acceptable has been slowly growing over the years, it has not yet topped 50 percent.[18]

And yet, from 1996 to 2008, nineteen polls by five different public opinion monitors have found that more than 80 percent of Americans believe gay people should have equal rights in terms of job opportunities. Indeed, a Gallup poll in May 2008 found 89 percent approval for allowing equal job opportunities for gays and lesbians.[19]

Assuming antigay animus largely or primarily expresses a moral sentiment, the public *must* be bracketing its moral opinion of homosexuality when it comes to at least certain issues, such as employment discrimination. As one poll analyst observes: "People have learned they need to be more tolerant of gays and lesbians. On that most scholars agree. This tolerance is believed to be rooted in a sense of fairness, not necessarily support for the group. Americans understand that, 'you treat people equally even if you don't approve of them. You do not fire people or discriminate against them because they are different.'"[20]

Moral bracketing is what allows people to say both that homosexuality is wrong *and* that antigay discrimination is wrong. How bad can that be?

Let me be clear—moral bracketing makes a lot of sense for the LGBT civil rights movement. The essence of moral bracketing is that it does not matter if a majority in this country does not like a particular minority (or does not like the activities of a particular minority), as long as the people in that minority and/or their behavior are not hurting anyone else. That approach is very helpful in the march towards equality for LGBT people.

And, as Synder makes clear in this volume, moral bracketing is not a politics that is devoid of *moral values*. To the contrary, it is an approach that values pluralism deeply and cherishes the ethical principles of respecting people's individualism and autonomy. Under a political approach respecting such values, it is understood that individuals living in a pluralist society will inevitably hold divergent normative and moral beliefs. The important role of law and government, therefore, is to safeguard equally and adequately the rights necessary for each individual to pursue his or her own normative view of "the good life"—but not otherwise to affirmatively advance one moral, normative view of "the good" over others.

And yet, the challenges that Sandel raised with regard to the ultimate utility of moral bracketing continue to resonate for me as an advocate for LGBT rights.

First, although many individuals who vote for a gay civil rights bill claim that they are not making a moral assessment about homosexuality, that position must be disingenuous at some level. The only way to justify prohibiting private employers, landlords, and business owners from discriminating against gay people is to have made the prior moral assessment that acting on one's homosexual orientation is not *so* harmful to the moral health of the community (because it might harm the individual or others) as to *justify* discrimination against such individuals in the public domain.

While people may not consciously acknowledge they have made this prior moral judgment, it is hard to see how such a judgment is not a necessary precondition for voting in favor of such laws. In other words, while people may describe their position in favor of such laws solely in terms of neutral tolerance, the path they have taken to arrive at that stage of neutral toleration might well have required a prior shift in their moral assessment of homosexuality. That shift was not necessarily to a position that gay sexual activity is morally equivalent to heterosexual sexual activity. But it was at least a shift to the position that gay sexual activity is not so morally problematic that employers may justifiably use that activity as the basis for granting or withholding job opportunities. Perhaps there would be some utility in enabling and/or forcing people to acknowledge they have reached that point in their moral assessment of homosexuality if they are supporting an antidiscrimination law.

Second, what quality of respect, and hence what degree of equality, can we realistically expect under a regime of neutral toleration? As long as advocates for LGBT rights ask simply for protection from discrimination in areas such as employment, housing, and most public accommodations, they seem to have significant support. But as soon as advocates demand full recognition of their families and children (for example, the right to civil marriage, the right to equal benefits, and the right to adopt children), the same legislative champions who were ready to vote for a gay civil rights employment/housing/some public accommodations bill are often nowhere to be found. It seems that once a law appears to connote approval of homosexuality—in an explicit manner, rather than sotto voce—most supporters become uneasy. They perceive that their constituents are not yet ready for them to vote for a law that presumes a moral equivalence between homosexuality and heterosexuality.

Finally, if we limit our arguments for equality to the moral value of neutral toleration, it will be harder for us to deal honestly with opponents of LGBT right who have moral objections to homosexuality. Once one acknowledges that some moral assessments necessarily underlie legislative enactments that provide equality for LGBT people, it is easier to understand how those who believe that homosexuality, or acting on one's homosexual orientation, is morally wrong might feel burdened in some way by such legislative enactments. As I describe more fully below in my discussion of Proposition 8, government should not alleviate those burdens in a way that would undermine the effectiveness of equality legislation for LGBT people. But a more open engagement with the moral assessments underlying such legislation would allow us to have a more honest and respectful conversation with individuals who have different substantive moral views.

None of these limitations, however, seemed serious enough to me to justify a change in course during most of the lifetime that I have been advocating for LGBT equality. I authored several articles between 1996 and 2004 noting the limitations of moral bracketing and calling for an internal (and essentially, academic) conversation about the substantive moral claims that might underlie the assertion of "gay is good." I did not, however, see any compelling need for a significant shift in the political or public strategy undertaken by advocates towards advancing LGBT equality. The turning point, for me, was in 2004.

Social conservatives have often asserted that "moral values" gave George W. Bush his second term as President. They point to the fact that exit polling indicated that voters ranked "moral values" as one of their foremost concerns at the ballot box in November 2004. Twenty-two percent of Americans said that, in deciding who ought to lead the United States, "moral values" mattered more to them than:

Education (4 percent)
Taxes (5 percent)
Health Care (8 percent)
Iraq (15 percent)
Terrorism (19 percent)
Economy and Jobs (20 percent)

Eighty percent of those respondents who said they chose their President based on moral values were Bush supporters.[21]

Were supporters of George W. Bush really more moral than supporters of John Kerry? What exactly was *meant* by moral values? How did people filling out those exit polls *know* what was meant? As more than one analyst has pointed out, not even the respondents themselves knew the answers to these questions. More than 44 percent of respondents answering the exit polls thought moral values meant specific issues like abortion and gay marriage. Others thought it referred to the candidates' personal qualities or religious affiliations.[22] But what the poll's use of the term "moral values" did was prohibit respondents from identifying the Iraq war, or health care, or jobs as *moral* categories. The poll itself contrived which issues were moral issues and which were not.

As it turned out, more sophisticated election analyses that took place in the months after the election indicated that opposition to "gay marriage" or abortion were not as important to voters in 2004 as conservatives liked to claim.[23] But to a certain extent, the damage had been done. The reality is that social conservatives have been incredibly successful with promoting *their* moral values (as moral values) in the public discourse. This success stems from the ability, specifically of the Religious Right, to promote its agenda on multiple levels.[24]

First, "moral values" has become a popularly understood code word for an entire set of conservative issues and beliefs, even identities and affiliations. Those who believe in moral values, or who vote "on their moral values," are presumed to agree about a number of social policies, religious beliefs, and political agendas. The term is used like a fraternity handshake to connote much more than its literal, dictionary meaning. And because the popular press has swallowed and regurgitated "moral values" according to the conception offered by its creators, we now have a popularly accepted understanding of what it means to "act in the public sphere upon one's moral values." By accepting this singular meaning of moral values, countless other meanings have been inherently excluded, as Babst's critique of heteronormativity in this volume suggests.

Second, the Religious Right has used the moral values messaging to galvanize the public. There has been a deliberate and comprehensive campaign by the Religious Right to create the terms "family values" and "moral values" as a simple, innocuous-sounding signal to voters—to include voters in the fraternity handshake without necessarily including them, or needing to include them, in the fraternity itself.

Third, the Religious Right's moral values messaging capitalizes, in a deliberate and brilliant fashion, on liberal fears of using morality-based language in political discourse. Conservative strategists know very well that liberals and progressives believe strongly in the separation of church and state and hence are often uncomfortable with the language of morality—so often conflated with religion—in politics. Some liberals and progressives make very clear that they stand for *values*, but still feel discomfort identifying their beliefs as *moral* values.

To me, it seems incredibly unfortunate to have one group—with such conservative positions on sexuality and gender no less—be permitted to get away with a monopoly on such a useful term as "moral values." After 2004, it seemed particularly essential to me to envision a strategy for taking that term back.

The campaign of Barack Obama for President in 2008 might ultimately turn out to be a turning point in terms of taking back the term "values." In *The Audacity of Hope: Thoughts on Reclaiming the American Dream*, in a chapter titled and devoted to Values, Obama notes how conservatives used the polling data on the ambiguous "moral values" term. But his response to their use is a clarion call to action based directly on values:

> I think Democrats are wrong to run away from a debate about values. . . . It is the language of values that people use to map their world. It is what can inspire them to take action, and move them beyond their isolation. The postelection polls may have been poorly composed, but the broader question of shared values—the standards and principles that the majority of Americans deem important in their lives, and in the life of the country—should be the heart of our politics, the cornerstone of a meaningful debate about budgets and projects, regulations and policies.[25]

I agree with Obama. And my inclination is to go for the whole package. The terms "values" and "moral values" are essentially interchangeable. They both refer to our vision of the good. They both refer to normative beliefs, assumptions, and presumptions about what is right and what is wrong. They both have relevance to "budgets and projects, regulations and policies." And many of them will impact issues of sexuality, sexual orientation, and gender.

Thus, we need a meaningful debate in this country about what "moral values" means in the context of LGBT equality. The chapters in this book offer a basic grounding for this debate, cutting across a range of scholarly disciplines. But we also need a blueprint for applying that grounding in a practical manner to the political sphere. In the following section, therefore, I lay out the premises and discursive moves of what I call the Moral Values Project, an enterprise I launched in 2005 to provide resources and a base for moral advocacy to achieve equality in the arenas of sexuality, sexual orientation, and gender.[26]

THE PREMISES OF THE MORAL VALUES PROJECT

Most of the discrimination that gay people experience in American society today derives from the assumption that gay is *bad*—or, at least, is *not as good as* straight. People (including public leaders) do not always say this openly and explicitly. But when one pushes the logic behind any denial of full equality to LGBT people, "morality" is always and perhaps necessarily the ultimate rationale.

Sometimes a discriminatory public policy or private action is based upon the belief that homosexuality or bisexuality—the sexual *orientation* itself—is not as good as heterosexuality. Other times, the public policy is based on the belief that even if an individual's sexual orientation may have been predetermined by God, nature, and/or nurture—and is therefore not itself a source of moral blame—it is bad (or "not as good") to *act* on a homosexual orientation as it is to act on a heterosexual orientation.

In contrast, the Moral Values Project holds these truths to be self-evident:

❑ sexual orientation is a *morally neutral* characteristic; and
❑ it is *morally good* to express one's gay sexual orientation by engaging in homosexual sex and being out as a gay person.

The Moral Values Project is then based on the following five premises:

Premise One: An individual's sexual orientation is a morally neutral characteristic and acting in a manner consistent with one's sexual orientation is a morally good act.

Sexual orientation, in and of itself, is a morally neutral characteristic.

The source of our sexual orientation—be it God, our genes, our childhood experiences, our ideological choices, or something else we haven't even discovered yet—does not matter. It does not matter because sexual orientation *itself* does not matter from a moral perspective, any more than it matters whether we have blue eyes or brown eyes, black skin or white skin.

Society, of course, can decide to make some things matter more than others. Thus, the color of our skin, or who excites us sexually, can be—and has been—*made* to matter more than the color of our eyes. But as a logical and inherent matter, sexual orientation, skin color, and eye color are all morally neutral characteristics.

By contrast, the choice to act consistently or inconsistently with one's sexual orientation is a morally laden act. The Moral Values Project believes that an individual who acts *consistently* with his or her sexual orientation acts in a *morally good* manner. A person who acts in that fashion will be able to feel happiness (including sexual pleasure) more authentically and will be more likely to live a life of honesty and integrity. By contrast, a person who acts inconsistently with his or her sexual orientation is more likely to experience unhappiness (including sexual deprivation and dissatisfaction) and is more likely not to have integrity in his or her life. A corollary of such choices is that the person who becomes the spouse of a person who is acting inconsistently with his/her sexual orientation is also more likely to experience unhappiness in his/her life.

Premise Two: We must force the conversation—in personal, political, and public media settings—that an individual's sexual orientation is a morally neutral characteristic and that an individual who acts consistently with his/ her orientation is acting in a morally good manner.

There are many people in American society who feel that homosexuality is just "not as good" as heterosexuality. Many of these people think that even if homosexuality itself is not a terrible thing, it would be better if people did not act upon their homosexual or bisexual orientations. Some people "know" why they hold such beliefs. Many others do not—they cannot articulate *why* being gay or having homosexual sex is not as good as being straight or having heterosexual sex. But whatever category a person may fall into, we have no hope of convincing her or him of the moral neutrality of sexual orientation, and/or of the moral goodness of acting consistently with one's orientation, if we do not engage in a conversation about those beliefs in the first place.

The second premise of the Moral Values Project, therefore, is that we must—in a consistent and perhaps annoying fashion—engage anyone who believes being gay, or acting on one's gay orientation, is morally problematic to explain to us *why* he or she believes that to be true. For those who use religion to explain the immorality of homosexuality, we must be able to deploy the teachings of religions that believe otherwise. For those who rely on a particular view of natural law, we must be able to explain the logical consequences of applying natural law to other areas of sexuality. (For example, it would require prohibiting all birth control and heterosexual oral sex as well.) For those who simply have a measure of disgust, we need to learn how to diplomatically uncover and then treat that visceral response.

Unfortunately, there are not many accessible scripts out there right now, for anyone—from an ordinary person talking to his family to a policy-maker talking to her colleagues—to explain why sexual orientation is a morally neutral trait and why acting consistently with one's sexual orientation is a morally good act. One of the goals of the Moral Values Project, therefore, is to formulate and broadcast such scripts in a manner that will meet a range of audiences.

Premise Three: An effort to achieve full sexual and gender equality in this country will benefit if the LGBT movement offers a vision of substantive moral goods that our society should advance.

The current political discourse for LGBT rights draws mainly on two compelling values: fairness and equality. We should not abandon this powerful discourse. But neither should we shy away from articulating *additional* substantive goods that members of our society also believe in, goods whose elaboration would benefit the struggle for full gender and sexual equality once we "connect the dots" for people.

To be specific, we believe a good society embodies, at a minimum, the following *four moral understandings:*

- ❑ It is good for people to feel safe.
- ❑ It is good for people to be happy.
- ❑ It is good for people to give and receive care.
- ❑ It is good for people to live a life of integrity.

The work of Robin West has been a particular influence on my understanding of the moral goods of safety and care. In books such as *Caring for Justice* (1999) and *Re-Imagining Justice: Progressive Interpretations of Formal Equality, Rights, and the Rule of Law* (2005), West has eloquently set forth the arguments for why government has an obligation to affirmatively support the ability of individuals to give and receive care and to feel safe. The moral understandings that underlie the Moral Values Project also find their resonance in Urvashi Vaid's statement in her book, *Virtual Equality*: "What principles define gay and lesbian morality? I see them as a commitment to honesty, demonstrated by the experience of coming out; a commitment to community, or a love that surpasses the definition of family and relationship we inherited from the heterosexual norm; and a commitment to joy, expressed in our affirmation of pleasure, both sexual and nonsexual."

Premise Four: Our government has the obligation, through its public policies, to create societal frameworks that advance a set of moral goods.

Our government has more than simply a negative responsibility towards us—that is, a responsibility not to interfere without good reason in our personal lives. It also has a positive responsibility towards us. Hence, government is not doing its job if it fails to ensure that its people, including its LGBT people, have the societal frameworks in which to be safe, happy, able to care for others and to be cared for, and live a life of integrity. Obviously, government cannot guarantee that we will always be safe, happy, find someone to care for, and who will care for us, and be able to live a life of integrity. But government can help create the *social frameworks* in which our *capacity* to feel safe, happy, cared for, and authentic is either supported or diminished. As Carlos Ball notes in his chapter in this book, this is a legitimate role that we can and should expect government to undertake.[27]

So how are the four substantive moral goods listed above faring in today's society for LGBT people? Not too well!

Safety: LGBT people know what it is like *not* to feel safe—whether we are walking down the street holding hands with our partner or being open about our partner, our family life, or our gender identity at the workplace.

It is a fact of life that when a person exhibits outward signs of being gay or is perceived as being gay, there is at least some risk that physical harm will be visited upon that person in return. Whether we envision an overtly butch lesbian, two men holding hands, or lesbians discussing their sexuality with the potential of being overheard, there is a risk that someone will "retaliate" against them physically.

And safety is not just physical. LGBT people lack the security of knowing that they will not be fired and lose their livelihoods simply because they are gay or transgender. They don't have the security of knowing that they won't be evicted from their apartments—thrown out of their homes—simply because their landlord may morally disapprove of homosexuality. And they don't have the security of knowing that their sexual orientation or transgender status won't be used against them in the receipt of public or private goods and services.

Happiness: While many LGBT people today are very happy, it is not because the government has made that easy.

Our current societal frameworks are not designed to help ensure that LGBT people will experience happiness. Happiness may mean being in a formally recognized relationship that one can share and celebrate with others. Or it might be as simple as being able to put a picture of one's lover on one's desk at work, just as one's straight colleagues do.

And happiness includes sexual pleasure. Gay people have had to articulate more explicitly than most—if only to ourselves—that sexual pleasure is often central to happiness and essential to becoming a fully actualized person. For some individuals, this is because they have forced themselves into abstinence or into having sex with people of the opposite gender. For others, it is simply the experience of feeling compelled to pursue sexual pleasure (and love and romance and other attendant things), even in the face of heavy resistance from the mainstream.

Care: Gay people know what it feels like *not* to be able to protect the ones we care for (and who care for us) in our communities.

Connections with others are key to our sense of self. For many of us, our connections are made within romantic and sexual relationships, and often include having children with these partners. We want to know that we can take care of our children just like straight parents take care of theirs, and we want to know that we can take care of our partners and that they can take care of us. We want this during our lifetime (when, for example, we want to be able to take time off from work to take our partner to the doctor) and we want this after our death (when, for example, we want our partner to be treated fairly by the Social Security system.)

Integrity: Gay people know what it feels like *not* to have integrity—to feel that we are hiding who we are and not being true to our full selves.

Kenji Yoshino discusses this experience in terms of "covering," a term he borrows from Ervin Goffman.[28] By "covering," Yoshino refers to an increasingly prevalent norm in society and antidiscrimination law, which tells gay people that is acceptable to be gay as a matter of fact, but that it is unacceptable for gay people to act out that identity—to show same-sex affection, to discuss their sexuality in any significant way, to engage in behaviors that are perceived as "gay." As Yoshino argues, this denial of integrity, this severing of the self, can exact significant physic damage on gay people and their relationships, and is ultimately stifling and harmful to society as a whole, particularly in a society in which we all, gay or straight, have some attribute that society pressures us to downplay in order to fit into the mainstream.

Premise Five: We as a society share these four moral understandings regardless of the source of the understanding (religious, spiritual, or secular) that any member of society might draw upon.

Some people may not initially identify these four beliefs as statements of *moral* understanding, perhaps because they do not consider themselves religious. Others might quickly view them as moral convictions because they are accustomed to understanding their religious beliefs as moral beliefs.

It is a central premise of the Moral Values Project, however, that morality does not derive from religious beliefs alone. A concomitant belief is that if our moral convictions happen to derive from religious beliefs, that fact neither detracts from nor enhances the power of such convictions.

The first necessary discursive move to be advanced by the Moral Values Project, therefore, is to change the public discourse so that morality (including morality in sexual matters) is understood as deriving equally and validly from secular, spiritual (but not affiliated with any particular religious denomination), *or* religious commitments and beliefs. Each of these sources should be understood as a legitimate and important basis for the creation of moral understandings.

Some religious people believe so strongly in the revealed truth of their beliefs that it is difficult for them to credit nonreligious beliefs as carrying equal weight and validity. Sometimes religious people simply believe this intuitively; at other times, they actually claim that the certitude provided by their religious beliefs provides greater intellectual support for their commitments.

There is no need to challenge religious people on the certitude of their beliefs. One of the (sometimes positive, sometimes negative) consequences of revealed truth is a sense of certitude. What does matter for political theory purposes, however, is that religious, secular, and spiritual beliefs should all be treated with *equal* respect and dignity in the public domain.

What this means, as a practical matter, is a commitment to the pluralism of various sources of "truth." Religious sources of moral values should be treated no better and no worse than secular sources or spiritual sources. A commitment to the First Amendment prescription of the separation of church and state necessarily precludes government from establishing and enforcing a religious theocracy. But it does not require a banishing of religious beliefs as a legitimate source of shared moral values in the public arena.[29] Conversely, the fact that a moral value is derived from a religious belief should not shield that moral value from contestation in the public domain.

The second discursive move is to explicate how religious, secular, and spiritual beliefs are often and ought to be *progressive* beliefs. The key discursive challenge here is to challenge the public perception that religious beliefs in the area of morality (read; "sexual morality") are by and large conservative and regressive. One way to do that is to highlight, in the public media, the diversity of religious beliefs about sexuality.

There are a growing number of religious denominations that believe that an individual who acts consistently with his or her given orientation is acting consistently with the precepts of that religion.[30] And there are many gay people who consider themselves religious.[31] The existence of religious denominations that support gay rights have figured prominently in amicus briefs submitted to the Supreme Court when it hears a gay rights case and in letters to Congress when it takes up a piece of gay-related legislation.

The challenge, of course, is to highlight the existence of these denominations and individuals whenever the media addresses the issue of gay rights. As Rabbi Sharon Kleinbaum, the Rabbi of Congregration Bet Simchat Torah in New York City, points out, it is both absurd and annoying to watch the typical talking-heads debate on television that pits someone like Reverend Jerry Falwell against someone like ACLU President Nadine Strossen. It is absurd because if we want to persuade individuals who are currently persuaded by Reverend Falwell, we need to offer them a gay rights advocate whose job is to "talk God."[32] And there are certainly many more clergy today who are willing to speak out on behalf of gay rights than ever before. It is annoying because it reinforces in the mind of the public that the "religious view" is "antigay," while the "civil rights view" is "pro-gay."

As unlikely a spokesperson as former Senator John Danforth captures the view I believe is essential with regard to the public perception of religious views on gender and sexual morality:

> In recent years, conservative Christians have presented themselves as representing the one authentic Christian perspective on politics. With due respect for our conservative friends, equally devout Christians come to very different conclusions. It is important for those of us who are sometimes called moderates to make the case that we, too, have strongly held Christian convictions, that we speak from the depths of our beliefs, and that our approach to politics is at least as faithful as that of those who are more conservative.[33]

I think it unlikely that the moderate Christian perspective espoused by Danforth would be consistent with the *progressive* Christian perspective that I would like to see highlighted in the media on LGBT issues. But I agree with Danforth that we must contest the public space currently accorded by the media to the "religious" viewpoint.

Rabbi Kleinbaum has a proposal for contesting that space that is somewhat drastic, but could be very effective. Whenever a media outlet has chosen a religious person to represent an antigay viewpoint, any advocate contacted to represent the pro-gay viewpoint should demand that a *religious* person be asked to present the pro-gay viewpoint. If the media outlet insists that it wants a lawyer (for example, because it is covering a marriage case brought by that lawyer or others), the advocate should require that the person presenting the antigay viewpoint should also then be a lawyer. Tit for tat. If the media outlet wants the issue to be religion, we can talk religion. If the outlet wants the issue to be law, we can talk law. But let's not let the *media* determine that the pro-gay side will talk law and the antigay side will talk religion.

Of course, as noted above, the ultimate discursive end of the Moral Values Project would be for the media to recognize that they must invite more than *religious* spokespeople (on either side of the issue) if they wish to address *moral* values in government. The true mark of success of the Moral Values Project will be when media outlets realize that to adequately cover the "moral values" front, they need *both* religious and secular people on *both* sides of a gay rights issue talking about morality.

LESSONS FROM PROPOSITION 8[34]

A robust Moral Values Project would facilitate substantive conversations about the positive moral value of acting on one's sexual orientation, as well as the positive moral goods of safety, happiness, caregiving, and integrity, everywhere from workplaces to radio shows to legislatures. Such conversations could, in turn, help shift the public's moral assessments of LGBT people in a manner that would advance true equality for LGBT people.

But conversations of this kind might also enlighten LGBT people and their allies why some people who believe homosexuality is immoral (either because of their religious or secular beliefs) experience themselves as "under siege" when society begins to extend equal protection to its LGBT citizens. As the passage of Proposition 8 in California in November 2008 made very clear, such fears can be exploited in a crass manner to deny gay couples access to equality. Hence, it behooves us to unpack those fears and figure out an appropriate response.

In May 2008, the California Supreme Court ruled that the state constitution required that gay couples be permitted access to civil marriage in California. The court reasoned that the state constitution's establishment of a fundamental right to marry (under the state's privacy and due process clauses) applied to two people of the same sex who wish to marry, and concluded that to receive equal protection under the law—also guaranteed by the state constitution—such couples had to receive the designation of "marriage" rather than the separate classification of "domestic partnership," already available in California for gay couples.[35]

But in November 2008, California voters passed Proposition 8, amending their California state constitution to block the access of gay couples to state civil marriage. The amendment added a new section 7.5 to Article 1 of the California state constitution with the following words: "Only marriage between a man and a woman is valid or recognized in California." Section 7 of Article I of the California constitution still proudly proclaims that no person may be deprived of liberty without due process of law and that no person may be denied the equal protection of the laws; section 1 of that article also still provides Californians with an "inalienable right" of privacy. But those sections can no longer be used as they were by the California Supreme Court, to provide gay couples with the liberty and privacy rights of equal access to civil marriage.[36]

What was particularly striking about the campaign to enact Proposition 8 was the extent to which proponents went out of their way to claim that the new provision would not take rights away from gay couples. In a Frequently Asked Questions document, for example, they raise the question, "Will Proposition 8 take away any rights for gay and lesbian domestic partners?" only to reply: "No. Proposition 8 is about preserving marriage; it is not an attack on the gay lifestyle. Proposition 8 does not take any rights away from gays and lesbians in domestic partnerships. Under California law, 'domestic partners shall have the same rights, protections, and benefits' as married spouses. There are no exceptions. Proposition 8 will not change this."[37]

But if the point of Proposition 8 was not to take rights away from same-sex couples, then what was its purpose? One argument advanced by its supporters was that Proposition 8 would simply restore the definition of marriage to what "human history has always understood it to be." But a secondary prominent argument for Proposition 8 was that providing access to marriage for gay couples would *reduce* the rights available to *others*. Supporters of Proposition 8 claimed, for example, that marriage recognition for gay couples in California would make life harder for parents in California who wanted to shield their young children from learning about homosexuals. From this vantage point, an essential selling point of Proposition 8 was that it would *protect* people from the excesses of extending rights to gay couples.

This "harm to others" argument was played out in two contexts: a range of religious entities could lose their tax-exempt status if they refused to perform marriages for same-sex couples or if they treated same-sex couples differently than they treated opposite-sex couples; and parents, particularly religious parents, would have no recourse when the public schools started teaching young students that homosexuality was morally acceptable.

The main legal case that Proposition 8 supporters used (and manipulated) in the education context was *Parker v. Hurley*, a case decided by a federal court of appeals in Massachusetts in January 2008.[38] Two sets of parents brought the case, David and Tonia Parker and Rob and Robin Wirthlin. The Parker's son Jacob had brought home from his public school kindergarten a Diversity Book Bag that included the book *Who's in a Family?* The book had pictures of different families, including interracial families, a family without children, a family with two moms, and another with two dads. In its final page, the book answered the question, "who's in a family?" with "the people who love you the most!" The Wirthlin's son, Joey, had came home from his public school second grade, talking about a picture book his teacher had read out loud that day, *King and King*. It's about a prince who is ordered by his mother to get married but who keeps rejecting the princesses he meets. Finally, he finds his true love—another prince!

The Parkers and Wirthlins were not happy. They did not ask the school to change the curriculum. But they did ask for a special accommodation, namely that no teacher or adult be permitted to expose children to materials or discussion about sexual orientation or same-sex unions without first notifying the parents and then giving parents the opportunity to pull their children out of such discussions. The school refused. Massachusetts state law explicitly gives parents prior notice and the right to "opt out" with regard to curriculum that involves human sexuality issues. But, as the school explained to the parents, these materials did not deal with human sexuality.

The parents sued, claiming their federal constitutional rights to raise their children as they wished and to practice their religion were being violated. The parents lost. The court found it difficult to perceive a real burden on the parents in light of the fact that the parents could continue to teach their children at home that same-sex marriages were immoral. And, as the court noted, while the federal constitution protects parents' rights to send their children to private schools, rather than public schools, it did not give parents the right to direct *how* a public school will teach their children.

In early October 2008, the parents' legal case came to an end when the Supreme Court chose not to hear their appeal. But their starring role as voices of doom for the families of America was just beginning.

The Family Research Council produced a video in September 2008, featuring the Parkers' story. In the video, the Parker parents described the book their son had brought home in the Diversity Book Bag as a book "about homosexuality and homosexual relations" and, as proof, opened the page of the picture book to the one showing a child with his two dads. The following month, Rob and Robin Wirthlin became a ubiquitous presence on the California TV scene. The supporters of Proposition 8 released a thirty-second ad that was shown innumerable times on television before the election. In the ad, a pretty young woman tells us that, contrary to what we may have heard, "Prop 8 has *everything* to do with schools." She then shows us a clip of an interview with Rob and Robin Wirthlin, who explain how "after Massachusetts legalized same-sex marriage," their son heard from the school how boys can marry other boys. "He's only in second grade!" exclaims Robin. Rob then explains that they tried to stop the school from teaching about gay marriage, but the court ruled they had no right to stop that or to pull their son out of class.

What does the right of gay couples in California to access civil marriage have to do with Robin's ability to teach her son Joey that gay marriage is wrong? *Nothing.* What does a change in society's views generally about how gay people should be treated in society, including with regard to marriage, have to do with Joey learning something about gay people in public school that his mother might not agree with? *Everything.*

It is critical that advocates for LGBT equality understand how the law operates in this area. It is not helpful to civil discourse that supporters of Proposition 8 blew their concerns out of proportion. But it still behooves those of us who seek to enshrine equality for LGBT people into the law to understand how the law might operate to place burdens on those who are out of step with changing social mores. It is only by understanding such impacts that we can even begin to consider what the appropriate accommodations, if any, might be.

Once society determines that discrimination on the basis of some category (race, religion, sexual orientation) is wrong, we expect our society to convey that norm in various ways. One important vehicle for transmitting our societal values to our children, including values of nondiscrimination, is the education our children receive in the public schools, funded with our tax dollars.

Indeed, in cases as early as 1925 and as recently as 1972, the Supreme Court has recognized the important role that public schools play in transmitting values and hence has protected the constitutional rights of parents to *shield* their children from exposure to values with which they do not agree by permitting them to educate their children outside of the public school system.[39] This was a right my Orthodox Jewish parents took full advantage of, sending me to ultra-religious Jewish schools throughout my elementary and high school years. But if parents choose to send their children to public schools, our system does not permit them to see the curriculum ahead of time and to remove their children from those aspects of the curriculum with which they disagree. One significant exception has been in the area of sex education. Many states, including Massachusetts, have made the policy choice that they will allow parents more specific control and discretion over that area and will often provide parents with prior notice of a sex education curriculum and the opportunity to "opt" their children out of such classes.

As our society changes its views about gay people and gay couples, therefore, new norms will arise that will appropriately be reflected in our schools. Diversity programs in public and private schools across the country, including programs that teach respect for gay people, have arisen, not as a result of the recognition of civil marriage (or even civil unions) for gay couples in these locations. Rather, they have been the natural outcome of a new and long overdue norm of nondiscrimination on the basis of sexual orientation that is beginning to take hold in our society.

The key legal point here is that it is not the legalization of same-sex *marriage* that is the root of the tension for parents like the Wirthlins. Those opposing Proposition 8 consistently argued that the legality of marriage for same-sex couples would not change anything in California schools with regard to curriculum, and they were correct in that regard. Law professors put out extensive legal statements to that effect and *The L.A. Times* published a sophisticated editorial making those same legal points.

But the audience targeted by the "Yes on 8" campaign was apparently not convinced. That is due partly, I believe, to the fact that gay rights advocates have not forthrightly addressed the natural tensions that have arisen as our social norms have begun to shift and thus have not grappled with how to address those tensions.

The same limitation exists with regard to the second main argument used by Prop. 8 supporters: that churches would be required to perform marriages for same-sex couples or lose their nonprofit tax status. This argument truly stretches the bounds of existing legal doctrine. But again, we need to understand how the basis of the fear operates in this area.

In the 1970s, the Internal Revenue Service revoked the tax-exempt status of Bob Jones University on the grounds that the school banned interracial dating among its students and hence did not serve a "charitable" purpose as required by law. In 1983, the Supreme Court upheld the IRS's position, despite the argument from Bob Jones University that its rule against interracial dating stemmed from a belief that the Bible prohibited such mixing of the races and, as a religious institution, Bob Jones felt compelled to comply with that understanding of the Bible.[40] (Bob Jones finally lifted the ban on interracial dating in 2000.)

No religious organization, other than Bob Jones University, has ever had its tax-exempt status revoked because of discriminatory rules that it applied on the basis of race or any other category. However, many state property tax exemptions provided to religious and other non-profit organizations are limited to property that is open to everyone in the public—and such exemptions have been revoked if the property is not, in fact, open to all.

For example, the Ocean Grove Camp Meeting Association of New Jersey, a Methodist organization, consistently described some boardwalk property it owned as open for public use. On that basis, it had sought and received federal, state, and local funds for maintenance of the property and it had received a property tax exemption from the state. The Ocean Grove association had a tradition of renting out its pavilion on the boardwalk property for weddings and other events that had no religious component.

But when a lesbian couple sought to rent the boardwalk pavilion for its civil union ceremony, the Methodist Ocean Grove association refused on the grounds that doing so would be contrary to its religious beliefs. The couple filed a complaint with the New Jersey Division on Civil Rights, citing a state law that prohibited public accommodations from discriminating on the basis on sexual orientation. The division ruled in the couple's favor. In addition, the state's Department of Environmental Protection revoked the portion of the association's property tax exemption that applied solely to the pavilion, since the tax exemption had been based on the premise that the property was available to the general public.[41]

When the legitimate liberty interests of gay people to live openly and honestly in society are recognized by society, as they need to be, such protections may sometimes come into conflict with the religious beliefs of individuals and organizations. We need to address these conflicts in an open and honest manner. It is the fair thing to do while we are asking our fellow citizens to thoughtfully consider and rectify the inequality that LGBT people have been subjected to in our society.

I have set forth elsewhere my preliminary thoughts on how to address such conflicts.[42] As a general matter, I believe that once a religious person or institution has entered the stream of commerce by operating an enterprise such as a doctor's office, hospital, bookstore, hotel, treatment center, and so on, the enterprise must be expected to adhere to a norm of nondiscrimination on the basis of sexual orientation and gender identity. This is essential so that any individual who happens upon the enterprise will not be surprised by a denial of service and/or by a directive to go down the street to a different provider.

But there are enterprises engaged in by belief communities (almost always religious belief communities) that deserve special solicitude, even if they otherwise operate in the general stream of commerce. These include schools, day care centers, summer camps and tours, that are sometimes for-profit and sometimes not-for-profit, but all of which are designed to inculcate values in the next generation.

If such an enterprise presents itself clearly and explicitly as designed to inculcate a set of beliefs in those who come in contact with the enterprise; if the enterprise clearly sets forth its belief that homosexuality, or acting on one's homosexuality, is morally wrong; and if the enterprise denies employment and services equally to individuals who are gay and to individuals who are heterosexual but who fail to profess the beliefs of the enterprise (i.e., that homosexuality, or acting on one's homosexuality, is morally wrong)—then I believe we are dealing with an enterprise that may need to continue excluding LGBT people from service and employment if it is to maintain its distinctive identity.

Obviously, LGBT people would be harmed if such enterprises are excluded from the purview of an antidiscrimination law. But in weighing the interests between the groups, I believe the harm to the enterprise in having the inculcation of values to its members significantly hampered (as I believe it would be if it were forced to comply with such a law) outweighs the harm to the excluded LGBT members.

I also think we need to consider the difficulties that arise with regard to *leadership* positions in enterprises that are more broadly represented in commerce. Many religious institutions operate the gamut of social services in the community, such as hospitals, gyms, adoption agencies, and drug treatment centers. These enterprises are open and marketed to the general public and often receive governmental funds. It seems quite appropriate to require that the enterprises' services be delivered without regard to sexual orientation and that most employment positions in these enterprises be available without regard to sexual orientation.

But the balance of interests, it seems to me, shifts with regard to the *leadership* positions in such enterprises. Particularly for religiously-affiliated institutions, I believe it is important that people in leadership positions be able to articulate the beliefs and values of the enterprise. If the identity and practice of an openly gay person would stand in direct contradiction to those beliefs and values, it seems to me that the enterprise would suffer a significant harm. Thus, in this limited circumstance, a legislature might legitimately conclude that the harm to the enterprise will be greater than the harm to the particular individuals excluded from such positions and provide a narrow exemption from a nondiscrimination mandate in employment.

These issues are not easy. But precisely because they are not easy, they deserve and demand our focused attention. While it may seem counterintuitive, I believe the best way to bring us to the point of full equality for LGBT people is to address head-on the tensions that arise when public schools teach tolerance and when public facilities owned by religious entities are asked to host commitment ceremonies for same-sex couples. Whatever we think the answers should be in any particular case, we will benefit more if we are in control of the answers and the message than if we pretend the tension is not real and legitimate.

A CALL TO MORAL ACTION IN POLITICS

Ultimately, the Moral Values Project is about formulating and embodying a strategy to advance a new moral agenda for this country.

People in society like to believe they are good. They like to go to sleep at night thinking that they are "good people"—or "good Americans" or "good Christians" or whatever they identify as. The Moral Values Project believes there is an important practical advantage in helping the many people who are not gripped by the Religious Right's current hold on morality to articulate why they, too, are "good" and "moral"—why they, too, act, vote, speak, and think *morally* when they support civil marriage for same-sex couples, when they believe in comprehensive sexual education, when they think Medicaid should pay for hormones for transgender people, and when they believe intersex infants should not be subject to cosmetic genital surgery.

The Moral Values Project wants to engage an alternative moral language, allowing more Americans to seize moral credibility. In doing so, we want to affirm the importance of moral values to the majority of the American public today. And we want to demonstrate that LGBT people care about moral values.

Finally, we want to call to task those who do *not* believe in the type of public policies we describe above. Like a modern-day prophet Isaiah, we want to call the people to understand how *they are falling short* when they support certain public policies over others. We want to play out in rich detail how the government currently *fails* to support the ability of LGBT people to feel safe, to feel happiness and pleasure, to care for others, and to be cared for, and to live a life of honesty and integrity—and how such failure ultimately lies at the feet of the American public. We don't want those people to go to sleep at night deluded into believing that they are "good people" (or "good Americans" or "good Christians" for that matter) if they have not supported public policies that advance the four moral understandings articulated by the Moral Values Project.

The goal of the Moral Values Project, is therefore twofold: it is rhetorical and intellectual. As a rhetorical matter, we seek to provide language for talking about the moral issues that surround gender and sexuality in society today. We hope that the language and discourse we create will be usable by religious, secular, and spiritual people. As an intellectual matter, we seek to make the case that we can engage in such moral discourse without losing the pluralistic underpinnings that have been so vital in advancing LGBT equality so far.

Government cannot guarantee us safety, happiness, care or integrity. But government can make it easier or harder for members of society to achieve these goods. A moral agenda should name these moral goods for what they are, and then highlight how government is failing to create the societal frameworks that would enable gay people to partake of these moral goods in a manner equivalent to that enjoyed by straight people. This agenda can then act as a mirror facing the average American, forcing each one of us to recognize that the "moral values" guiding our political decisions today fail our most basic moral convictions. And then, like a modern-day Isaiah, we can call the people to do better.

NOTES

1. Michael J. Sandel, Moral Argument and Liberal Toleration: Abortion and Homosexuality, 77 Cal. L. Rev. 521 (1989) (hereinafter "Moral Argument"). This law review article was modified and subsequently published as "Moral Argument and Liberal Toleration," in *New Communitarian Thinking: Persons, Virtues, Institutions, and Communities*, Amitai Etzioni, ed. (Charlottesville and London: University of Virginia Press, 1995). Sandel expanded on these themes in *Democracy's Discontent: America in Search of a Public Philosophy* (Cambridge: The Belknap Press of Harvard University Press, 1996.) I am not asserting that no political philosopher made these arguments prior to Sandel's 1989 article. But Sandel's article is the one that made an impact on me, and it remains, from my perspective, one of the clearest articulations of the limitations in traditional liberal philosophy, as described by Carlos Ball in this volume.

2. R. Claire Snyder-Hall, Marriage Equality and the Morality of Liberalism: The California Decision. This approach is most widely associated with John Rawls and Ronald Dworkin. John Rawls, *Political Liberalism* (New York: Columbia University Press, 1993), pp. 173–211; Ronald Dworkin, Taking Rights Seriously 90-100 (1977).

3. Carlos Ball, Against Neutrality in the Legal Recognition of Intimate Relationships. Carlos Ball's fullest explication of this approach is in his excellent book. Carlos A. Ball, *The Morality of Gay Rights: An Exploration in Political Philosophy* (New York: Routledge, 2003). I first made this argument in Feldblum, Sexual Orientation, Morality, and the Law: Devlin Revisited, 57 *U. Pitt. L. Rev.* 237 (1996).

4. Sandel, Moral Argument, *supra* n. 1, at 521.

5. *Id.*

6. Bowers v. Hardwick, 478 U.S. 186, 191 (1986).

7. Sandel, Moral Argument, *supra* n. 1, at 535 (quoting Hardwick v. Bowers, 760 F.2d 1202, 1212 (11th Circ. 1985), rev'd 478 U.S. 186 (1986) (footnotes omitted).

8. 394 U.S. 557 (1969).

9. 381 U.S. 479 (1965).

10. See Feldblum, Moral Conflict & Liberty: Gay Rights and Religion, 72 *Brooklyn L. Rev.* 61 (2006) (describing Justice Blackmun's reaction to the mail he received from gay people to his dissent in *Hardwick*). As Linda Greenhouse convincingly argues,

Justice Blackmun's passion for his dissent in *Hardwick* may have been due in part to his commitment to protecting the constitutional right of privacy for intimate decisions that he announced in *Roe v. Wade*. See Linda Greenhouse, *Becoming Justice Blackmun: Harry Blackmun's Supreme Court Journey* (New York: Times Books, 2005).

11. Sandel, Moral Argument, *supra* n. 1, at 536.

12. *Id.* at 536–37.

13. *Id.* at 537.

14. *Id.* at 538.

15. See Chai R. Feldblum, Sexual Orientation, Morality, and the Law: Devlin Revisited, 57 *U. Pitt. L. Rev.* 237, 308–10 (1996) (describing testimony on the Employment Non-Discrimination Act). Moral bracketing of this kind has dominated the strategic approach for developing support for the federal gay civil rights bill, starting with the first bill offered by Congresswoman Bella Abzug in the 1970s and extending to the latest bills introduced. See Chai R. Feldblum, The Federal Gay Civil Rights Bill: From Bella to ENDA in U. Vaid, J. D'Emilio & W. Turner eds., *Creating Change: Sexuality, Public Policy, and Civil Rights*, (New York: St. Martin's Press 2000) (chronicling moral bracketing strategy in developing support for gay rights civil rights bills. I did a focused deconstruction of another hearing on ENDA, in which a Democratic member of the House committee taking testimony posed the substantive moral question in a dramatic fashion. See Chai R. Feldblum, The Moral Rhetoric of Legislation, 72 *N.Y.U. L. Rev.* 992 (1997). The same moral bracketing in political discourse dominates the rhetoric of those opposing bills to prohibit marriage equality for same-sex couples. See Chai R. Feldblum, Gay is Good: The Case for Marriage Equality and More, 17 *Yale J. L. & Feminism* 139, 140 (2005) (deconstructing moral bracketing in the debate on the Defense of Marriage Act (DOMA) and the federal marriage amendment). For analysis of equality and neutrality as regards religion and sexual orientation, see the discussions in the Gill and Marcosson contributions to this volume.

16. Interview by Michael Boucai with Matt Coles, Director, ACLU Gay & Lesbian Rights and AIDS Project, New York City (Oct. 24, 2005).

17. Interview by Michael Boucai with James Esseks, Litigation Director, ACLU Gay & Lesbian Rights and AIDS Project, New York City (Oct. 24, 2005). ENDA, the Employment Non-Discrimination Act, prohibits discrimination on the basis of sexual orientation (and gender identity, in some formulations of the bill) in private employment.

18. See Karlyn Bowman & Adam Foster, Attitudes About Homosexuality and Gay Marriage, American Enterprise Institute, p. 4. In 2007, 83 percent of liberals, 50 percent of moderates, and 23 percent of conservatives considered homosexual relations to be morally acceptable. Available at www.aei.org/publications/pubID.14882,filter .all/pub_detail.asp (last visited August, 26, 2008).

19. *Id.* at 11.

20. EDK Associates, *Values Based Research Needs to Promote GLBT Rights: Opinion Leader Interviews and Public Opinion Experts* (October 2001) at 12.

21. See www.cnn.com/ELECTION/2004/pages/results/states/US/P/00/epolls.0 .html (visited March 1, 2009).

22. See http://people-press.org/reports/display.php3?ReportID=233 (visited March 1, 2009).

23. See Kenneth Sherrill, *Same-Sex Marriage, Civil Unions, and the 2004 Presidential Election* 2, *available at* www.thetaskforce.org/downloads/ MarriageCUSherrill2004.pdf.

24. For an in-depth analysis of how the term "family values" originated and gained currency among conservatives just before the onset of the Reagan Revolution, how it provided an attractive and sufficiently vague ("broad") slogan around which to rally—and ultimately associate—a wide range of disparate claims, see Alyssa Rayman-Read, *From Pulpit to Politics: How "Family Values" Led Evangelicals out of Crisis into Coalition* (2004), available at www.moralvaluesproject.org. Rayman-Read uses the term "Religious Right" and I adopt that for these subsequent paragraphs that draw significantly on Rayman-Read's analysis.

25. Barack Obama, *The Audacity of Hope: Thoughts on Reclaiming the American Dream* (New York: Three Rivers Press 2006), p. 52–53.

26. www.moralvaluesproject.org.

27. For an explication of the political theory on government and capabilities, see Martha Nussbaum, *Women and Human Development* (Cambridge: Cambridge University Press, 2000) pp. 75-83.

28. Kenji Yoshino, *Covering: The Hidden Assault on Our Civil Rights* (New York: Random House, 2006).

29. For the legal rendition of this argument, see Michael J. Perry, *Why Political Reliance on Religiously Grounded Morality Does Not Violate the Establishment Clause*, 42 Wm. & Mary L. Rev. 663, 672 (2001).

30. See generally John C. Green, *Antigay: Varieties of Opposition to Gay Rights*, *in* The Politics of Gay Rights 121, 123 (eds. Craig A. Rimmerman, Kenneth D. Wald, & Clyde Wilcox, 2000) ("some of the strongest advocates for the gay community are found among the theological liberals in all [religious] groups.")

31. A majority of gay people surveyed in a 2001 poll indicated that religion is important in their lives. Less than one-fifth said it was not important at all. Kaiser Family Foundation, *Inside-OUT: A Report on the Experiences of Lesbians, Gays and Bisexuals in America and the Public's Views on Issues and Policies Related to Sexual Orientation* at 34 (2001). *See also* EDK Associates, *Values Based Research Needs to Promote GLBT Rights: Opinion Leader Interviews and Public Opinion Experts* at 16 ("Gays and lesbians are as likely as heterosexuals to report frequent church attendance and devotion to faith."); Sean Cahill, *Same-Sex Marriage in the United States: Focus on the Facts* at 377 (2004) ("Many [gays] are deeply religious or spiritual. . . . Eighty-five percent of 2645 African-American gay people surveyed in summer 2000 reported a religious affiliation. Only 15 percent indicated they were atheist/agnostic or skipped the question." It is interesting to note, however, that gay people are significantly more likely than the general population to profess no religious faith whatsoever; whereas approximately 15 percent of gay and bisexual people say they are atheist, agnostic, or had no religion, the figure is approximately 6 percent for the general population. Kaiser Family Foundation at 34.

32. Interview by Michael Boucai with Sharon Kleinbaum, Rabbi, Congregation Beth Simchat Torah, Washington, D.C. (Nov. 2, 2005). See also Interview by Michael Boucai with Sylvia Rhue, National Black Justice Coalition, Director of Religious

Affairs and Constituency Development, Washington, D.C. (Oct.18, 2005) ("The appropriate messengers of religious messages are religious people.").

33. John C. Danforth, *Onward Moderate Christian Soldiers, New York Times*, June 17, 2005.

34. This Section is excerpted from The Selling of Proposition 8, which first appeared in the Harvard Gay & Lesbian Review, Jan–Feb. 2009.

35. In Re Marriage Cases, 183 P.3d 384 (California 2008). In October 2008, the Connecticut Supreme Court similarly ruled that the state constitution required that gay couples be permitted access to civil marriage in Connecticut. Relying solely on the equal protection guarantee provided by the state constitution, the court concluded that gay couples had to receive the designation of "marriage" rather then the separate categorization of "civil unions," already available in Connecticut for gay couples. Kerrigan v. Commissioner of Public Health, 957 A.2d 407 (Conn. 2008).

36. Given the sweeping nature of the amendment made by Proposition 8, a number of groups have challenged the validity of Proposition 8 on the grounds that it was a revision of the state constitution, not an amendment, and hence was required to have undergone additional procedural steps before being put to the voters.

37. www.protectmarriage.com/ (last visited March 1. 2009).

38. Parker v. Hurley, 514 F.3d 87 (1st Circuit 2008).

39. Pierce v. Society of Sisters of the Holy Name of Jesus and Mary, 45 S.Ct. 571 (1925); Wisconsin v. Yoder, 406 U.S. 205 (1972).

40. Bob Jones v. U.S., 461 U.S. 574 (1983).

41. Bernstein v. Ocean Grove Camp Meeting Association, State of New Jersey, Office of the Attorney General, Department of Law and Public Safety, Division on Civil Rights, Docket No. PN34XB-03008.

42. Feldblum, Moral Conflict and Liberty: Gay Rights and Religion, 72 *Brooklyn L. Rev.* 61 (2007).

Index of Cases Referenced

Andersen v. King County, 19, 21, 43, 43n2, 44n27, 47n108

Baehr v. Lewin, 15n7, 44n21, 127, 134n27
Baker v. State of Vermont, 44n23, 127
Bob Jones v. U.S., 232n40
Bowers v. Hardwick, xvii, 20, 25–26, 28, 31–32, 34, 43, 44n15, 46n69, 206
Brown v. Board of Education, 112

Church of the Lumumi Babalu Aye v. City of Hialeah, 156n40
Corporation of the Presiding Bishop v. Amos, 143
County of Allegheny v. ACLU, 68, 73n70
Cruzan v. Director, Missouri Department of Health, 34

EEOC v. Catholic University , 147, 157n51
Employment Division v. Smith, 67, 73n67, 144–49

Gonzalez v. Roman Catholic Bishop of Manila, 146
Goodridge v. Department of Public Health, 19, 21–22, 29–36, 40–41, 43, 43n2
Griswold v. Connecticut, 20, 26, 29, 34, 40–41, 207

Hernandez v. Robles, 19, 21–22, 26, 29–37, 43n2

In re Marriage Cases, xii n2, xii n3, xiii n9, 45n31, 101, 116, 134n30, 232n35

Kedroff v. St. Nicholos Cathedral of the Russian Orthodox Church in North
  America, 146

Lawrence v. Texas, xviii, 19–22, 24–29, 31–35, 41–43, 44n9, 101–2, 113, 127

Index

About the Contributors

Gordon A. Babst is associate professor of Political Science at Chapman University in Orange, California and the author of *Liberal Constitutionalism, Marriage, and Sexual Orientation: A Contemporary Case for Dis-Establishment*. His research interests include the dilemmas of pluralism in the context of the separation of church and state, and the intersection of political theory and globalization studies.

Carlos A. Ball is professor of Law at the Rutgers University School of Law (Newark), the author of *The Morality of Gay Rights: An Exploration in Political Philosophy* (Routledge, 2003), and a coeditor of *Cases and Materials on Sexual Orientation and the Law* (West, 2008). His articles have appeared in the *Cornell Law Review*, the *Georgetown Law Journal*, the *Minnesota Law Review*, the *North Carolina Law Review*, and the *UCLA Law Review*, among other journals.

Chai R. Feldblum is a professor of Law at Georgetown University Law Center, where she teaches in the areas of sexuality, gender and the law, legislation and administrative law, and disability law, and where she directs the Federal Legislation Clinic. Her publications include *Moral Conflict and Conflicting Liberties* (2008); *Gay is Good: The Case for Marriage Equality & More* (2005), and *Rectifying the Tilt: Equality Lessons from Religion, Disability, Sexual Orientation and Transgender* (2003). She has served as a legislative lawyer consultant to the Human Rights Campaign and the National Gay & Lesbian Task Force, has been a key drafter and negotiator on the Employment Non-Discrimination Act, and founded the Moral Values Project in 2005.

Emily R. Gill is Caterpillar professor of Political Science at Bradley University in Peoria, Illinois, and the author of *Becoming Free: Autonomy and Diversity in the Liberal Polity* (Kansas, 2001). Her research interests focus on the tensions cause by cultural, religious, and sexual diversity in liberal democracies.

Valerie Lehr is the Vice President of the University and Dean of Academic Affairs, and professor of Government and Gender Studies at St. Lawrence University. She is the author of Queer Family Values (Temple University Press, 1999), as well as a number of essays on gay and lesbian family politics and, most recently, the rights of queer youth.

Sam Marcosson is a professor at the University of Louisville's Brandeis School of Law. professor Marcosson did his undergraduate work at Bradley University, where he earned a B.S. in political science, and received his J.D. from Yale Law School. He is the author of *Original Sin: Clarence Thomas and the Failure of the Constitutional Conservatives* (2002).

Jason Pierceson is associate professor of Political Science and Legal Studies at the University of Illinois at Springfield and is the author of *Courts, Liberalism, and Rights: Gay Law and Politics in the United States and Canada*. His research interests include public law, legal and political theory, and the legal and political issues relating to sexuality.

R. Claire Snyder-Hall, is associate professor of government and politics in political theory at George Mason University and director of the Master of Arts in Interdisciplinary Studies program. Her publications include *Citizen-Soldiers and Manly Warriors: Military Service and Gender in the Civic Republican Tradition* (1999), *Gay Marriage and Democracy: Equality for All* (2006), and the coedited special issue of *Hypatia: Journal of Feminist Philosophy* entitled "Democratic Theory" (2007), as well as numerous articles and book chapters. She is currently working on third wave feminism. Snyder-Hall holds a Ph.D. from Rutgers University and a B.A. cum laude from Smith College.

Ronald Steiner is director of Graduate, Summer & Joint Degree Programs at the Chapman University School of Law, where he also teaches Legislation, Law & American Culture, and an Advanced Tort Seminar on Private Law as Public Policy. He received a B.A. in English from Lafayette College, an M.A. in political science from the University of Delaware, and a Ph.D. in Political Science from the University of Minnesota. His dissertation, The Interpretation of Treaties and the Constitution of Native American Identity (1993), explored the intellectual and historical foundations of federal Indian law. He received his J.D. from the University of Southern California, where he graduated Order of the Coif. He served in 1999 and 2000 as Deputy Counsel on the California Governor's Blue Ribbon Advisory Panel on Hate Groups.

Karen Struening is the director of the Skadden, Arps Honors Program in Legal Studies at the City College of New York. She teaches constitutional law and other legal studies courses in the Department of Political Science at City College and is the author of *New Family Values: Liberty, Equality and Diversity* (Rowman & Littlefield, 2002). Her research interests include constitutional and family law. professor Struening serves on the Board of Directors of the Council on Contemporary Families.